VICTORI ~~~~

BATTLES OF THE

SECOND WORLD

WAR

C. E. Lucas Phillips

SAPERE
BOOKS

VICTORIA CROSS BATTLES OF THE SECOND WORLD WAR

Published by Sapere Books.

20 Windermere Drive, Leeds, England, LS17 7UZ,
United Kingdom

saperebooks.com

ISBN: 978-1-80055-275-3.

TABLE OF CONTENTS

THE OBJECT OF THE EXERCISE 7
1: 'THE MOST ENVIABLE ORDER' 10
2: ORDEAL IN CRETE 21
3: THE BATTLE OF THE ATLANTIC 68
4: CRUSADER 93
5: GAZALA 161
6: RUWEISAT 194
7: WADI AKARIT 214
8: DAVID AND GOLIATH 232
9: GURKHAS AND YORKSHIREMEN AT IMPHAL 265
10: THE MIDGETS AT SINGAPORE 303
APPENDIX A: ROLL OF VICTORIA CROSS AWARDS 1939-45 321
APPENDIX B: AWARDS SINCE 1945 331
APPENDIX C: PRINCIPAL WITNESSES 332
APPENDIX D: SUBMARINE TERMINOLOGY 336
APPENDIX E: OUTLINE ORGANIZATION OF AN ARMY IN THE FIELD 338
APPENDIX F: A BRIEF NOTE ON THE INDIAN ARMY 340
A NOTE TO THE READER 341

THE OBJECT OF THE EXERCISE

This book sets out to record a number of actions or series of actions in the Second World War which were made memorable by multiple awards of the Victoria Cross.

The object has been to paint a picture of each performance in the full colours of its tactical setting, correlating the part with the whole, so that each shall appear, as it should do, as something more than an episode suspended in a vacuum. Thus we may better apprehend its worth and its meaning. Each action is chronicled fairly extensively, as far as its circumstances concern the Victoria Crosses won therein. In the process we catch glimpses of many other deeds of heroism, some of which, the reader may think, also deserved the VC, so that the thread of valour will be seen to sparkle throughout the whole tapestry. I have found the choice of which events shall be described to be an exacting task. To have attempted a study of all the 182 VC awards of that war would have resulted in an assemblage of very short and merely anecdotal passages not much different from the official citations in *The London Gazette*, which very often are by no means satisfactory descriptions. A great many VCs, especially those of the air and the sea, were won for isolated incidents, so that a description of them all would become merely episodic, and it is almost impossible to make any kind of selection where all are of equal merit. The reader may be surprised to find that only one VC was awarded in the Battle of Britain, and will learn the reason why.

Furthermore, in the process of selection I have by-passed actions already fully chronicled in other publications (including some of my own), such as the St Nazaire Raid, the

Dambusters, the Battle of El Alamein, Arnhem, the Dieppe Raid, Cassino and others.[1] Thus the incidents that have been selected here are, in the main, those that are not particularly well known to the general public, such as the fascinating and curiously neglected *Crusader* operation (five VCs), the lonely flights of the pilots of Coastal Command in the Battle of the Atlantic (five), the model and audacious one-day Battle of Wadi Akarit (three), the remarkable Battle of Crete, unique in the world's history, and the operations of 17th Indian Division in the mud and squalor of Imphal (four). *Crusader*, intimately associated with Tobruk, has been recorded at some length (though still far from completely), since its confused and irrational manoeuvres provide a rich example of how the defects of generalship (on both sides) were remedied by the fortitude of the regimental soldier. General Carver's *Tobruk* gives a more detailed account of this military melee, though not of the VCs.

There is a rather long Desert sequence, due to the remarkable circumstances in which Charles Upham won not only the Victoria Cross but also a Bar to it, in each case not for isolated acts but for prolonged leadership, starred with a whole series of Homeric accomplishments in deadly personal combat, from Crete in May 1941 to Ruweisat in July 1943. It is quite impossible to write any book about the Victoria Cross without the inclusion of this rare and superlative achievement. Moreover, this sequence has provided an opportunity for including such outstanding feats of heroism as those of Private Waken-shaw, Sergeant Elliott and several others.

---

[1] The St Nazaire Raid has been recounted in detail in the present author's *The Greatest Raid of All* and the great Desert battle in his *Alamein*.

Wherever possible, I have obtained first-hand evidence for all these occurrences, not relying too much on material already published unless it is of unimpeachable authenticity. It will occasion no surprise that the best informants have often been those who did not themselves win the Cross. A list of the principal witnesses and other sources used will be found in Appendix C, but I must especially mention *The Story of the Victoria Cross*, by Brigadier the Rt Hon. Sir John Smyth, Bt, himself a VC, who has achieved the feat not only of recording every VC won since 1854 but also of giving short descriptions of a great number of them.

For readers not familiar with military matters there are a few short explanatory notes in the appendices.

1: 'THE MOST ENVIABLE ORDER'

Fear, we are told, is the oldest of animal emotions; so we are taken aback when we hear Leonardo da Vinci declare that 'courage is death, fear is life'. We are tempted to leap from our chair and retort with the Gurkha maxim that 'it is better to die than be a coward'.

Fear certainly lurks in the bosoms of most of us, but is overcome by those springs within us that are not animal. To the man in battle, and often to others also, the overcoming is an express and positive duty. Fear for the lives of others than ourselves is still more difficult to overcome, since it demands a more deliberate and calculated confrontation with danger when we could easily satisfy our consciences with excuses for inaction. The Reverend Theodore Hardy, chaplain to the 8th Battalion of the Lincolnshire Regiment in the First World War, won every possible decoration for a soldier in battle — the Military Cross, the Distinguished Service Order and finally the Victoria Cross — in a whole series of life-saving deeds, beyond the scope of his duty, that take our breath away. He also won death.

We do well, therefore, to honour all brave men and women who hazard their lives for their country, their cause or to save others. The measure of our estimation lies in the fact that the Victoria Cross is the highest of all honours that the Sovereign can bestow, taking precedence even of the Order of the Garter. The Duke of Windsor, when Prince of Wales, proclaimed it to be 'the most democratic and at the same time the most exclusive of all orders of chivalry — the Most Enviable Order of the Victoria Cross'.

No doubt it was to a large extent the 'democratic' image that fired the public imagination and set the seal of popular approbation on Queen Victoria's inspired ordinance. Not only was heroism at last recognized and publicly acclaimed, but also, at a stroke, contrary to the accepted notions of centuries in a society still largely aristocratic, the ordinary seaman and the private soldier were assayed and stamped with the same hallmark as the admiral and the general. There was only one standard, the human standard of valour in deadly peril. And as time went on the arms of the Queen-Empress extended themselves still more widely to embrace people who were not even British, not even Christians, not even white-skinned. The Muslim sepoy could be hailed as a hero in the same breath as the Christian Admiral-of-the-Fleet.

In this truly remarkable and original idea Queen Victoria was not animated by any concept of boosting morale or stimulating her sailors and soldiers to higher endeavour. A professional admiral or general might have thought in such terms, but not the Queen. As sovereign of a vast empire, she felt a deep sense of personal gratitude to those who were brave in her cause. Unable herself to be tested in battle, she had a warm admiration, a particularly womanly admiration, for those who faced the test with manly courage, and she crystallized the feelings of her heart in the new and transcendent honour named after herself. In so doing, she epitomized also the admiration of the nation and the Empire.

Before the VC was instituted in 1856 no awards for gallantry in battle existed except the Distinguished Conduct Medal, which itself was not always given for gallantry. Since then various other honours have been instituted, such as the Distinguished Service Order (also not always given for gallantry alone, except it be to a junior officer), the several awards particular to each of the three fighting Services, and some high-ranking civilian awards, of which the most admired is the George Cross. We may well think, therefore, that some of the early winners of the Victoria Cross (if we judge merely by the citations) would today have received one of these lesser decorations. Thus the standard of heroism required to qualify for the Victoria Cross has become more exacting than of old, yet all who have won it, according to time and circumstances, must be reckoned among the bravest of the brave. In such a brotherhood there are no degrees, no gradings or comparisons. There may, indeed, be examples of which one may say 'That hardly sounds like a VC'; but in all such examples death has set its crimson seal upon what might otherwise have earned a lesser honour. Death in action, it is often said, is in itself the highest honour. 'When a man dies gloriously in war,' declared Socrates, 'shall we not say that he is of the golden race?'

Many other factors closely affect whatever criteria one may apply in the assessment of brave deeds in battle. Darkness, isolation and extremity of circumstance impose particularly severe strains. What is done in a fiery assault, when the blood is hot, must be measured against cool, long-sustained endeavour in the face of great odds. Leadership and example, whether by corporal or colonel or their equivalents in the other Services, weigh heavily in the scales. So also is the balance tilted when the performance has some influence on the tactical situation.

On all these grounds such performances as those of Sergeant Turner, the Halifax bus-conductor, and Subedar Netrabahadur Thapa, the Gurkha officer extraordinary, qualify for high places in the Valhalla of the Brave; yet we must guard against making comparisons where grounds for comparison so rarely exist. Who would dare to make critical comparisons between

Guy Gibson, Leonard Cheshire and Hugh Edwards (those heroes of the Royal Air Force), and the great submarine commanders John Linton, David Wanklyn and Tony Miers? All were examples of long-sustained leadership of the highest order in imminent and constant peril. Continuous and inspirational leadership similarly formed the basis of the awards of the double VC to Charles Upham, and distinguished the achievements of 'Jock' Campbell and Bob Foote. Sharp contrasts, however, mark the ice-cold nerve of the midget submariners, who were never seriously under fire at all, and the sacrificial fights of Gerard Roope, of HMS *Glowworm*, and Fogarty Fegen, of the armed merchantman *Jervis Bay*.

Many others have deserved the Victoria Cross, but not won it. For there usually have to be witnesses and written testimony, which is carefully scrutinized. Thus, among the many gallant young pilots who went up single-handed to fight and win the Battle of Britain, only Flight Lieutenant James Nicholson, attacking a German squadron over the New Forest while himself enveloped in flames, could be given the award. For all those others, many of whom went to their deaths in the sky, there were no witnesses.

So also, Lieutenant Jock Young, of the Assam Regiment, when sent out to hold a lonely post deep in the Burma jungle and told to hold out 'to the last man', ordered his company to withdraw when their annihilation by the Japanese was certain, but stayed behind himself with a tommy-gun and a pile of grenades. When his Indian officer demurred he said: 'No argument, subedar sahib. It is an order. I was ordered to fight to the last man and I shall obey those orders. You will withdraw to Kohima and I shall stay.' Only a few frightened villagers witnessed his final immolation in a whirlwind of bursting grenades and machine-gun fire.[2]

The reader will no doubt find other such examples in these pages. He may well ask himself as he studies these incidents: 'What actuates a man to do such things?' One may understand how an officer, a NGO or a Petty Officer, having a duty of leadership, will feel himself impelled to pursue that duty against the bitterest odds. But what actuates the humblest man with no such responsibility for leadership? What moved Private Beeley, of Winchester, and Private Gurney, of Australia, to leap up, when their companies were pinned down to the ground by fire, and charge the enemy alone? What spurred Private Wakenshaw, from the back streets of industrial Gateshead, to go on serving his gun when his arm was blown off and all his comrades lay dead around him?

To such questions the psychologists have found no satisfying answer. Perhaps Robert Bridges in *The Testament of Beauty*, is nearest the mark when he affirms that

> in pride of his calling
> good warriorship welcometh the challenge of death.

Not every man would shape the thought in such lofty terms, but there are plenty of authentic examples of men who enjoy battle, who take pleasure in dancing on peril's edge, who cheerfully fight to the cannon's mouth and 'for whom life has no relish save in danger of death'. Brigadier John Currie, when his staff-officer went to ground in a burst of shell-fire, laughed and said: 'Why are you lying down, man? Why don't you get up?' General 'Strafer' Gott tartly asked a lieutenant-colonel under machine-gun fire: 'What are you ducking for?'

Private Clifford Portsmouth, a South African, is a remarkable witness to this relish for battle. In an action in the Western

---

[2] Related in detail in the author's *Springboard to Victory*.

Desert he attacked and destroyed an enemy machine-gun nest, killing seven men, then wiped out with grenades another party hiding in a rock cistern, went on to knock out a second machine-gun and an anti-tank gun, gathered in a bag of prisoners and finally reported to his platoon commander, Lieutenant K. H. Douglas, saying with a broad grin: 'Sir, what a wonderful war!'[3]

Others in their manifestations of courage are inspired by zeal for the cause. Charles Upham was certainly one of these, as was his CO, Howard Kippenberger, who shut up his law books to join up for his second war, and lost both feet (without winning the VC). Our psychological probing for the *fons et origo* of this aspect of human behaviour therefore finds no positive answer. Environment, upbringing and physique have little to do with it. 'Honour appeareth in the meanest habits.' Until, like gold, men are tried in the fire one cannot be sure. Your man of 'big assemblage', strong-thewed, renowned in the fields of sport, may, like Falstaff himself, prove to be a poltroon when the bullets fly. Certainly men of large stature, such as Bernard Freyberg, Lord Gort, 'Jock' Campbell and Private Speakman, have been shining examples of valour; but one is impressed by how many small men have won the VC, such as Jackie Smyth, the Nelsonic figure of Carton de Wiart, one-eyed and one-armed, and the midget submariners to be met in these pages.

All sorts and conditions of men have won the Victoria Cross, from the ages of 15 (Boy Cornwall at the Battle of Jutland was 16) to over 60. In the Second World War the youngest was Sergeant John Hannah, RAF, who was only 18 when he won his VC in a raid over Antwerp. Several in this book were 40 or over. If there is a common denominator among them, one

---

[3] Louis Duffus: *Beyond the Laager.*

would say that, with few exceptions, they are men of quiet, composed dispositions, wearing with the utmost modesty the halo that inevitably surrounds them. Nearly all are men of fine character and personal integrity.

Field-Marshal Montgomery, in conversation with the author some years ago, remarked: 'Though other considerations have their importance, the one, dominant factor in winning a battle is morale; and the VC is the outcome, as well as the outward symbol, of a high state of morale in the individual and nearly always in the unit also. Men who win the VC certainly help to win battles.'

Not that the Victoria Cross is always won in victory. Far from it. The greatest bravery is often shown in adversity, illuminating the black shadows of defeat with gleams of honour. Even in the lamentable Malayan Campaign of early 1942 the sombreness of total defeat was in part redeemed by acts of singular heroism, in which four Victoria Crosses were awarded — to Squadron-Leader Arthur Scarf, Lt-Colonel Arthur Cumming, Lt-Colonel Charles Anderson of Australia and, in circumstances of extraordinary daring, to Lieutenant Thomas Wilkinson, RNR, who engaged a Japanese cruiser with his flimsy little Chinese river-boat, armed with only one small gun. Other examples of the VC won in adversity will be found in these pages.

The Emblem of Valour

The Victoria Cross was instituted by Queen Victoria by Royal Warrant in 1856, with retrospective effect from 1854. Since then various other Royal Warrants have governed the conditions of its award and today it is open to all, without distinction of rank, sex or race, who serve with the armed forces. Four civilians have won it, three being civil servants during the Indian Mutiny and the fourth a civil chaplain in the Afghan War of 1879. Except for two occasions in the early days, it has been awarded only in operations against the enemy and, since the institution of the George Cross and George Medal, it is unlikely that it will ever be awarded otherwise.

The Cross itself is very simple in design, not at all spectacular. It is made of bronze, originally from Russian guns captured in the Crimea, and is cast in a form inexactly described as a Maltese Cross (heraldically, a cross *patté*), upon which is imposed the royal crown and lion, under-charged with a scroll inscribed 'For Valour'. The ribbon used to be blue for the Royal Navy and crimson for the Army, but since 1920 it has been plain crimson for all three Services. When the ribbon alone is worn it is ornamented with a small replica of the Cross. It is the only battle distinction that can be awarded after death, and in the last war such posthumous awards amounted to 87, virtually half of the total. If a man is killed in a feat not considered to merit the VC, he is eligible for no honour except 'Mentioned in Despatches'. The only other award that can be given posthumously is the George Cross, which is not given for operational conduct in battle, though it can be awarded for non-combatant gallantry.

Since its institution there have been 1,351 awards of the Victoria Cross, nearly half of them won in the war of 1914-18. In the Second World War there were only 182. Since then nine VCs have been won, of which four were in Korea and four by Australians in the Vietnam war (serving to remind us that the Viet Cong were the Queen's enemies). Only some 140 holders of the VC are still alive as I write.

Three men have achieved the phenomenal glory of winning the VC and Bar. Two of them were doctors of the Royal Army Medical Corps (a corps brightly embellished with VCs and other awards for bravery) — the handsome Arthur Martin-Leake, who won his VC in the South African war and the Bar in 1914; and Noel Chavasse, who won both awards in the First World War, the Bar posthumously. The third winner of the double VC is the remarkable New Zealander, Charles Upham, whose deeds are set out in this book.

The register of VCs includes three examples of father and son — Lord Roberts (the celebrated 'Bobs') and his son Frederick Hugh, Walter Congreve and his son William, Charles Gough and his son John.

Four pairs of brothers have won it — Hugh Gough, brother of the aforesaid Charles (so making three VCs in one family), Reginald and Euston Sartorius, Alexander and Victor Turner (the latter famous for his stand at Alamein), and Roland and George Bradford (the former of the Durham Light Infantry and the latter of the Royal Navy). Worthy to be bracketed with them are Derek Seagrim, of the Green Howards, who won the VC in the Western Desert, and his brother Hugh, of the Indian Army, who won the George Cross in Burma; both were killed. Mrs J. N. Randle had the sad but proud distinction of being wife and sister to two posthumous VCs — her husband Jack, of the Royal Norfolks, and her brother Leslie Manser, of the RAF.

Many memorable battles have been signalized by a brilliant cluster of VCs. The record is held by the fierce action at Rorke's Drift in the Zulu War of 1879, for which no fewer than eleven were awarded, all 'good' ones, seven being to officers and men of the South Wales Borderers. In the famous Zeebrugge-Ostend Raid in 1918, nine were awarded to the Royal Navy and Royal Marines, while at Gallipoli in 1915 the Lancashire Fusiliers won their celebrated 'six VCs before breakfast'.

In the Second World War, with which we are here mainly concerned, perhaps the most spectacular example was provided by the raid on St Nazaire in 1942, for which five VCs were awarded. It was remarkable for being the only occasion on which a soldier has won the VC for an action at sea, when Sergeant Thomas Durrant, Royal Engineers, manning a little Lewis gun in a motor launch, defiantly engaged a German frigate at close quarters, continuing to fight when his body was riddled with bullets. Of the events related in these pages, five VCs were also awarded in the remarkable desert battle known as *Crusader*, another five (RAF and RN) in the long-drawn-out battle of the Atlantic, and four in the operations described at Imphal in the Burma campaign.

A special provision of the Royal Warrants allows the Victoria Cross to be awarded to recipients elected by the officers and men themselves, where all are equally brave and distinguished. This has been done on several occasions, notably at Rorke's Drift and Zeebrugge, but the practice has fallen into desuetude. On the other hand, awards are still made to a selected officer or man in recognition not only of his own bravery but also of that of his comrades. This was to be seen, for example, in the awards for the St Nazaire Raid to Lt-Commander 'Sam' Beattie, who, when commanding HMS *Campbeltown*, rammed the dock gates with uncanny precision under very heavy fire, and to Able Seaman Savage posthumously. The former was awarded 'in recognition not only of his own valour but also of that of the unnamed officers and men of a very gallant ship's company'. The award to Savage, who was a Volunteer Reservist in one of the fleet of motor launches in the raid, was made not only to himself 'but also for the valour shown by many others' in the small boats of Coastal Forces. One may think that other citations could well be put in similar terms, as in the case of aircraft crews.

A scrutiny of the Roll in Appendix A shows how extraordinarily far-flung was the conflict that raged in the Second World War and how richly it was infused by the bravery of the fighting Services of Britain and her associated peoples. The register of honour is headed by the Burma campaign, in which 31 VCs were awarded. The North African campaigns come next with a tally of 27, of which 21 were won by Eighth Army in the Western Desert before meeting First Army in Tunisia.

In the North-West Europe campaign of 1944-5 (starting in Normandy) there were 22 and in Italy 20. In the far-scattered islands of the Pacific 11 were won, nearly all by Australians. Six were awarded for the three weeks of the Dunkirk campaign, and three for the Dieppe Raid. Others were won in Greece, Malaya, Somalia, Abyssinia, Eritrea, Hong Kong and Syria. Twenty-four were won in the oceans of the world and 26 by the air forces of Britain and the Dominions.

Of the peoples engaged in this mighty conflict, the Services of the United Kingdom naturally predominate, with VCs. The Indian Army (including its British officers) follows with 30, of which ten were won by Gurkhas. Australians won 17, Canadians 12, New Zealanders nine and South Africans three. One Rhodesian, one Dane and one Fijian make up the distinguished roll.

2: ORDEAL IN CRETE

(Unless otherwise attributed, all quotations in this chapter are from various New Zealand records.)

Prelude in Greece

In 1940, after Germany had ravished the greater part of Europe, the British Empire and Dominions stood alone against Hitler and Mussolini. Throughout the Continent, freedom was either extinguished or on the defensive. America was Britain's friend, but not yet her ally. Russia was in cynical treaty with Germany for their respective aggressions. Mussolini, thirsting for a share of glory and eager to snap up whatever scraps the Nazi lion might leave for him, searched the map for easy fields to conquer.

He selected two. In September, clutching at 'the chance of 5,000 years', he sent Marshal Graziani to seize Egypt with a powerful force from the Italian colony of Libya, and in the following month, having previously grabbed Albania, he used that territory as a base for an assault upon Greece, which he invaded without warning or provocation.

The Greeks, however, poorly equipped though they were, gave them a hot reception and pushed them back deep into the mountains of Albania. An even worse fate enveloped Italian arms on the other side of the Mediterranean, where, in the Libyan desert, Graziani's host collapsed in ruin before an audacious counter-offensive by Richard O'Connor's almost absurdly small British force. Farther afield the Italian possessions of Abyssinia, Somaliland and Eritrea were crumbling fast as the small British columns thrust into their fastnesses.

Thus by the end of the winter of 1941 Mussolini's gleaming vision of a vast African empire had grown dim indeed and cries of bitter lamentation issued melodramatically from the Italian radio. Hitler, watching his ally's distress, saw in it a long-desired excuse to achieve his own aggrandizement by going to his ally's help. Having already sent a strong German force under Lt-General Erwin Rommel to bolster the Italians in Africa, he dispatched through the intimidated Balkans a far more powerful expedition which swiftly overwhelmed the hesitant Yugoslavs in a *blitzkreig* of calculated savagery and swung into Greece on 6 April.

Obligations of honour compelled Britain to send help to Greece when the German threat became imminent. Severely weakening our defences in Africa (and so permitting Rommel to gain his first success), we rushed a force of British, New Zealand and Australian troops across the Mediterranean; but before they were fully deployed the German blow fell with great force and speed on the exposed Yugoslav flank. The Greek divisions on the left, far too weak to resist such an onslaught, disintegrated.

Thereupon the Greek Government, having decided that it had no option but to capitulate, asked the British to re-embark in order to save their country further ravagement, and thus, on 24 April, the British had to begin another 'Dunkirk'. In that harrowing experience the Royal and Merchant Navies, ever ready in gallantry, lost two warships and five transports under the incessant hammer-blows struck by the bombers of the Luftwaffe, who from now onwards dominated the sky in immense numbers. Yet, of the 53,000 troops in Greece, 41,000, plus another 10,000 RAF, Greeks and Yugoslavs, were brought safely off in five days and nights. Among them was the brave young King George of Greece.

The evacuation from the shores of Greece was made memorable by the first of the Victoria Crosses to be won by New Zealanders in the Second World War.

Sergeant Jack Hinton, a driver in civilian life and a man of strong, rugged features, was then aged 31. On 28 April he was in the New Zealand Division's reinforcement unit. The unit was awaiting embarkation at the port of Kalamata, on the southern shore of the Peloponnesus, together with some 6,000 other NZ, British and Australian troops, mostly non-combatants without arms.

The situation was tense. A squadron of British warships was due to arrive after dark to take off the stranded troops, but German armoured columns of the 5th Panzer Division were racing across the Peloponnesus to forestall them and at 8 o'clock, just as the troops began to move down to the harbour in the gathering darkness, the advance guard of the Panzers, composed of armoured cars, motor-borne infantry, guns and mortars, crashed in and reached the quays.

Then occurred a dramatic outburst of what might be called a mass fighting spirit. Someone seemed to have passed an order to the embarkation parties to 'retire to cover', but, in spite of their unpreparedness, many small parties reacted with instinctive offensiveness. One, and perhaps the mainspring for this outburst, was led by Sergeant Hinton, who shouted: 'To hell with this, who'll come with me?'

Quickly organizing covering fire, he launched himself with great daring against one of the big 6-inch guns near the quayside. When he was a cricket-pitch length from its muzzle the gun fired in his face. The shell missed him and he immediately threw in two grenades with such accuracy that the whole gun detachment was wiped out. Followed by a crowd of eager Kiwis, Hinton made for the other gun, but the detachment fled before him and took refuge in nearby houses. Hinton went after them, smashed in windows and doors and went in with the bayonet. He repeated the performance in a second house.

All along the quays and in the town other parties began to hunt down the Panzers in the dark. A German official account tells of their two 6-inch guns and their anti-tank guns firing 'shot after shot' and of how 'the British come out from side streets, jump from house to house, shoot from the windows, welling up in every garden and lane'.

A series of confused and deadly affrays went on for several hours, but the British counter-attacks were pressed home with such determination, by rifle, bayonet and grenade alone, that, by 1 a.m. on the 29th, the Germans had been driven right out of the town, leaving a hundred dead or wounded in the streets and another hundred or more captured.

The way was thus open for the embarkation to go forward, but, unhappily, the ships standing by offshore were led, by a series of misunderstandings, to believe that all was lost and they made out to sea again. Only a few hundreds were taken off next morning and the remainder were obliged to submit to the Nazis. Among their number was the gallant Hinton, who was sharply wounded early in the fighting and who learned of the award of his Victoria Cross six months later while a prisoner of war.

The 'Kiwis'

At this, our first mention of the New Zealanders, we should pause in our narrative for a moment to look at a formation of which we shall see a great deal and which before long was to attract the admiration of friend and foe alike.

The 2nd New Zealander Division, wearing its fern-leaf emblem, was composed of men who had a particularly fine fighting spirit. They were commanded by that great warrior, Major-General Bernard Freyberg, who in 1914 had taken service in the British Army, had risen astronomically from subaltern to brigadier, had been wounded nine times, bearing 27 scars, and had won the VC and the DSO with two bars. He was to be wounded three times more in the campaigns to come. Of massive and athletic physique (and therefore often nicknamed 'Tiny'), he was described by Winston Churchill as a man of 'unconquerable heart'. He saw every situation through the eyes of a front-line subaltern and, though not distinguished as a tactician, had a remarkable 'feel' of the battlefield.

In addition to Freyberg, one other officer was already wearing the crimson ribbon. This was the tall and wiry Lt-Colonel L. W. Andrew, CO of 22 Battalion, who had won it in the First World War as a corporal. His battalion was to win another before long. The man on whom our main interest will be centred, however, was a junior officer of mature years, who was to achieve the phenomenal distinction of winning two VCs. He was to do this not by single acts alone but in each instance by a long and sustained sequence of brilliant and fearless leadership. We have therefore to follow him through three chapters of this book.

Charles Upham was at that time a second-lieutenant. Aged 30, he was in every way a remarkable person. The son of a lawyer in Christchurch and educated at Christ's College in the English public-school tradition, and later at Lincoln Agricultural College, he became first a farmer and then a land valuer. This conventional upbringing partially concealed certain mainsprings of his character which were not released until touched off by the trigger of battle. Though of small stature, he was strong and wiry, with a very fine head marked by a large, firm, resolute mouth. Like so many other men in these pages, he was a heavy pipe-smoker. Unlike them, he was obstinate, pugnacious, independent, blunt, tactless, hard-swearing, highly strung, careless in his dress.

Upham was described by a fellow-countryman as a 'well-educated rough diamond'. Outwardly rough he may have been, but diamond he certainly was. Beneath his dour exterior lay an utter integrity and a fine and generous spirit. He seems to have been infused from the beginning with a strong patriotism for the Empire and hatred for Nazi Germany, and to him all Germans were, as in the 1914 war, 'Huns'.

The war moulded Charles Upham into a magnificent fighting machine. 'War', he said, 'means fighting', and from the moment of his enlistment in the ranks in 1939 he dedicated himself entirely to mastering the tools and techniques of fighting at his own level. He became expert in the handling of rifle and bayonet, Bren-gun and, above all, the hand-grenade. When he became a sergeant and later a junior officer, he engrossed himself also in the tactical handling of a platoon. In everything that he did he was intense. Devoted to the interests and training of his platoon, he was indifferent to his own personal comforts, was scornful of wounds and sickness and, whenever there was a dangerous job to be done, he did it himself. In fine, he was a superb junior leader. He was impatient of formal military drills and duties but, when necessary, performed them admirably. So also, when called upon, he could shed his untidy habits and turn himself out as smartly as anyone.

To these qualities Upham added an acute modesty: when in later years he won Empire-wide fame as a double VC, he became acutely embarrassed and shut himself up like a clam.

Upham spent all his service in 20th NZ Battalion, which was fortunate to be commanded in the early operations by another remarkable figure in Howard Kippenberger, a lawyer by trade but a natural-born soldier, who was followed by the able Jim Burrows.

Unequal Odds

Though our effort to rescue Greece won the applause of President Roosevelt, it was a bad moment for Britain. Our forces throughout the Middle East (whom General Sir Archibald Wavell directed from Cairo as Commander-in-Chief) were severely strained, fighting several campaigns simultaneously in distant territories, committed to the defence of an enormous area and constantly nagged by Churchill to make military bricks without straw.

All was not yet lost for Greece, however. There was still the venerable Minoan island of Crete, a much-prized jewel of the Greek crown, and an island of much strategic value to both sides. Thither we withdrew some 19,000 of our forces from Greece and, together with the standing garrison of the island (14th Infantry Brigade), began hurried preparations for its defence and to embark upon a battle such as there has never been in the world's history.

Crete was within hopping distance of enemy-occupied Greece, but nearly 400 miles from Alexandria. Physically it was no more than a chain of rocky mountains erupting suddenly from the sea, reaching up to more than 8,000 feet in Tennyson's 'many fountained Ida' and haunted by memories of ancient culture and mythology. It was the birthplace of Zeus himself. Lying east to west it was about 160 miles long, with an average width of only about 35 miles.

Crete

The rough-hewn spine of mountains that ran its whole length was disposed in a manner peculiarly difficult for its defence. Its knuckly crest hugged the southern shore, so that the slope here was very sharp, the sea at its foot very deep, with no landing places other than a few tiny fishing harbours.

Northwards the mountain slope was more gradual, though riven into deep and rocky corrugations by small sparkling streams, until it flattened out somewhat to provide access in a few places for ships and aircraft. Thus the northern shore was the more exposed and vulnerable, especially as it looked directly towards Greece. In General Freyberg's words, Crete 'faced the wrong way'.

Along this northern shore were the only four gates that offered much promise to an aggressor. At about the centre was antique Heraklion, which possessed the best airfield and port, and so was a major danger spot. Farther west was Retimo, with a small airfield and possible landing beaches. Westward again was Suda Bay, where the Royal Navy had a very important refuelling base. Finally, there was a small airstrip of red earth, littered with wrecked British aircraft, close to the small village of Maleme; though the least important, this, in the event, was to prove the critical point. We must particularly note also a picturesque town poised on the rocky coast, its gleaming white walls embowered with poplars, tamarisk and jasmine. This was Canea, the capital of the island. The Canea-Suda area was to be the Germans' chief objective.

Connecting these towns on the north coast was the one and only good road, the few routes that straggled over the mountains from north to south being rough and tortuous tracks. Communications for an army were thus very difficult.

A land of antique beauty composed in tones of soft green and silver-grey overlying Devon-red soil, Crete was planted (to the vexation of those who had to fight in it) with innumerable olive groves, vineyards, almonds and small patches of cornfield, with clusters of the tall, green spires of cypress, thickets of bamboo and hedges of prickly pear here and there, and generous sprinklings of the many beautiful wild flowers for which Crete is famous. Movement was constricted and fields of fire limited. Hill and valley were thickly studded with picturesque villages and hamlets of white stone, squat, flat-roofed and adorned and scented with jasmine, oleander, myrtle and tamarisk. They were inhabited by kindly and sturdy souls, all of whom, to the surprise and resentment of the Germans, were ardently devoted to the British, and many of whom, when the bitter days came, were to face the Nazi firing squads, often 20 at a time, in barbarous retribution for aiding a British soldier. In Crete was to be written one of the blackest pages of Nazi infamy.

Full and reliable information on the German intention to invade the island quickly came to the British Intelligence from their active and daring agents. The operation was directed by Colonel-General Wilhelm List, commander of 4th Air Fleet. Under him were two powerful air corps. The 8th Air Corps, commanded by General von Richthofen, mustered no fewer than 700 bombers and fighters. The 11th was led by General Kurt Student, a leading practitioner of the new technique of airborne invasion, under whom were another 550 aircraft and 22,750 combat troops of high quality. These troops included the 7th Air Division, all parachutists of dark and sinister repute, and the crack Assault Regiment, representing the elite of Nazi Youth, organized in three battalions of parachutists and one of glider-borne troops. Student was also given 9,000 mountain troops, with more at call, some of whom would be landed by transport aircraft and others by sea. The technique was that the parachutists and glider-borne troops should seize the airfield and the ports, whereupon the mountain troops would pour into the footholds so secured. It was by far the largest and most formidable aerial force ever hitherto assembled, and for this great chance Student's soldiers, baulked of their hopes of invading England the year before, were eagerly waiting. Indeed, the invasion of Crete had been planned in outline six months before.

On the British side the omens were far from propitious. Wavell himself flew in from Cairo and accepted a good defence plan prepared by the Royal Marine Major-General Eric Weston, who had flown in a week or two before, but at the special request of Churchill he appointed Bernard Freyberg as the overall commander.

The situation confronting Freyberg was bleak. He had only two well-equipped formations at hand. One was the British 14th Infantry Brigade, excellent troops,[4] and the other was a Royal Marine force of 2,000 men with the cumbersome title of Mobile Naval Base Defence Organization, recently arrived. Its combat elements consisted only of coast-defence and antiaircraft artillery, very good material but not organized or trained for infantry work. They were commanded by Eric Weston, tall, gaunt, brainy, very brave, but slightly temperamental, with the breezy Lt-Colonel Jack Wills as his senior staff officer.

The troops evacuated from Greece, however, were destitute of everything but their clothes, though most of the infantry had managed to keep their rifles. No guns, no mortars, no machine-guns. Even after borrowing from the Royal Marines and the Welch Regiment, there were crippling shortages in vehicles, signal equipment and entrenching tools. More serious still was the loss of all fighting aircraft. At the start there were some 40 RAF fighters on the island. These faced the overwhelming odds with their customary devotion, but by the 19th they had been reduced to seven, which were then withdrawn at Freyberg's own request. Thus, beyond the range of fighter aircraft from Egypt, the garrison faced the grim prospect of having to fight the coming airborne attack without air support of their own. The three airfields became serious liabilities, openly inviting Student's troops. Furthermore, the garrison had to be prepared to face invasion by sea also, a threat which severely strained their resources and which was to

---

[4] Then 2nd Leicestershire, 1st Welch, 2nd York and Lancaster, 2nd Black Watch.

keep them 'looking over their shoulders' when the airborne attack began.

Preparations were hurried forward with the few means available. Lacking picks and shovels, the resourceful troops dug weapon-pits with their steel helmets. Wavell, at his wits' end for men and the tools of war, managed somehow to scrape together a few reinforcements from beyond the Mediterranean, brought at fearful hazard and with heavy losses by the Royal Navy and by many a gallant merchant ship. A hotchpotch of about 48 makeshift field-guns was landed, mostly captured enemy weapons, and many lacking even their sights. A squadron of the 3rd Hussars from the besieged garrison of Tobruk arrived at Suda under Major Gilbert Pack, equipped with 16 outworn light tanks, described by Roy Farran, one of their Troop leaders, as 'armoured perambulators'. Their ship was bombed and sunk at Suda; other hands failing, the hussars themselves turned stevedore and, while the bombs still fell, rescued their tanks from under water, but their precious wireless sets were lost. Six of the tanks went to Heraklion.

The gunners without guns, the drivers without vehicles, the sappers without tools, the signallers without radio or telephones were issued with rifles and formed into makeshift infantry units. In the NZ Division (which lacked one of its three brigades) most of these were assembled into an extempore brigade, called 10th Brigade, commanded by Howard Kippenberger, known as the 'infantillery'. Most were good material but quite ignorant of infantry work.

Thus at length a garrison was built up which on paper numbered 30,000 British and Dominion troops, many of them untrained in the use of arms, together with 11,000 extremely raw, wretchedly equipped Greeks. Thinly spread out over 100 miles, the garrison was totally inadequate and for movement had to rely mainly on their legs. The administrative difficulties were enormous, including the feeding of 15,000 Italian prisoners captured by the Greeks in Albania.

Nevertheless, by the second week of May, Freyberg was able to report that he was hopeful, though not fully confident, that the island could be held. Setting up his Force HQ in a quarry in the neck of Akrotiri peninsula, he appointed Brigadier Edward Puttick to command the attenuated NZ Division in his stead and, in pursuance of Weston's plan, disposed his forces in four sectors. The main elements (as finally deployed when the battle had begun) were:

> MALEME SECTOR (stretching from the airfield to Canea, an area 12 miles long by two): 2nd NZ Division.
>
> SUDA SECTOR (General Weston): 1st MNBDO, two battalions of 19th Australian Brigade under Brigadier G. S. Vasey, 1st Welch Regiment, some companies of the Rangers (9 KRRC) and 1,250 'infantillery'. Among the last-named we should note especially 280 men of the Northumberland Hussars, under Major R. W. Rogerson, and about the same number of the Lancashire Hussars under their able and fearless CO, Tim Hely.
>
> RETIMO: Australian units under the inspiring command of Lt-Colonel Ian Campbell.
>
> HERAKLION (Brigadier B. H. Chappel): 14th British Infantry Brigade (less 1st Welch), some more Australians and some 'infantillery'.

In each sector there were two or more Greek battalions, together with British or Australian anti-aircraft units, mostly unequipped for defence against infantry attack. The British 7th General Hospital, in tents and caves, was on the coast west of Canea, in the NZ sector, and a naval tented hospital was situated south of Canea.

Meanwhile the German air squadrons steadily stepped up their offensive measures. Virtually unopposed, 8th Air Corps bombed the island at will, destroying British aircraft on the ground, powdering everything with red dust, and dominated the sea approaches also. Fourteen British and Greek ships were sunk in Suda Bay, over which hung a monstrous pall of smoke, thickening and extending daily.

Petty Officer Sephton

It was, in fact, at sea that the first VC of Crete was won, serving to remind us that at all times His Majesty's ships, together with many gallant British and other merchant ships, were facing deadly risks and enduring fearful strains to support the garrison. Every day, long and bitter battles were fought with the swarms of Nazi bomber aircraft of all sorts that harried them all the hours of daylight. On 18 May there occurred one of those incidents that showed the Luftwaffe Nazi pilots at their worst. On the whole, the German soldier on land (when in combat with British forces) respected the Red Cross emblem. But not the German airmen. They had already sunk four hospital ships in the evacuation from Greece. They also on several occasions bombed and machine-gunned sailors struggling in the sea after their ships had been sunk. Now they attacked another hospital ship, the *Aba*, just off the coast of Crete.

The *Aba*, full of wounded and sick, was on passage for Palestine. In accordance with the Geneva rules, she was painted white, with the Red Cross emblem prominently displayed on several parts of her hull and superstructure. She was thus extremely conspicuous, as she was intended to be, and there could be no possible mistaking of her status. Yet, on the afternoon of that day, she was attacked by a flight of Stuka dive-bombers, which dropped eight heavy bombs on her, but all missing. *Aba*'s captain sent out a call for help and in response Rear-Admiral Glennie, commanding a patrol force several miles away, dispatched HMS *Coventry* and two other light cruisers to her aid at full speed.

HMS *Coventry* was an old First War light cruiser converted into an anti-aircraft ship, temporarily commanded by Lt-Commander Dalrymple-Hay. She had a main armament of ten 4-inch high-angle-fire guns and several of smaller calibres. The fire of these guns was controlled by the gunnery officer (Lieutenant Horace Law) from an air defence position above the bridge, for which purpose he had at his service large and elaborate optical apparatuses known as directors, manned by teams of picked hands. Here a complex of instruments focused on the target, observing its range, height and bearing, and, by electric circuits, directed the fire of the guns on the aircraft's predicted position in the sky.

One of the directors was installed on top of the fore-mast tripod and the other in a steel tower close abaft the mainmast; both stood high above the deck and so were extremely exposed. In *Coventry* one of these director-towers was commanded by Lieutenant J. M. Robb, and the hands manning the instruments were Chief Petty Officer Davenport, Petty Officer Alfred Edward Sephton, Able Seaman Stanley Fisher and Corporal Bill Symmons (Royal Marines).

Sephton, who will claim our chief attention, was a rating of the Regular service, just 30 years old, with 14 years' service. He was tall, slim, strong and typical of the best class of the lower-deck sailors that the Navy turns out — quiet, clean-cut, of equable disposition, expert at his own level and dedicated to the Navy since boyhood. He was one of six children born to a sergeant-major of the Royal Artillery and had been brought up in Wolverhampton in a happy and well-ordered family. Besides his other qualifications, he was a diver and had been captain of the football team of HMS *Ajax*. To his shipmates he was known as John. On this occasion Sephton was director-layer in one of the towers and, as such, was the key man in his crew.

Steel-helmeted, the close-packed crew of the director waited and watched in their high tower as *Coventry* moved at speed in the hot afternoon sun. Sephton and Fisher were sitting back to back. All eyes were searching the brilliant blue vault of the heavens. As *Coventry* approached *Aba* they saw at a distance that an enemy aircraft was circling very low over the hospital ship, glinting like polished steel against the sky. At the same time the radar reported the approach of more aircraft, and very soon afterwards a formation of eight Stukas appeared and made straight for *Aba*. Dalrymple-Hay manoeuvred so as to give her the best protection and *Coventry*'s guns went into action, putting up a deterrent barrage; whereupon the enemy aircraft broke formation and swung aside to attack the warships.

A short but violent action ensued, the incidents following each other with lightning rapidity. The Stukas peeled off in pairs from their flight formation and then, hawklike, stooped for their dives in pairs. The first two came at *Coventry* from astern, one on each quarter, with the declining sun behind them, very difficult to see and to keep within the field of a telescope.

Every gun in *Coventry* that could bear engaged them, their muzzles almost at the perpendicular, the blasts of the 4-inch guns under-scored by the excited chatter of the multiple pompoms, the sky stippled with shell-bursts and streaked with tracers. With considerable daring the Stukas dived steeply through the barrage and dropped their bombs. Huge fountains of water were thrown up on either hand, drenching the gun crews on deck. A few men were hit by bomb splinters and some ammunition was set on fire, but the ship was not hit. As the Stukas pulled out of their dives, however, just above *Coventry*'s mastheads they opened fire with their heavy machine-guns on the director-towers.

At the first burst Sephton was very severely wounded in the back, the bullets penetrating to the stomach. He flopped forward on to his telescope, but immediately pulled himself erect again and with a great effort of will brought himself back to the eye-pieces. His vision was swimming and he said to Davenport: 'I can't see.' He clung on none the less and continued to direct the fire of his guns, bracing himself against the director. 'In mortal pain and faint with loss of blood,' declares the official citation, 'he stood fast to his duty without fault.' Dripping with blood, he clung on and kept his guns on their targets to such good effect that the aim of the Nazi pilots was so badly shaken that not a single bomb hit the ship. After further attacks, made with less and less determination, they broke off the engagement and flew away. Though none of them was seen to be immediately shot down, fragments of aircraft were seen to drop off and later reports suggested that few of them reached home.

Throughout the action Sephton bore himself with the utmost gallantry and devotion and his courage did not cease with the last shot. Fisher had also been wounded behind him and had similarly clung to his post, but as both lay on the platform waiting to be carried down the steel ladder, Sephton insisted that Fisher should be taken down first. Sephton's wounds, however, were mortal and his citation ends with the tribute that 'thereafter until his death his valiant and cheerful spirit gave heart to the wounded. His example inspired his shipmates and will live in their memory.'

He died very soon afterwards in the sick-bay and was committed to the deep. After the death of his parents his Victoria Cross passed into the hands of his eldest sister, Mrs Eva Bull. A collector offered her £2,000 for it but, she said to the author, 'Money does not buy honour.' Instead, she gave the Cross to Coventry Cathedral, in whose safe keeping it still is, as well as a memorial plaque to the other old hands of HMS *Coventry*.

Meanwhile ashore the garrison waited among the olive groves. The Germans bombed them daily and the fighters darted in and machine-gunned them from treetop level. The weather was very hot. Around them stretched the brilliant peacock-blue of the Mediterranean. They bathed and were refreshed. Their morale was exceedingly high. The hospitable Cretans loaded them with armfuls of oranges. On Akrotiri Peninsula, high above Suda Bay, the Northumberland Hussars, armed now with rifles instead of anti-tank guns, looking out from the tomb of Venizelos, thought the scenery 'theatrically beautiful'. Those who knew their classics saw in imagination the caves and rocky clefts of the mountains peopled with the mysterious creatures of mythology.

The ancient gods were now to witness a combat such as would have staggered even Homer's legendary heroes.

Assault by Air

The attack came on 20 May. It was launched with all the concentrated power and intensity of a German *blitzkrieg* and was directed first of all against the Suda and Maleme sectors. From the airfields of Greece and its adjacent islands 1,280 aircraft took off. Sixteen thousand men, the pride of Nazi youth, were put into the air in relays. Ten thousand were parachutists. Seven hundred and fifty of the crack Assault Regiment were glider-borne. Five thousand stood by in big transport aircraft. Yet another 7,000 embarked in small ships. The orders to the airborne troops were to capture Suda Bay and all three airfields on the first day.

In Crete the day began with the usual dawn bombing about 6 a.m. When it was over, the troops stood down and went to their breakfasts. They had scarcely finished when they became aware that a 'profound throbbing' was disturbing the peace above the peacock sea. 'The heavens shook,' said the Northumberland Hussars, 'as with the Wrath of God.' A few moments later 450 bombers swept in and began to pulverize the ground all the way from Maleme to Suda Bay. Under the weight of their blows 'the ground trembled as in a continuous earthquake'. An immense pall of red dust and smoke enveloped the scene. The sky became perforated with balls of smoke as the British anti-aircraft guns opened fire, and with long streaks of denser black as here and there the enemy aircraft were shot down. The British 7th General Hospital and the NZ 6th Field Ambulance near Canea were bombed and machine-gunned at 0 feet despite their huge Red Cross emblem clearly displayed.

Even before the bombing had stopped, fleets of huge, wide-winged gliders swept in, towed by big, three-engined bombers and each carrying about ten men; their very silence, said Kippenberger, was 'inexpressibly menacing'. Immediately on their heels other enemy squadrons flew in very low and the azure sky became densely stippled, as though with confetti, as showers of white and coloured parachutes broke open and drifted to the ground among the clouds of red dust. The

German attacks, prosecuted in wave after wave, were pressed home with great resolution and daring, regardless of very heavy losses in aircraft and men, including the commanders of both the 7th Air Division and the Assault Regiment.

So began the first battle of its kind in history. For a brief moment the garrison, all the way from Maleme to Suda, stood spellbound at the astonishing spectacle. Then, with the same spontaneity as the troops at Kalamata had shown, every man grabbed his rifle and fell upon the invaders. Whenever they dropped within or close to a defended area there occurred what the official histories described as 'a great slaughter' as the parachutists, clad in green-and-yellow camouflage overalls and carrying Schmeisser machine-pistols, hung in the air or were caught in the vulnerable moments of landing; many were trapped in trees, on roof-tops, in cactus bushes and on telegraph wires. Others were hunted down as they tried to assemble together in formed bodies and to collect their heavy weapons from their coloured parachutes. The Cretans, men and women, armed with everything from shotguns to carving knives, joined fervently in the lethal hunt. On the extreme west of the island the boy-soldiers of the isolated 1st Greek Regiment wiped out a whole company of parachutists, killing 53 and capturing the rest. The 8th Greeks also had a good killing in the hills south of Prison Valley.

In the New Zealand sector the cry went up from olive grove to vineyard: 'The bastards are landing.' By platoons and sections the Kiwis pounced on them among the olives, the vines, the rocks and the houses. Lieutenant Roy Farran, of the 3rd Hussars, led out a troop of his ancient light tanks and joined the New Zealanders. Not least of the remarkable incidents in this sector was the behaviour of the prisoners in the NZ Field Punishment Centre under Lieutenant Roach.

Releasing them from custody at the last moment, he issued them with rifles and ordered: 'Get out there at once.' The defaulters burst upon the invaders with an ardour that later won the remission of their sentences. Capturing several German machine-guns and commandeering a donkey for transport, they turned the guns effectively upon the enemy. It was here that the burly Sergeant Clive Hulme, of the provost staff, began the remarkable series of feats of daring which was to lead to his Victoria Cross, as will later be recorded.

With the object of gaining quick possession of Suda Bay and its port, the Germans directed particularly strong attacks on the Akrotiri Peninsula and west of Suda Town. In the latter area the Royal Marines, in the words of Jack Wills, 'polished them off pretty quickly' and marched off some 400 prisoners to Canea town jail. The extempore infantry of the Lancashire Hussars, under Lt-Colonel Tim Hely, locked up another large party in the dungeons of an old Turkish fort.

Against Akrotiri, clearly a key position, 150 men of the Assault Regiment were launched in 15 gliders under Captain Altmann. All were killed or captured by the amateur infantry of the Northumberland Hussars and the more expert men of the Welch Regiment. Most of the gliders were shot down in the air, Captain Evans, of the Welch, personally dropping four with a Bren-gun. Those Germans who succeeded in landing fought with great spirit and treated honourably the few British whom they temporarily captured.

South of Canea, however, a glider-borne force overran a section of Royal Marines anti-aircraft guns, which had no means of defence against infantry. They then lined up the unarmed gunners and shot them to death. After this act of butchery the Nazis occupied the gun emplacements and adjacent houses with five machine-guns and a large stock of grenades, which they threw with great accuracy. Later they were attacked and overcome, after determined resistance, by a scratch force of marines led by Major D. H. W. Saunders, handsomely supported by the carrier platoon of the 1st Welch under Sergeant Beney.

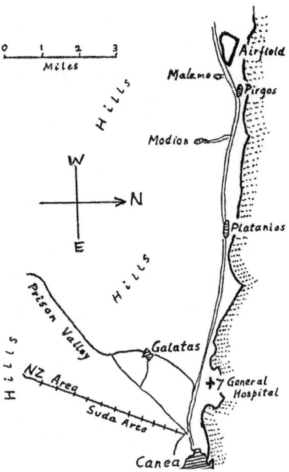

Crete: the New Zealand Sector

One German company landed in the undefended area adjacent to the General Hospital and the NZ Field Ambulance near Canea. Violating the Red Cross emblems clearly displayed, they attacked both, shot the unarmed CO of the Field Ambulance (Lt-Colonel J. L. H. Plimmer) and, at pistol point, drove out the 300 patients, many of them barefoot and in hospital pyjamas, even using them as a shield while trying to join up with another party; until they met swift retribution at the hands of a rescue party sent out by 18th NZ Battalion.

Throughout that morning, and indeed throughout the whole eleven days of the battle, the sorest trial that the garrison had to endure was the incessant low-level machine-gunning by the German aircraft. For all the hours of daylight they ranged the battlefield at will, screaming down to 0 feet, blazing at every disclosed position, swooping down on any movement, and even chasing single men. Even Freyberg had on several occasions 'to run for my life'. The incessant harassment became in time a severe strain, but in the absence of the RAF there was little to be done but endure it.

In the afternoon came the turns of Heraklion and Retimo. Both were subjected to the same treatment as the other sectors — heavy bombings followed immediately by parachute landings — and in both the results were the same. The British and Australians, all troops of high quality, reacted with energy and spirit. The invaders were firmly held off, with heavy losses. At Heraklion, out of 2,000 parachutists dropped, 1,440 were killed or captured. At Retimo the enemy made a dangerous penetration towards the airstrip but Ian Campbell, by instant and repeated counter-attacks, regained control and kept it. The town itself was gallantly held by the armed Cretan police.

Thus by evening of the first day the enemy assaults had so far completely failed. Everywhere the olive groves, vineyards and village streets were thick with German dead. In the New Zealand sector, however, two sensitive spots developed where the enemy were able to begin assembling in formed bodies. One of these was in what became known as Prison Valley, a wide, open plain, a little south of the tactically important village of Galatas, ideal for parachute landings and dominated by the large white, rectangular prison, equally ideal as a firm base for the invaders and in the charge of a pro-German governor. Here some particularly raw Greek troops were quickly scattered and about 1,500 Germans began cautiously to come together. Their objective was Canea-Suda, which they were required to capture that same day. They were foiled in their possession of an important hill by a blond, well-turned-out young English captain attached to the Greek Military Mission, named Michael Forrester, of the Queen's Regiment, who quickly reorganized a company or so of the 6th Greek Regiment and, 'tootling a tin whistle', led them in a 'mad bayonet charge' up the hill. Somewhat oddly, the Germans fled at their approach.

The other area penetrated proved to be far more dangerous. A German force dropped to the west of the vital Maleme airfield in an area unoccupied by the New Zealanders. Another dropped in the hills just to the south, similarly unoccupied. Each party gradually assembled in formed bodies, collected their mortars and machine-guns from the coloured parachutes and began to exert pressure against 22nd NZ Battalion under Lt-Colonel Andrew, VC. As elsewhere, the 'fog of war' enveloped the battlefield, accentuated by the physical fog of red dust from the continuous bombing, by the acute shortage of signal equipment, and by the snarling Messerschmitts that continuously swept the ground with machine-guns. The dispersed platoons became pinned to the ground and by evening, all attempts at contact failing, events forced Andrew to the conclusion (mistakenly) that his two westerly companies, including that holding the airfield itself, had been overcome.

Darkness fell. The German aircraft ceased their harassing. The sounds of battle gave way to the raucous night-song of the frogs and the braying of frightened donkeys. The dead lay at peace among the wild flowers. At midnight, with permission, Andrew withdrew 22 Battalion to a line east of Pirgos, leaving the Maleme airfield open to the enemy.

The Airfield Lost

From that moment things began to go wrong. No attempt was made that night to restore the situation at Maleme. Freyberg and his brigadiers were faced with an unprecedented tactical situation. There was no 'front', except the immensely long and dangerous coastline. They had not been well advised on the technicalities of airborne operations and had been led to believe that the big troop-carrying transport aircraft that would follow the parachutists could land more or less anywhere, which was certainly untrue of the rugged terrain of Crete. Accordingly, Maleme did not appear to them to be of paramount importance and Freyberg was obliged also to keep troops in hand for an invasion by sea, which, he was advised from Cairo, could be expected the next night.

In fact, up till midnight the Germans had virtually lost the battle already. Their strength was almost spent; not a single airfield had been captured for their troop-carrying craft and their losses had been huge. They were within an ace of abandoning the operation, but that night Student, sitting anxiously in the Hotel Grande Bretagne in Athens, decided to make a final effort next day, throwing in the last of his parachutists in an attempt to capture Maleme, which he did not yet know had been evacuated but which seemed to offer the least desperate chance; Heraklion and Retimo clearly seemed denied.

At midday on the 21st he accordingly dropped a force of some 360 men in the area east of Pirgos, with orders to capture Maleme, but once more they were quickly gobbled up by the New Zealanders, only 80 escaping to take refuge in Pirgos. Transport aircraft that landed on the beach were shot to pieces by the makeshift artillery and by some tanks of 3rd Hussars.

By now, however, Student knew that Maleme had been unaccountably evacuated and he immediately began to exploit the golden opportunity. Soon after 5 o'clock squadrons of big Junkers, handled by daring pilots in the face of fire, began to fly in a battalion of mountain troops and heavy weapons. A new and dangerous phase began as the German strength rapidly built up.

That night the New Zealanders made their overdue counterattack on the airfield. It was entrusted to two fine battalions — the Maoris and 20 Battalion, now temporarily commanded by Major Jim Burrows in Kippenberger's stead. Charles Upham, though still suffering from dysentery contracted in Greece, marched with him and was now about to begin that series of exploits which was to lead to his first Victoria Cross.

The airfield had to be taken before daylight, after which it would be impossible to escape decimation by the ground-strafing aircraft. Mischances, however, delayed the move forward of 20 Battalion, who were in a reserve position, and they did not join hands with the Maoris until far too late. From the joint start-line to the airfield lay three miles of difficult terrain known to be infested with scattered nests of the enemy. The axis of advance was the main road via Pirgos, with 20th on the right of it, the Maoris on the left and three of Farran's light tanks on the road itself.

The battalions moved off into the dark, not knowing what enemy they would encounter, until they suddenly clashed with them at a few yards' range. A series of deadly encounters ensued among the houses, in ditches, behind hedges and trees. The German airborne troops were equipped with an exceptionally high complement of machine-guns and other heavy weapons and so commanded twice the fire-power of a normal infantry unit. The automatic fire, Upham said, was the heaviest he ever encountered. Leading the weak 15th Platoon in 20 Battalion's C Company under Captain Den Fountaine, Upham was just to the right of the road, with Farran's tanks to his left, but of little use at night.

Upham encountered the first resistance about a mile from the start-line, while moving over an open field. A heavy machine-gun suddenly burst into life from behind a big tree 50 yards ahead, and four of Upham's platoon were hit. The remainder fell prone and crawled forward on Upham's orders. He then executed a typical infantry manoeuvre, at which he had made his platoon expert. From a range of about 25 yards the sections opened fire on the enemy gun-flashes and the shadows around the tree, while Upham himself, alone, loaded with grenades, crawled round by a flank until he was very close in rear of the enemy, their dark forms now distinguishable. Then he rose to his feet, bowled two grenades and dashed in, throwing another and firing his revolver. When his platoon ran up they saw the small wiry figure of their officer standing beside the machine-gun, with eight parachutists lying dead around him.

Upham was now in a condition that was typical of him in close action: highly stimulated, shouting loudly, swearing heartily. It is said that he always became enraged when any of his men were killed by 'the bastards'. He proceeded to repeat the same action a few minutes later.

On the roadside a house, with a shed attached, stood out against the night horizon. From both house and shed, streams of tracer streaked through the dark as two enemy machine-guns spotted the platoon. The platoon went to ground and opened fire while Upham, running this time with bent head, gained the back of the house and crept round to the shed. Stealthily he planted a grenade within the entrance and moved back round the corner. When the grenade detonated he shouted excitedly to his men: 'Come on, boys!' As his platoon rushed up, a dozen Germans, some without trousers or boots, ran out of the house with hands up, and inside the shed eight lay dead or wounded.

The night was wearing on. There was no time to lose if the airfield was to be retaken before daylight. All along the front of the two battalions similar fierce little actions were being fought, the night alive with the chatter and the tracers of machine-guns and the bursts of grenades. As so often in night fighting, the Germans tended to fire high, so Upham got down on hands and knees and led his platoon boldly forward underneath the streams of tracer. Again and again he repeated his typical manoeuvre.

Thus struggling, the forward companies of 20 Battalion reached the village of Pirgos, half a mile from the airfield, dangerously shrouded with thickets of bamboo and strongly held by some 200 Germans of 2nd Parachute Brigade. Dawn had arrived, the sky oyster-grey. A sticky house-to-house fight ensued in the village and the quadruple bursts of two captured Bofors guns were heard assailing Farran's tanks from behind the wall of a cemetery. One, as we shall see, was silenced by the leading tank but the other soon threatened 15th Platoon.

While three men sneaked forward to cover him, Upham crawled up a ditch on his belly and tossed over his grenades accurately, killing the gunner. The whole dangerous village was cleared and 20 Battalion saw Maleme airfield ahead of them.

Daylight, however, put an end to the attempt to recover it. The right-hand company of the 20th had in fact reached the edge of the airfield, now strewn with burning and crashed enemy aircraft, but to cross its exposed surface in daylight was impossible. Every minute large transport aircraft were landing the troops of 5th Mountain Division and their fire power was rapidly increasing. Burrows, himself right forward with Upham's platoon, called a halt and ordered Upham to send 'two very good men' to the isolated right-hand company with orders to withdraw to an assembly point. It was a dangerous mission, across half a mile of open fire-swept ground and it was typical of Upham that he went himself, taking with him his gallant sergeant, David Kirk. Killing several more Germans on the way, they gained the right flank safely and Upham, lighting his pipe, stayed with the company and guided them back.

Throughout the whole night's fighting Upham had shown first-class junior leadership in a most impressive display of aggressive infantry action, and he had begun to win his VC.

Immediately after this in the same village of Pirgos, an act of gallantry by Farran's leading tank met with no reward. It was commanded by Sergeant Skedgewell, with Trooper Charles Wilds as gunner and Trooper Cook as driver. Reaching a road junction at the entrance to the village, Skedgewell very properly halted, according to his training. To have driven headlong into the narrow streets of a defended village would have been foolhardy. Taunted by a New Zealand officer, however,

Skedgewell did so and ran into the kind of trap that awaits tanks or cavalry in such a place.

As he passed the corner of the cemetery wall, he was assailed at point-blank range in his sensitive broadside by the two captive Bofors guns concealed in a typical defilade position. The tank was holed and Wilds was very severely wounded, one of his legs being nearly severed. With great courage he instantly swung round and replied with his 0.5-inch machine-gun, with which he knocked out the first gun and killed its detachment.

Although nearly fainting, he then turned to the second gun, while Cook tried to swing the tank to face the enemy. Before he could do so the tank was hit again amidships and set on fire. Skedgewell, in Farran's words, 'was smashed up in his seat' and Cook was hit in the foot. Wilds, in a dying condition, continued to engage the second gun and silenced it sufficiently for Cook, who, despite the acute pain in operating the foot controls, somehow managed to drive the burning tank out. A flight of Messerschmitts then screamed down on the tanks, their machine-guns blazing. The three men were extricated with great difficulty and agony, but Skedgewell and Wilds died before the stretcher-bearers could get them to a doctor. Wilds was later recommended for the Victoria Cross but got nothing. Being dead, he was ineligible for anything else.

The loss of the airfield virtually meant the loss of all Crete. Another hour of darkness would have given the Kiwis possession. If the danger of invasion by sea could have been discounted, the counter-attack could have been made much earlier. In fact, that very night a force of destroyers under Rear-Admiral Glennie utterly routed an invasion fleet aiming for Maleme, while another intended for Heraklion was forced to run for home. The flashes of the guns and the flames of the burning transports were clearly seen all along the NZ sector.

The pity was that the situation had not been restored 30 hours earlier, before the Germans had discovered the withdrawal of Andrew's battalion.

The encircling threat from Prison Valley now began to develop also. This was Kippenberger's sector, hilly and exposed, but he had no trained infantry under his command. The darkening picture was again enlivened in a moment of crisis by the blond Michael Forrester and his Greeks in one of the most stimulating incidents of the battle. Kippenberger was assembling some troops to counter-attack a hill that the enemy had captured when, to his utter surprise, a strange new force burst dramatically upon the scene and relieved him of the necessity. With a 'terrific clamour' and with Forrester leading 20 yards ahead, a motley crowd, in which a company of 6th Greek Regiment was mingled with village men and women, arrived with shotguns and all sorts of antiquated weapons, charged up the hill, 'running, bounding and yelling like Red Indians', and at their approach the Germans again unaccountably turned and fled.

Enemy airborne forces were now pouring in at Maleme and on the beaches. Artillery was being landed. The heat was sweltering, passing 100°. The earth was fouled by the blackening corpses of men and donkeys, swarmed over by clouds of bluebottles. A great stench arose to drown the scents of jasmine and myrtle. Overall lay a powdering of red dust from the blastings of innumerable bombs. Early on Sunday, 23 May, the fourth day of the battle, General Student himself arrived and went forward to put spurs into the unenterprising troops in Prison Valley, which now became the critical area of the battlefield and where the parachutists of 7th Air Division had been joined by 5th Mountain Division, both lavishly equipped with heavy machine-guns and mortars. Here the most vital ground was the picturesque hilltop village of Galatas, whose grey stone walls overhung the scene like a medieval castle. That same afternoon the New Zealanders were subjected to a formal infantry assault, behind a machine-gun barrage from low-flying aircraft, by the equivalent of six battalions, aimed chiefly at Galatas from both south and west. It slowly penetrated Kippenberger's paper-thin line of infantillery and on the extreme coastal flank a dangerous situation arose. The 20th Battalion was quickly pushed in to secure that flank and among them was Charles Upham.

Two days earlier Upham had been wounded in the left shoulder by two mortar-bomb splinters while holding a forward position, and he now wore his arm in a sling. As he took post on Ruin Ridge he was hit again by a spent bullet that lodged in his right foot, but he ignored it. The enemy could be plainly seen preparing to attack. Very soon afterwards they did so, but on 20 Battalion's front were firmly repulsed with heavy loss. On the sector held by Upham's platoon no fewer than 40 enemy dead were counted.

On their left hand, however, the enemy succeeded in making a penetration which they exploited with their customary initiative. Burrow's battalion was in danger of being cut off on the coast and the whole line was threatened with disintegration. Orders came by runner (the only means of communication) for the forward companies to fight their way out to a position north of Galatas, which the enemy was now threatening. Upham then acted in a way that was characteristic of him. He stayed behind to warn other platoons and sent his own back under Sergeant David Kirk, under whose gallant leadership they fought through an enemy company, killing or wounding another 44.

Upham was left alone, with a scattering of enemy all round him. In his right arm he carried a rifle but his left was useless and his foot in some pain, but he was always scornful of wounds and sickness. He picked his way back carefully through some olive trees and had not gone far before he was shot at and saw two Germans moving towards him, armed with submachine guns. As he paused they fired two more shots. At the same instant Upham tripped over an obstruction in the ground and fell flat in some long grass as though shot. Taking advantage of the cover, he crawled awkwardly to the nearest olive tree and cautiously worked his way up into its branches. The two Germans, now only some 30 yards away, were still moving towards him, apparently expecting to find his dead body. Somehow he had to manipulate his rifle with one hand — hold it firm, aim, fire, operate the bolt and fire again. His first shot must be a 'dead cert' and his second must follow as fast as possible.

He rested the rifle in a fork of the tree, ready loaded and cocked. Very coolly, he waited until the leading German was only six yards away. He fired and killed him. The other dashed forward, machine-gun up. Upham's second shot killed him at a range of one yard and the man's body struck the muzzle as he fell.

Night Charge at Galatas

At Heraklion and Retimo, meanwhile, the British and Australians had firmly held their own, but by the evening of the 25th things on the main front were going ill. The New Zealanders were by now dog-tired. Many of those untrained as infantry were drifting from the field. Galatas had been captured. The line seemed about to crack. The Kiwi Concert Party, the band, the storemen and every other available body were put in to plug the gaps. North of the lost village Kippenberger, 'more tired than I have ever been in my life', yet quietly smoking his pipe, was trying to rally the waverers and desperately improvising a scratch force to recapture the village. Roy Farran came up with two 'armoured perambulators', offered his services to the Kiwis and without hesitation clattered alone into Galatas to reconnoitre, his guns blazing into the houses. He found the village 'stiff with Jerries' and reported accordingly to Kippenberger.

Then took place one of the most stirring episodes in the New Zealand annals. In the fading light, the sky turning to dusky violet, some 200 men from various battalions formed up in two parties. With them were a few more Englishmen, conspicuous among whom was the blond Michael Forrester, hatless and carrying a rifle and fixed bayonet, 'itching to go'. From some obscure well-spring of human emotion, tired though they all were, an extraordinary sense of exhilaration swelled within the little force. After days of retiring they were at last to attack. There lay Galatas, 200 yards ahead. Without artillery, without mortars, without preliminaries and with only a single order, the forlorn hope went straight for it as night was falling.

Farran led the way with his two tanks. Behind him, contemptuous of the fire directed at them from the village, the inspired force, breaking into a double, burst out spontaneously into a deep-throated roar which was heard 400 yards away above all other noises of battle. To Lieutenant Thomas it set the blood tingling with an exhilaration like the roar of a big football crowd. To Lt-Colonel John Grey it was 'a deep-throated, beast-like noise'; to Corporal Adams 'a most ungodly row of chaps charging and yelling'.

Farran penetrated right to the centre of the village, but as he rounded a corner there was a blinding flash as his tank was hit by an anti-tank shot, as Skedgewell's had been at Pirgos. Other shots followed rapidly. Farran, his gunner and driver were all badly wounded. Escaping painfully through the driver's hatch, they lay on the roadside as the New Zealanders stormed in like men possessed. Farran shouted: 'Come on New Zealand! Clean them up, New Zealand!'[5]

The Kiwis needed no exhortation. With 'blood-curdling shouts', they swarmed in among the houses. The Germans fought hard, pouring out automatic fire of every sort at muzzle-point from windows, doors and roof-tops, but were overwhelmed by bayonet, rifle-butt, grenade, pistol and bare fist in the roughest of rough-houses. 'Thunder and lightning', said a German account later, 'was in every corner and cranny.' Rooms in which the grenades burst were 'like butcher's shops'. In the main square an enemy force was hastily drawn up for organized resistance, but the New Zealanders went right through them and scattered them in rout.

That day added one more sentence to Sergeant Clive Hulme's citation, as we shall shortly see.

Rear-guard VC

The gallant effort at Galatas was of only temporary avail and the 26th proved to be the day of crisis. South of Prison Valley the 8th Greeks had very gallantly held at bay for three days an enemy flanking force sent across the hills to capture Suda and so cut off the whole British force, but late on the 25th the Greeks were assailed by three battalions of mountain troops and inevitably dispersed. Another Greek battalion stood in the way but forsook the field. The British left flank, held by

---

[5] Roy Farran: *Winged Dagger.*

Vasey's Australians, lay open. This was a blow to the heart. There was yet another withdrawal towards Suda and Freyberg was at last obliged to admit defeat. He signalled to Wavell that his main forces now in the Suda area had 'reached the limit of endurance'. He began preparations for a complete evacuation from the whole island, and placed General Weston in command of all operations in the Suda area.

Unhappily misunderstandings confounded higher councils, now almost destitute of means of communication. Brigadier Puttick, needing to see Freyberg, had to go four miles on foot. Freyberg himself was travelling pillion on a motor-cycle ridden by the Northumberland Hussar Lieutenant M. B. Payne, an accomplished trick rider. While awaiting permission from Cairo (and thence from London) to evacuate, Freyberg insistently ordered a line to be held west and south of Canea, in order to protect some vital shipping due in at Suda that night. Those orders Weston strove to enforce. He moved 1st Welch Regiment up on to the coastal flank west of Canea, with some companies of the Rangers and the Northumberland Hussars in the rear, and ordered the New Zealanders and the Australians to stand where they were.

Tall and cool, Weston went about the field in his jeep, trying to pick up the tangled threads of his new responsibilities and scorning the bombs, which he said were 'nothing to bother about', and scorning likewise the bullets that some Australians shot at him in fear that his movements might invite the marauding Stukas.

He found the New Zealand and Australian brigadiers strongly opposed to Freyberg's order. They considered a further withdrawal essential and, in the confusion that prevailed as the night of the 26th drew on, they withdrew on their own account at about midnight to the position on the outskirts of Suda known as 42nd Street. Hely, commanding the remnant of the Lancashire Hussars, was disconcerted to find an Australian unit streaming back through his ranks in the dark and was obliged to conform.

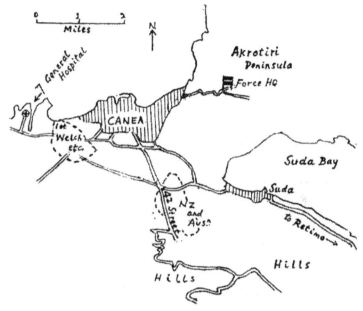

Crete: the Suda Sector on 27 May

The consequences of this independent action were lamentable. The Welch and the units with them on the right flank were isolated and left in the air by the brigadier appointed to command them. Their CO, Lt-Colonel Duncan, discovered that his left flank was wide open. He sent out several patrols to find contact, but they never returned. Two dispatch riders were sent out independently during the night by Jack Wills, Weston's staff officer, with orders for withdrawal, but they never reached Duncan. Accordingly, Duncan stood and fought where he was.

Early on the 27th the Germans gave the Welch a terrific hammering from aircraft, guns and mortars, followed at once by an infantry assault by 4,500 men. Quickly finding Duncan's open flank, they flooded through and also punctured his front in the gaps between his thin-spread companies. To avoid complete collapse, he ordered withdrawal to a position near Suda. After an heroic battle of seven hours in fierce heat, the battalion fought its way out stubbornly step by step, seven officers and 250 men finally getting through. Duncan, himself manning a Bren-gun, took post with a small rear-guard at a critical bridge and fought to the last before being taken prisoner. Elsewhere a sergeant and a dozen men still fought on, surrounded by the enemy, for another whole day. No wonder the enemy themselves proclaimed the Welch to be 'elite troops'. 'They would not surrender,' wrote a German reporter.

The stand of the Welch, forlorn hope though it was, served to give a respite to the New Zealanders and Australians at 42nd Street, and next day, in a dashing and spontaneous attack, they were able to put to flight a German mountain brigade. The move for total evacuation of the island now began. The only practical place — and that a very precarious one — was the very small fishing harbour at Sfakia, on the steep south coast, a 40-mile march across the mountains by a rough and tortuous track. Unhappily, Freyberg could find no means of communicating the order to the garrisons at Retimo and Heraklion. The latter were fortunate to be able to get orders radioed direct from Cairo, 400 miles away, and were evacuated by a small naval force under Rear-Admiral Rawlings, but suffered terrible losses when attacked by the German bombers at sea. The Australian garrison at Retimo, fighting to the last round under the valiant Ian Campbell, had unhappily to be left to their fate, which befell them several days later.

On the main sector the withdrawal operation to Sfakia was put under Weston's command, an operation which 'he personally fought with great gallantry', in the words to the author of Tim Hely, who joined his staff. A good many of the non-combatant units were now in a low state of morale and behaved badly, but the fighting spirit of others was undimmed, exhausted though they were after nine days' continuous fighting with little sleep, food or water. The fine bearing of the Welch, despite their rough handling, was an example to all. The Australians, New Zealanders, a hastily organized battalion of Royal Marines led with conspicuous ability by Major Ralph Garrett, and a newly arrived commando unit under Colonel Robert Laycock formed rear-guards that leap-frogged each other in turns, step by backward step, supported by such tanks of 3rd Hussars as remained, while 42nd Field Company, RE, blew up the mountain track at successive stages. The Germans detached their 100th Mountain Brigade to destroy them, but, as we shall see later, the rear-guards were never penetrated.

The first rear-guard action in the hills brought to a climax a long series of gallant exploits which was to result in the award of the Victoria Cross to a soldier of 23 NZ Battalion.

Sergeant Clive Hulme was a powerfully built, broad-shouldered countryman of 30 years. He was the provost (military police) sergeant of 23 Battalion but at the beginning of the Crete campaign had been detached to serve in the division's Field Punishment Centre. He had thus to be a tough fellow. To these qualities he added an astonishing gift for initiative and leadership, a cool head and remarkable skill at arms. These attributes he had displayed since the beginning of the battle on numerous occasions, either alone or leading small patrols. A dead shot, his speciality was stalking enemy snipers, at which he displayed all the craft of an Indian hunter. Very much an individualist, he fought one-man battles, wandering about the battlefield in search of prey.

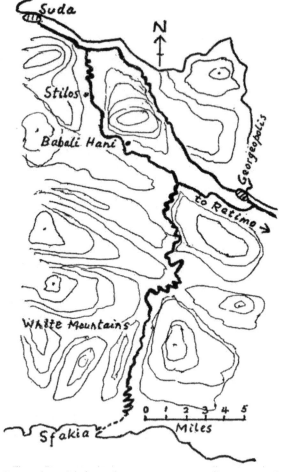

Crete: the withdrawal route, contours diagrammatic

As soon as the enemy parachutists had dropped from the sky on 20 May, the prisoners in the FP Centre, as we have noted, were issued with rifles and led forward by Lieutenant Roach to join 23 Battalion. From there they at once dominated one of the German's main dropping zones. Again and again Hulme took the lead in hunting down the enemy, sometimes alone, sometimes with one or two of the defaulters. He roamed the country on his own initiative, stalking German snipers, invariably with success. At the end of the second day 126 German bodies were counted in this area, most of whom had fallen to Hulme and his patrols.

Three days later Hulme rejoined his own battalion and by this time had acquired from dead parachutists a camouflage blouse and a cap which could be pulled down over the face, revealing only the eyes, and these further assisted the stalking of snipers. Finding a small party of New Zealanders taken prisoner and guarded by only one sentry, and reluctant to shoot for fear of hurting his own countrymen, Hulme stalked the sentry from behind, jumped on him and killed him with a German bayonet.

He played a conspicuous part in the charge at Galatas: his platoon having been held up by an enemy post located in a school, he attacked alone and wiped it out with grenades. On withdrawal next morning, having heard that his brother had been killed, he determined to avenge his death. He therefore dropped behind the withdrawing troops, took cover, waited for the enemy to reappear in the village and shot three of them.

When a conference of senior officers was taking place at a critical moment just before the last battle outside Suda, they came under fire from a hill above them. Hulme at once donned his camouflage clothes, climbed to the back of the hill and spotted a party of four Germans who were harassing the conference. He shot their leader at once. When the others turned to see where the fire had come from, he turned also and was so mistaken for a comrade. When they turned back again he shot two in quick succession and got the fourth just as he was about to return his fire. On his way back Hulme met a fifth German on the hillside and dropped him dead also.

By the time that the retreat began, the story of Hulme's exploits was on everyone's lips. Now, on 28 May, he was to crown his long record with yet one more gallant feat.

A rear-guard position was taken up by 5th Brigade at the straggling village of Stilos, in the foothills of the White Mountains, where the rising southward road crossed a sunken river-bed. It was manned by the remnants of five battalions, including the 23rd. Desperately tired after their last battle and a gruelling night march, the battalions arrived very early in the morning and, after making their dispositions, bedded down to snatch some rough sleep.

Hardly had they put their heads down when they were roused sharply by two officers who, feeling uneasy, had gone out to reconnoitre and, on reaching a stone wall that ran along the crest of a ridge, had discovered a company of Germans, coming out of the sunken river-bed about 400 yards away. The Germans had spotted them also, and their machine-gun bullets whizzed over the ridge.

The 23rd leapt to their arms and Major Thomason, the acting CO, shouted: 'Sergeant Hulme, get some men on top of that hill!' Hulme himself was the first to arrive, but he was only just in time, for the enemy were also racing to possess the ridge. When he reached the wall which ran along the crest they were only 15 yards away. He opened fire at once and, when reinforced, drove the enemy down the hill again. He then calmly sat on the wall and picked off the enemy in the valley below one by one.

Soon afterwards the Germans began to mortar the New Zealanders severely, whereupon Hulme sallied out, penetrated the enemy position, killed all four of the mortar crew and put the mortar out of action. From this position he then worked his way round the left flank and killed three more Germans. Shortly afterwards, while attacking a fourth, he was himself severely wounded in the shoulder.

Throughout the action Hulme's spirited initiative materially assisted the success of the rear-guard action. His VC was awarded for 'most outstanding and inspiring qualities of leadership, initiative, skill, endurance and most conspicuous gallantry' throughout the whole nine days of fighting so far. His total 'bag' of enemy stalked and shot, as witnessed and recorded, amounted to 33.

The Last Brush

The melancholy retreat went on. The way up the barren, treeless, unpeopled mountains became steeper and steeper, the serpentine track more and more rough. The weather was very hot. An extreme scarcity of water brought on the agonies of thirst. The wounded were in acute distress. Ambulances were scarce. Numbers of wounded were carried on stretchers the whole dolorous way, a task as gruelling for the stretcher-bearers as for the wounded. The more seriously wounded, together with their devoted doctors, had to be left behind to fall into the hands of the enemy. Three hundred stretcher cases from the General Hospital were left in caves to save them from the vicious German air pilots who, on several occasions in the retreat, swooped down on ambulances crowded with wounded and shot them to pieces with machine-guns at 0 feet, leaving them bloody, charred and stinking wrecks.

At length the mountains were topped and the steep drop down to Sfakia began. The corkscrew track fizzled out altogether a few miles from the beach and nothing remained but a steep footpath twisting down a ravine among wild rhododendrons, now in full bloom. The sea was in sight. The last rear-guard action was fought, in which Sergeant-Major Childs and Corporal Summers, of the 3rd Hussars, greatly distinguished themselves in the bold handling of their tanks.

On the critical day of 30 May, Freyberg called his senior officers to a conference in a cave above Sfakia beach and gave final orders for the evacuation to begin that night. Not long afterwards shots were heard alarmingly close to the cave. A strong enemy patrol, with mule transport, mortars and machine-guns, having infiltrated through a ravine known as Rhododendron Valley, was seen moving down towards Sfakia itself.

Fortunately 20 NZ Battalion was at hand, and so was Kippenberger. He acted quickly, sending one company to block the ravine frontally, and another to clamber up a very steep rocky spur and take the enemy in the flank on the west. There followed another model little operation by Charles Upham, the last and least in the series that won him the VC, which was awarded essentially for gallant example and leadership throughout the battle. To him now fell the main flanking operations.

The task might well have given pause to many men in full pride of their health, for the spur that they had to climb was 600 feet high and almost cliff-like. All were dog-tired and Upham himself was suffering from his wounds. The bullet that had lodged in his right foot seven days before was still there. Most men would have been satisfied to climb the ridge at its nearest point and bring down fire from there. Not so Upham. He determined to get in behind the enemy, seal their way of escape up the ravine, and wipe them out.

In the heat of the day he started his climb. Dropping off a platoon halfway, he climbed on painfully with only three or four men, covering two stiff miles in two hours. When it seemed that their trembling legs would carry them no farther Upham clambered up on the razor-edged crest of the ridge and beheld the Germans moving about the rhododendrons in the bed of the ravine below. He counted 22 of them, the remainder of a force that had been brought to a halt at the mouth of the ravine. He ordered Private Brown to climb up beside him with a Bren-gun. There, lying precariously across the crest, with the upper part of his body hanging down the reverse slope, Brown opened fire with devastating effect and Upham himself finished off what was left. The whole German force of about 50 was thus wiped out.

That night the dark shapes of four destroyers, under the command of Rear-Admiral E. L. S. King, were discerned at sea and the evacuation from Sfakia beach began. It was resumed on the next night (31 May), with agonizing heartburnings for those who had to be earmarked to stay behind, for the number of ships that could be spared was very small. The orders from Cairo were that priority should be given to the New Zealanders and Australians, so that only a few hundred troops from Britain escaped the prison camp. Through a misunderstanding on the last night, however, the whole of an Australian battalion was unhappily left on the beach.

Many of those left behind, such as Roy Farran and Pipe-Major Robert Roy, of the Black Watch, made daring and skilful escapes. None, perhaps, was more remarkable than that of Ralph Garrett, who, collecting a mixed party of five officers and 13 other ranks, put to sea in an abandoned landing craft and, after ten gruelling days, took them safely back to Egypt over 420 miles of the Mediterranean.

In the records of the Victoria Cross the twelve days of fighting in Crete against enormous odds account for three awards, but the weft of valour runs strongly throughout its heroic fabric. Notwithstanding the errors of their commanders, the courage of the fighting soldiers had never faltered. Had the New Zealand Division been at full strength, with all its artillery, it is quite certain that the German attack would have failed entirely. So also would it have failed if the garrison had had air support. As we know now, it would have indeed failed, straitened though the garrison was, if Maleme could have been held for another 24 hours. The huge price that the Germans paid in men and aircraft was a severe blow to them. The battle report of the 11th Air Corps deplored the 'exceptionally high and bloody losses' in picked soldiers of the highest quality. The 7th Air Division had been virtually destroyed. The flower of their officers lay dead. The wreckage of 250 aircraft and nearly all the gliders scarred the countryside all along the north coast. Another 148 had been damaged. After the war 4,000 German graves were counted from Maleme to Suda, another 1,000 at Heraklion and Retimo. Many more of the thousands of wounded died in Greek hospitals and nearly 1,000 were drowned at sea. Crete, said General Student after the war, was the graveyard of the hopes of the German airborne forces. The threat of similar assaults on Cyprus, Malta and even Alexandria (which Student dreamed of) was forestalled.

Furthermore, the loss of Crete was strategically not a serious blow to the British. To have attempted to hold it would have imposed far too great a strain on all three Services at the expense of operations in a larger field. The Fleet had already lost nine cruisers and destroyers, all sunk by dive-bombers, and another 17 had been damaged. Two thousand sailors had been killed. But Admiral Cunningham, the naval C-in-C, when asked for this last effort, had uttered the immortal words: 'It takes the Navy three years to build a new ship, but it will take 300 years to build a new tradition. The evacuation will continue.'

3: THE BATTLE OF THE ATLANTIC

Battles might be won, territories gained, enterprises prosper, but all were of no avail if Britain should lose the mastery of the ocean routes by which alone she was able to maintain life. For nearly 300 years the structure of British overall strategy had been built on the rock of that principle. Not the Dutch, the French nor the Spaniards could shake it. In the First World War the Germans, breaking the long and honourable traditions of the sea by indiscriminate attacks on all kinds of shipping, often without any attempt at rescue, made a very dangerous attempt but failed. In the Second World War their attempt swelled to raging proportions and had profound effects.

As we have seen in Chapter 2, in the summer of 1941 Britain and her imperial family stood alone against the massive strength of Nazi Germany and Fascist Italy. Our land forces, though weak in effective numbers, had begun to mop up Mussolini's distant African empire in a most satisfactory way, but at the heart of the Empire, amid the torrent of violent events that swept across the world, a long and bitter battle was being raged by sea and air. The fall of France in June 1940 had been followed by the historic Battle of Britain, in which a handful of fearless young fighter pilots of the Royal Air Force had saved Britain from the invasion that Hitler had been preparing. Repulsed in the air, Hitler in his chagrin determined on a policy of starving Britain into surrender by strangling her ocean life-lines. In an historic directive of December that year he ordered: 'The main effort of the Navy will remain unequivocally directed against England.' And in the next month he proclaimed Britain's early ruin by Germany's combined sea and air power, announcing that 'In the spring our U-boat war will begin.' The most significant result was that the main emphasis of the German naval offensive shifted from European waters far out into the Atlantic.

Thus began the long and deadly conflict designated by Mr Churchill as 'the Battle of the Atlantic'. It was launched and maintained not only with the customary German thoroughness but also with ferocity and ruthlessness. Though he possessed some of the finest and most modern of the world's warships, Hitler ordered that they were to avoid anything in the nature of a fleet action with the British, and degraded them to the rank of mere commerce raiders, preying upon unarmed merchantmen. The like policy applied to the much more deadly submarine U-boats, of which Germany began to build ever-increasing numbers, and before long they were able to range right across the Atlantic to the shores of Canada and America. In the air long-range Condors (Focke-Wulf 200) reconnoitred far out to sea, spotting merchant convoys sailing to or from Britain, attacking them with bombs and reporting their positions to the lurking U-boats.

For such tactics the German Navy was ideally situated, for it now had at command every European port from the Bay of Biscay to the north of Norway. Not only could they harry all our coasts and bomb all our ports and cities but also they could sally out from Norway on a course 1,000 miles to the north of Scotland, raid the Atlantic and, at need, home into Brest, St Nazaire, Lorient or La Pallice. Britain, with straitened resources and with commitments stretching over nearly the whole of the globe's surface, was in mortal peril. Outside observers thought that we stood no chance. Winston Churchill himself said afterwards: 'It was the only thing that really frightened me.'

Yet we overcame it all, by ingenuity, by new tactics and by dauntless courage. Not least of the men of courage were the merchant seamen, of many nations besides our own, and the 20,000 brave men in 1,000 small craft who tackled the insidious menace of the magnetic mines strewn around our coasts.

Coastal Command

In this chapter, however, we shall be concerned mainly, though not wholly, with the remarkable achievements in the Battle of the Atlantic of that branch of the Royal Air Force known as Coastal Command, in whose ranks four Victoria Crosses, all but one of them posthumous, were to shine amid a constellation of other awards. Theirs was essentially a maritime role, cast in the most intimate partnership with the Royal Navy. Their prowess was perhaps less loudly acclaimed than the heroic deeds of the fighters and bombers. As in the Navy, eternal vigilance was their rule of life, and in their patient, exacting and often monotonous sorties over the bleak stretches of ocean, always on the *qui vive*, and at all times open to sudden perils, they achieved much to which no glamour was attached. Day after day and night after night they kept ceaseless watch and ward all round the shores of Britain and far out into the Atlantic and Arctic Oceans, shadowing and reporting the movements of enemy warships, hunting down U-boats, escorting convoys of merchantmen and even attacking enemy warships in port.

Coastal Command also administered the photo-reconnaissance aircraft which, ranging deep into enemy country, provided a constant stream of information of far-reaching importance, with special versions of the Spitfire and

Mosquito. In Chapter 8 we shall see how they helped in the attack on the great *Tirpitz*.

Originating as No. 10 Group, Coastal Command became so designated in 1936 under Air Marshal Sir Arthur Longmore. At the outbreak of the Second World War in 1939 the Commander-in-Chief was Air Marshal Sir Frederick Bowhill, with his headquarters at Northwood, Middlesex. From small beginnings it rapidly expanded until ultimately there were nine groups, covering all our shores and extending to Iceland, Gibraltar and (in due course) the Azores. All worked in close comradeship with the Navy, usually sharing the same headquarters.

The aircraft with which their squadrons were first equipped for their diverse duties were mainly that gallant and handsome old warhorse, the Sunderland flying-boat, a few Hudsons, ten squadrons of Ansons, some long-range Blenheims and a few others of obsolescent type. All but the Sunderland had very limited radii of action and killing power.

As the war progressed, all but the Sunderlands and Hudsons were superseded by such craft as the Catalina flying-boat with its enormous endurance, the Wellington, the Beaufighter, the Halifax, and, at last, a few of the Very-Long-Range version of the Liberator, the *prima donna* of Coastal Command, which had a decisive influence on the Battle of the Atlantic.

These aircraft were manned, of course, mainly by young men of the United Kingdom, but there was fine material also from the great Dominions, together with Dutchmen, Poles, Norwegians, Danes and Czechs. Later in the war some American squadrons were also put under Coastal Command. The weapons with which they attacked the enemy at first were bombs and torpedoes, but later the naval depth-charge was found to be by far the most effective weapon against enemy submarines, which were Coastal's principal quarry. It was dropped in salvos of four to eight from point-blank range — 50 to 150 feet. Rockets and 40-mm 'cannon' were also mounted.

With these weapons Coastal ran up an exceptionally high score against the enemy. Its pilots killed 189 enemy submarines, shared in the killing of another 24, severely damaged 121 others, sank 366 other enemy ships and damaged many more. To pick out individual squadrons would be invidious, for luck was a determining factor, but we may note that 120 Squadron killed 16 U-boats and shared three more kills with the Navy. The highest individual score was that of Squadron-Leader T. M. Bullock, who killed four.

First Atlantic VC

The scroll of VCs in the Battle of the Atlantic was initiated before that battle waxed to its full intensity, by a heroic deed of self-sacrifice in the Nelsonic tradition, on the part of a naval officer of mature years, who was almost due for retirement when the war broke out.

The depredations of the enemy in 1940 had already been sufficiently serious. On several occasions German surface warships and heavily armed merchantmen, each with a reconnaissance aircraft, had raided right across the North and South Atlantics, seeking out the most helpless prey, while the U-boats lay in wait for all shipping approaching the British coasts. In a single week in September 27 ships of 160,000 tons had been sunk, most of them on course for Canada. In the next month U-boats slaughtered another convoy, sinking 20 ships out of 34.

It was at the end of that month that the German pocket battleship *Scheer*, commanded by Captain Theodor Krancke, broke out into the Atlantic through the Denmark Strait, north of Iceland. She was a long, lean, fast ship of 10,000 tons armed with six 11-inch guns and eight 5.9s. A week later she was lying in wait for one of the convoys from Halifax, Nova Scotia, the chief departure point for convoys from Canada.

The Germans were well informed of their departure dates, and the convoy that Krancke hoped to slaughter was numbered HX84, consisting of 37 ships, which sailed from Halifax on 28 October. Their only escort was HMS *Jervis Bay*, a converted passenger liner of nearly 14,000 tons, built for the Australian run and owned by the Aberdeen and Commonwealth Line. She was armed with seven 6-inch guns, four forward and three aft, of ancient vintage and very limited range. They were manually loaded and their fire was governed by a somewhat primitive gunnery control system. The ship naturally stood very high out of the water, but all the more so for having been loaded with thousands of empty oil drums in order to maintain her buoyancy when her thin plates were penetrated by a shell. She was, of course, no match for any well-found man-of-war.

Jervis Bay was commanded by Captain Edward Stephen Fogarty Fegen. He was 48 years old and came of an Irish family from Tipperary which for generations had served the British Navy, his father an admiral and his grandfather a captain. He was a big, deep-chested, powerful man, with strongly moulded features, a thrusting chin and a quiet disposition, well known for his exceptional gifts for leading and training cadet officers and young seamen, in many of whom he inspired a personal affection. Fegen had served throughout the First World War in destroyers and other small ships, and some years afterwards, by a quirk of fate, was appointed to command the Australian Naval College at Jervis

73

Bay. He had been awarded the Lloyd's medal, and a life-saving medal from the Dutch Government, for saving the crew of a Dutch ship wrecked off the China coast. His crew now in the *Jervis Bay* numbered some 254 officers and ratings. Some were naval reservists, others merchant seamen who had been signed on to the Navy. Many were young lads, others quite elderly men.

Early in the afternoon of 5 November 1940 the *Scheer*'s reconnaissance seaplane reported eight ships to the south-east and Krancke set off to intercept them. At half past two, however, he sighted a single merchantman, the *Mopan*, a fast banana boat, sailing independently and not as part of the convoy. Having by threats prevented her from making any wireless report, Krancke took off her crew of 68 and sank her by gunfire. He had just about completed this act of legitimate piracy in the old tradition when, at about 5 p.m., his look-outs sighted a forest of masts appearing over the horizon. It was convoy HX84, sailing in nine columns. In the centre was *Jervis Bay*.

Uncertain of the identity of the distant warship, Fegen began to close her and challenged her by lamp. When he was certain that she was hostile, his reaction was instantaneous. He had no hope whatever of overcoming the powerful German ship, yet his duty was to protect his convoy as best he could. He might succeed in doing so if he could engage the enemy long enough for the convoy to scatter, as they now began to do on the convoy commander's order. With no other thought in his mind and knowing perfectly well what the result must be, Fegen at once increased speed, went to the head of the convoy, placed himself between them and the enemy, dropped a trail of smoke floats to conceal the convoy, and went straight for the *Scheer*, hoping that he might decrease the distance sufficiently for his guns to take effect.

He did not have the chance. *Scheer* opened fire with her 11-inch guns at ten miles. *Jervis Bay* replied with her 6-inch cocked up at full elevation, but all her shells fell far short. She was soon hit and thereafter continued to be hit by almost every salvo. After several salvos the bridge itself was hit, together with the forward steering, in a fearful smother of smoke, fumes, wreckage and blood. Fegen was badly wounded, most of his left arm being torn off by a large shell splinter. But he held his post out on the remaining wing of the tottering bridge, ordered the after-steering to be manned, and still held his course straight for the enemy. Another shell wrecked the gunnery control room, but such of *Jervis Bay*'s remaining guns as could bear continued to fire independently.

When the bridge had become a useless wreck and was on fire, Fegen clambered down in great pain and covered in blood. He ordered the after control to be manned, but was himself too weak to climb into it. So he stood outside it on the boat deck, clinging to the rail, where he observed that some of his convoy were still in sight, and accordingly gave orders for more smoke floats to be dropped. The ship, which had a great deal of wood in her construction, was in flames in several places.

A minute or two later the after control room was destroyed by a direct hit, killing all within. Water came flooding in below and the engines stopped. The ship was out of control but one of her guns was still firing. Fegen began to make his way forward, when the ship was hit again and Fegen killed.

The unequal fight lasted some 25 minutes. Even when *Jervis Bay* had become a motionless, burning hulk, *Scheer*, instead of ignoring her and going in chase of the merchantmen, continued to pound her to pieces with one broadside after another. Thanks to her extra buoyancy, she remained afloat for a remarkably long time and held the *Scheer* for almost a full hour, while the scattered convoy got away in the gathering night. She did not sink until 8 p.m., with the loss of nearly 200 officers and men. Before that time the senior surviving officer had given the order to abandon ship. Krancke made no attempt to rescue the survivors as they clung to broken rafts and pieces of floating wreckage, but later that night the Swedish *Stureholm*, under her fat and jovial master, Sven Olander, returned at great risk and picked up some 60 of them.

The exemplary self-sacrifice of Fogarty Fegen and his shipmates was not in vain. The hour's delay brought darkness to the help of the dispersing merchant ships and all but five escaped as the *Scheer* turned and hunted them by star-shell and searchlight. To the hands of the unfortunate five Krancke did not extend the same clemency as he had to those of *Mopan*. He smashed their ships to pieces and left the seamen to their fate in the cold waters of the Atlantic night.

The spirit of the merchantmen themselves rose to the heroic occasion. The London tanker *San Demetrio*, carrying 7,000 tons of petrol, was set on fire by the *Scheer* and was abandoned, but next morning a boatload of her hands, under Second Officer Hawkins, boldly reboarded her. Chief Engineer Pollard got her engines and pumps going and the flames were doused. The shell-holes were plugged and the petrol sealed off. Then, without compass, chart or sextant, Hawkins brought his precious ship safely home.[6]

The Victoria Cross that Fegen so well deserved was awarded with exceptional speed 'For valour in challenging hopeless

---

[6] A detailed account of the action is given in *The Jervis Bay*, by George Pollock.

odds and giving his life to save the many ships it was his duty to protect'.

Flying Officer Campbell

The threat presented by the big enemy warships brought forth the second VC of the Battle of the Atlantic and the first for Coastal Command.

By April 1941 the enemy campaign against our shipping was raging in its full intensity. In the preceding months the *Scheer* had made another sortie. The 8-inch-gun cruiser *Hipper*, in a savage attack near the Azores, sank seven unescorted merchantmen, making no attempt to rescue the survivors. The great battle-cruisers *Scharnhorst* and *Gneisenau*, in a wide-ranging foray of two months, had sunk or captured 22 more ships, of 115,000 tons. These were in addition to the mounting depredations of the U-boats. In the first three months of 1941, 304 ships, totalling 1,250,000 tons, had been sunk. Two-thirds of these were British ships, the remainder of Allied or neutral countries. Frightening figures indeed, and the total for the year was to top 4 million tons.

At the end of March *Scharnhorst* and *Gneisenau* returned to Brest to repair the many wounds inflicted on them by naval and air action. They were very soon spotted there by the reconnaissance aircraft of Coastal Command, though their identities were not at first certain, and were kept under surveillance whenever the bad weather of that month allowed. It was of high importance that they should not again be allowed to break out into the Atlantic and Bowhill ordered 22 Squadron to attack the battle-cruisers at first light on 6 April.

No. 22 Squadron, wearing its badge of a Maltese cross, was an old First World War unit commanded by Wing Commander F. J. St G. Braithwaite. It was equipped with Beaufighters, armed with torpedoes, but often employed in laying mines in enemy waters, in both of which roles it had already shown considerable prowess. The main body of the squadron was stationed at North Coates, in Lincolnshire, but had a special detachment at St Eval, in Cornwall, and it was this detachment that was detailed for the Brest attack. The task allotted to it was of the utmost peril. Brest was the most heavily defended of the ports occupied by the Germans. It was also extremely difficult to attack from the air, lying within a semicircle of commanding hills, bristling with anti-aircraft guns. The only practicable approach was from seaward, but any low-flying aircraft would be hard put to pull out fast enough to clear the hills. An attack by torpedoes would mean going in at just above sea-level in face of the fire not only of the cruisers themselves but also of three anti-aircraft ships specially stationed to protect them and all the land batteries. In all, the anti-aircraft guns numbered no fewer than 270.

Six Beaufighters were detailed for the mission. They taxied out at St Eval in the dark of a cold night soon after 4 a.m. Two of them failed to take off in the wet ground. Navigational difficulties then beset three of the remaining four. One failed to locate Brest, another did not arrive until 7 a.m. and was obliged to turn away in face of the blistering fire, a third did not arrive until 9 a.m., when it was far too late.

Very different was the experience of Flying Officer Kenneth Campbell and his gallant crew in aircraft 'X', though the facts did not become known for some time and his posthumous award of the Victoria Cross was not announced until nearly a year later. His crew consisted of Sergeant J. P. Scott as navigator (a Canadian from Toronto), Sergeant R. W. Hillman as gunner and Sergeant W. Mullis as wireless operator.

Campbell himself was 24 years of age, dark, good-looking and with features full of character and intelligence. Born at Saltcoats, Ayrshire, he had been educated at Sedbergh, in the far Yorkshire fells, a school that had the remarkable record of producing two other winners of the Victoria Cross in this war — Brigadier 'Jock' Campbell and Second-Lieutenant Ward Gunn, who both won it in the *Crusader* battle. After school Kenneth Campbell had read Natural Science at Clare College, Cambridge, and had taken his degree just before the war began. He had been a member of the Cambridge University Air Squadron and thence was commissioned into the RAF Volunteer Reserve when war broke out.

Sergeant Scott brought the aircraft accurately to the target area just as day was breaking. There was a dawn mist but as soon as Campbell, flying very low, crossed the spit of land south-west of the harbour entrance and swung in towards his target a terrific barrage of fire erupted. Campbell's attack was in fact directed against *Gneisenau*, which he saw lying alongside the quay on the north shore, protected by a stone mole that curved round from the west. He appreciated perfectly well that, even if he succeeded in penetrating the searing barrage, the Beaufighter would find it almost impossible to avoid crashing into the high ground beyond the harbour.

These hazards he accepted without hesitation and indeed cheerfully. There was a hope that he might slip through the barrage by sheer speed. He came down to 0 feet and made straight for *Gneisenau* with 270 guns blazing at him. With extraordinary daring he flew right across an anti-aircraft ship at below masthead height, scarcely above the muzzles of her guns, almost singed by their blast. Then he skimmed over the mole and, at 500 yards' range, he ordered Hillman to fire his torpedo and saw it strike home in a great fountain of smoke and water.

Almost immediately afterwards the Beaufighter, shot to pieces, plunged into the sea, with the loss of all her gallant crew. Their bodies were extracted from the wreckage by the Germans and buried in Brest cemetery, one being in an unidentifiable condition.

Gneisenau was severely damaged below the water-line. A report made after the war asserts that, had the blow been delivered at sea, *Gneisenau* would probably have been a total loss. She was fortunate to be able to return at once to the dockyard whence she had come only the day before. Four days later she was attacked again and suffered four direct hits by Bomber Command. Both she and her 'twin' *Scharnhorst* continued to be harried from the air by both Bomber and Coastal Commands all that year and never again ventured into the Atlantic.

Campbell's Victoria Cross was a remarkable example of an award based on civilian or quasi-civilian testimony. The facts were gradually pieced together from our Intelligence agents and French patriots in the harbour who witnessed the incident.

The Battle of Wits

The Battle of the Atlantic continued to rage at full intensity for the rest of 1941, all through 1942, and well into 1943. By the beginning of that year the Germans had a fleet of more than 400 submarines, of which more than 110 were constantly at sea, hunting in 'wolf packs'. Both figures were soon to rise higher still. On the other hand, great improvements had been made in the escorting of Atlantic convoys, and important new techniques had been evolved. The United States and Stalin's Russia were by now our allies, the former enthusiastically so, the latter passively and cynically, giving little or no recognition to the blood and treasure that we expended from our straitened resources in order to help her.

In January 1943 the combined Chiefs of Staff of the Western allies laid down that the Battle of the Atlantic should have first priority for that year, and next month Air Marshal Sir John Slessor was appointed Commander-in-Chief of Coastal Command.[7] By then a most impressive advance had been made in fighting methods, and these he continued to foster. In the early days aircraft had been of little use against U-boats except to locate them and to drive them down into deep water. Their bombs were not lethal. It was not until the bomb was replaced by the depth-charge that the air arm became a killer and it then became the most deadly of all submarine hunters. In Slessor's first year Coastal Command sank 84 U-boats.

A keen and deadly battle of wits was being waged between the U-boats and the Royal Air Force. In the early days the German submarines (like the British) normally remained below the surface by day but came up at night to recharge their batteries and to ventilate the foul air within. This convenient custom was upset when Squadron-Leader H. de V. Leigh devised the 'Leigh light' which was a naval searchlight mounted in the aircraft, working with an improved type of search radar. The U-boats could now be attacked from the air when surfaced at night as well as by day. As time went on, the Germans produced a 'search receiver', an anti-radar warning device that temporarily discounted the advantages of the Leigh light. The RAF replied, however, with a new type of ASV — the anti-submarine radar — which the enemy were unable to outwit.

---

[7] Following Air Marshal Sir Philip Joubert de la Ferté, who had followed Bowhill.

Coastal Command's adoption of the depth-charge prompted the Germans to new tactics also. Habitually a submarine dived on being attacked, but this was of no avail against the underwater blast of the Torpex depth-charge. Admiral Doenitz, the German Grand Admiral, then ordered his U-boats not to dive when attacked, but to stay on the surface and fight the aircraft by gunfire. For this purpose he equipped his boats with a formidable armament of four or five fast-firing guns of 40 and 20 mm. This was serious, because the aircraft could be attacked at a distance of several miles, without means of reply, and was highly vulnerable when it swung into its final straight run-in just above sea-level, which it usually did from astern, following in the U-boat's course.

There were long faces in Whitehall. Should they revert to the far less accurate high-level bombing? But Slessor had faith in the courage and skill of his air crews. 'We shall probably lose more aircraft,' he said, 'but we shall certainly kill more U-boats. Coastal Command will continue to attack with depth-charges at low level.'

The results of these tactics will now be seen in the awards of three more Victoria Crosses.

The Enemy as Witness

Among the most sensitive parts of the Atlantic were the waters off West Africa. By this route passed our shipping to and from South Africa, the Middle and Far East, and Australia. Freetown, in Sierra Leone, hot, sweaty and malodorous, was very important as a port of call, and as a terminal for traffic to and from the Americas. The German surface ships and submarines haunted it continuously and found many victims.

One of the RAF squadrons guarding those waters in 1943 was 200 Squadron. Stationed at Yundum, in Gambia, it was commanded by Wing Commander W. H. Ingle and equipped with Hudsons and Liberators. Formerly a Coastal Command unit, the squadron was not now under Slessor's command but was still employed in a Coastal Command role, under Air Headquarters West Africa, in Freetown. In early August, in addition to its normal duties of reconnaissance, escort and attack, the squadron had a special requirement to keep guard over the cable-laying ship *Lady Denison-Plender*. The heat and humidity were at their tropical worst.

Newly commanding one of the squadron's Liberators was Flying Officer Lloyd Allan Trigg, a man of modest and rather reserved disposition, with slender, clean-cut features. A New Zealander, educated at Whangarei High School, he was 29 years old and married with two sons. He had been farming in Mangonui but it had been his boyhood ambition to join the Royal New Zealand Air Force and this he was able to do, in the ranks, soon after the war began. Transferred to England, he was commissioned in January 1942. Trigg had already given quite outstanding service on convoy escort and hunting submarines, having completed 45 operational sorties, displaying both skill and courage of a very high order. This service had won him the Distinguished Flying Cross.

At half past seven in the morning of 11 August he took off from Yundum on a reconnaissance specially ordered by Air Headquarters. It was his first operational sortie in a Liberator, and unhappily it was to be his last. His crew consisted of Pilot Officer G. Goodwin (as second pilot), Flying Officers R. Marinovich and J. Townshend and Flight Sergeants T. Soper, R. Bonnick, A. Bennett and L. Frost. On this occasion the aircraft was armed with bombs. Trigg was given a defined area to patrol, but at 11 a.m. was diverted to hunt for a U-boat which had been spotted by a Catalina flying-boat and attacked without success.

After searching for some hours, Trigg found the enemy boat, surfaced. He at once turned and bore down to attack. He was accosted by accurate shell-fire at a range of some miles. The aircraft was hit several times. It burst into flames, which enveloped the tail, and its destruction by fire was certain.

Trigg would have been fully justified at that point in breaking off the engagement and ditching in the sea. He chose not to do so and swung in low and straight to make his run-in. It was the most crucial minute, when the pilot could not manoeuvre and presented an easy target. Every split second multiplied the likelihood of instant destruction. Despite the flames and the shell-bursts, Trigg executed a masterly attack. With the enemy projectiles actually streaming into his open bomb-doors, he skimmed over the submarine at 40 feet and released his bombs accurately astride it, with devasting effect. Immediately afterwards the blazing aircraft crashed into the sea and all eight of the crew were killed.

Hours later an aircraft on Air-Sea Rescue spotted a rubber dinghy crowded with men. It was the Liberator's own dinghy but the men in it were survivors of the sunken enemy submarine. Their testimony it was that formed the basis for the citation of Trigg's Victoria Cross. It was a very rare case of the enemy providing the evidence; otherwise there would have been no VC.

In Northern Waters

By August 1943 a dramatic change had come over the Atlantic scene. Whereas the total of Allied shipping losses in March had reached the appalling figure of just on 700,000 tons (120 ships), by August it had sunk to 120,000 tons (25 ships). The

Battle of the Atlantic had been virtually won, and thereafter the figures continued to dwindle. A very dangerous gap in the waters south of Greenland, formerly beyond the reach of land-based aircraft, had been closed in the spring by the RAF's new Very-Long-Range Liberators, by a squadron of the Royal Canadian Air Force operating from Newfoundland and by the provision of escort aircraft carriers. Coastal Command's killings rose dramatically. From May till the end of July its pilots were killing three U-boats a week and in August one a day. A more offensive policy by Slessor bore good fruit. The purely defensive methods of convoy protection had to be maintained, but he now began a more offensive campaign in the Bay of Biscay, assaulting the U-boats after they had left their protected harbours and before they reached the convoys. The morale of the U-boat crews was badly shaken.

Thus the dawn of 1944, when Air Marshal Sir Sholto Douglas became AOC-in-Chief of Coastal Command, opened with brighter skies. The Allies were on the march towards winning the war. Weighty considerations, however, still governed the course of our policy in northern waters. By those distant and frigid wastes enemy ships of all sorts could make their way into the Atlantic from Norwegian ports, or they could steal out to prey upon the convoys that Britain, in very severe conditions, sent to the Russians by way of the Arctic Ocean. The *Scharnhorst* had just been sunk by a British fleet in a bitter winter battle off North Cape, and the giant *Tirpitz* had been immobilized by the daring midget submarines (as related in Chapter 8), but U-boats were still a constant danger. The virtual denial to them of the Bay of Biscay ports forced them to conduct most of their operations from Norwegian ones.

For the protection of these northern waters, Coastal Command, in close association with the Navy, maintained

British, Canadian and American squadrons in Scotland and in Iceland. They had given splendid service in very arduous conditions of ice, snow and fierce gales, with heavy losses to the enemy. Here there had been a unique occasion in 1941, when a U-boat, having been attacked, surfaced and surrendered to a Hudson of 269 Squadron, and was escorted until a surface ship came to take her in tow.

It was from Iceland that the next Victoria Cross was to be won, again posthumously. Here was based No. 162 Squadron of the Royal Canadian Air Force, formed at Yarmouth, Nova Scotia, commanded by Wing Commander C. G. W. Chapman and stationed at Reykjavik. It was equipped with an aircraft known as a 'Canso', which was a Catalina flying-boat to which was rigged a wheeled undercarriage, thus making it amphibious. In June of this year the squadron had had an amazing run of successes, when they spotted six U-boats, sank four and helped in the sinking of a fifth. It was in this 'straight flush' that the fight about to be recorded took place.

One of Chapman's Cansos was commanded by Flight Lieutenant David Scott Hornell. A native of Mimico, Ontario, he was 24 years of age, very good-looking, with a military moustache and a cheerful disposition. He was married and employed by a Canadian rubber company. He had enlisted in the Royal Canadian Air Force at the outbreak of war and in due course was commissioned and qualified as a pilot. By June 1944 he had already carried out 60 operational sorties.

On the 24th of that month Hornell was sent out on another routine anti-submarine patrol. In his crew were Flying Officer B. C. Denomy as co-pilot and Flying Officer S. E. Mathieson as navigator. His wireless operator/air gunners were Flying Officer G. Campbell, Flight Sergeant S. R. Cole and Flight

Sergeant Bodnoff, and his engineers were Sergeants R. G. Scott and F. St Laurent.

The day was bright and clear. After some hours over the rough but sunlit sea, a U-boat was sighted north of the Shetlands on the port beam, moving on the surface at speed at a distance of about five miles. It was 7 o'clock of the long northern evening. Hornell at once turned and prepared to attack. The U-boat altered course and then opened accurate fire at about 3½ miles. In disregard of it, Hornell closed the enemy and at 1,200 yards ordered his gunners to return fire. One gun jammed but the other secured hits on and around the conning-tower, and the U-boat jinked sharply to starboard. It then reopened fire and two large holes were torn in Hornell's starboard wing. He took evasive tactics by undulating action, but the aircraft was now very difficult to control. In manoeuvring to begin his run-in to attack he was again hit at 800 yards and the starboard wing burst into flames from spilt petrol and oil. An easy target now, the aircraft was hit again and again and was vibrating violently.

Notwithstanding his inevitable fate, Hornell pressed home his attack with great skill and determination as the flames spread to the petrol tank. Flying straight up the submarine's track at 50 feet, he made a perfect strike, his depth-charges straddling the submarine, the bows of which were thrown high out of the water before she sank.

Now, however, Hornell had to save himself and his crew. With a supreme effort at the controls he managed to gain a little height and turned into the wind. But the vibration was increasing in violence, the flames spreading rapidly and the engine fell off. There was nothing more that he could do. Coolly and skilfully he brought her down to the surface of the sea in a heavy swell, about a mile from the U-boat. Full of holes and blazing furiously, she sank rapidly.

After ordeal by fire came ordeal by water. Hornell ordered his crew, wearing Mae Wests, to abandon ship, but only one dinghy was found undamaged. This could not hold all eight of the crew, so they took turns in it, while the others dropped into the icy, heaving sea, holding on to the sides of the dinghy. This ordeal lasted all the northern night, throughout which Hornell, though himself growing weaker and weaker and gradually losing his sight, sustained his comrades by his cheerful and inspiring leadership. Once the dinghy capsized in the rough sea and was righted only with the greatest difficulty. Men's strength began to give out. Scott and St Laurent died and their bodies were lost.

The 'flash' signal that Hornell had made on sighting the U-boat was never received by his squadron, but by pure chance a homeward-bound Catalina of 333 Squadron sighted the lone dinghy and, a short distance away, a group of other dinghies giving refuge to the survivors of the enemy submarine. The Air-Sea Rescue service went into operation. A Sunderland flew out, but could not alight in the rough waters. An airborne lifeboat was dropped, but it fell 500 yards downwind. Hornell prepared to swim out to it, but was in no condition to do so and was restrained with difficulty. Soon afterwards he went completely blind.

Not until 21 hours had passed did the rescue launch arrive, to find the survivors almost at the end of their tether. Hornell died immediately after he was picked up. All, British and Germans, were taken to the Shetlands, where the gallant Hornell was buried in Lerwick cemetery. His Victoria Cross, awarded unusually quickly, was presented to his widow by the Earl of Athlone, Governor-General of Canada.

Flying Officer Cruickshank

Less than a month later the cold northern waters were again the setting for the winning of a VC by a Coastal pilot. Enemy submarines were still active, either trying to get round into the Atlantic or intent upon harassing the Russian convoys. One of the RAF squadrons carrying out surveillance of these was No. 210 Squadron, commanded by Wing Commander L. W. Burgess and stationed at Sullom Voe in the Shetland Isles. Another First War squadron, originally No. 10 Naval Squadron, it wore the badge of a Welsh griffin rampant. A versatile and peripatetic unit, it had seen much hard service in the Atlantic, the Arctic and off the coasts of North Africa. Equipped with Catalinas, one of its crews had distinguished themselves by trailing the great *Bismarck* when she broke out into the Atlantic in 1941. The squadron had already bagged seven U-boats and was about to bag its eighth.

The pilot responsible for this feat was Flying Officer John Alexander Cruickshank, an Aberdonian of 24 years, behind whose slim-line moustache lay a somewhat dour personality. In civilian life he was a bank clerk. His crew consisted of Flying Officer J. C. Dickson as navigator, Flight Sergeants J. S. Garnett and F. Fiddler as second and third pilots, Flight Sergeant S. B. Harbison as flight engineer, Warrant-Officer W. C. Jenkins and Flight Sergeant H. Gershenson and F. J. Appleton as wireless operators and gunner, and Flight Sergeant A. I. Cregan as rigger.

Just before 2 o'clock in the afternoon of 17 July Cruickshank took off in his Catalina on an anti-submarine patrol. It was a long patrol, far out to sea. Eight hours later it was still not yet night-time in those far northern waters, but the light was becoming dim when the radar picked up a contact.

89

Cruickshank homed on to it and at 1,000 feet sighted a stationary vessel on the surface at a distance of about six miles. Cruickshank took his craft up into the clouds and subsequently sighted the vessel again at about two miles. It was now travelling fast and turning to starboard. Cruickshank's crew thought that the vessel might be a friendly one and fired the recognition cartridge, followed by the letter of the day. The answer that they promptly received was a box barrage from the vessel's guns and it then turned hard to port and began a series of violent zigzags.

Cruickshank followed round, making a complete circle. Now that the vessel was obviously hostile, he shaped course to come in astern of her at two miles, flying up the line of her track. He dived down to 50 feet and began his attack. The U-boat was travelling very fast and opened up a heavy but inaccurate fire. At 1,000 yards the Catalina replied with her 'cannon', scoring hits on the conning-tower. She then skimmed over the submarine and the controls for releasing her depth-charges were operated, but failed to work.

Cruickshank at once climbed to 800 feet, turned to port and came in again from dead astern up the submarine's track for a second attack. It was now stationary again and firing hot, accurate flak. The Catalina was hit again and again. Dickson was killed, Cruickshank himself severely and repeatedly wounded, with two serious wounds in the chest and ten in the legs. Three others of the crew were wounded also. Undeterred, Cruickshank pressed home his attack and, from 50 feet, straddled the U-boat with six depth-charges just as it tried to evade by turning to port.

By now Cruickshank was shot to pieces and in a state of collapse, having sustained yet more wounds. Immediately the attack was accomplished Flight Sergeant Garnett took over as second pilot at the same moment as the Catalina ran into a bank of sea fog. A violent explosion told of the death of the U-boat and Garnett set course for home.

There followed an agonizing return flight of five hours, with one dead man and four wounded on board and the air in the Catalina soured by the fumes of high explosive and the smell of blood. Cruickshank was bleeding profusely but after a time recovered a little from the initial shock and insisted on resuming command and retaining it until assured that the damaged aircraft was under control, that the right course had been set and the necessary signals made to base. Only then did he consent to have his wounds dressed, but he refused morphia lest it should impair his faculties. For the remainder of the flight he remained unconscious or semi-conscious, breathing with the greatest difficulty, but once more insisted on resuming command as the aircraft neared home, realizing that the landing of the damaged aircraft would be a hazardous task for the less experienced Garnett, himself suffering from a hurt. He therefore had himself carried forward and propped up in the second pilot's seat, where, for a full hour and in great agony, he gave orders as necessary, insistent that the Catalina should not be brought down until the conditions of light and sea made it possible.

Garnett having brought the aircraft safely down on to the water, Cruickshank continued to direct it while it was taxied and beached in a place where it could be easily salvaged. It arrived at about 3.30 a.m., having been out some 13½ hours. A long series of signals had been going on all the time, the shore base helping by giving the aircraft directions and advice. A rescue team awaited them and a medical officer at once went on board and gave Cruickshank an instant blood transfusion. When the war was all over and his wounds healed at last, he received his Victoria Cross from the hands of King George at Holyrood Palace.

4: CRUSADER

The Western or Libyan Desert extends westwards from the Nile and southwards from the Mediterranean for perhaps two million square miles. We think of it usually as a very hot, arid, desolate waste, almost devoid of life. And so it is for most of the year, but in the brief winter, when the events of this chronicle took place, a totally unexpected change takes place. The flawless, burning sky becomes filled with vaporous clouds, which discharge themselves suddenly upon the desert's face, turning what seems to have been sand into a muddy morass that is often impassable even by tanks. The nights turn bitterly cold. The dawn becomes blistered by a malevolent wind that searches viciously through the warmest winter clothing. Worst of all are the monstrous swirling sandstorms, thick as a thousand blankets, which envelop all creation in a shroud of misery.

Such were the conditions in which was fought the long and bewildering battle known to the British side under its operational name of *Crusader*. It remains one of the least known of the battles of the Second World War, although five Victoria Crosses were won during the nineteen days of its dust-veiled turbulence. The overall generalship on both sides (with one notable exception) was deplorable, but in simple soldiership it outmatched even the later Battle of Alamein. No battle in the two and a half years of the fluctuating Desert war was more bitterly or bloodily contested. In its fiery heat, which was that desolate shelf of sand and rock known to the British as Sidi Rezeg, a small force of British soldiers, in a scarcely credible feat of heroism, held at bay the repeated onslaughts of

German tanks, guns and infantry for three days. Here also, a little later, the New Zealanders won, lost and won again its death-strewn desolation.

Scarcely less memorable was the valour of the besieged garrison of Tobruk, the relief of which was one of the purposes of *Crusader*. Before coming to that main operation, we ought therefore to take note of the first of the seven VCs to be recorded in this chapter, three of which were won at Tobruk.

First Australian VC

Tobruk, a small seaport on the Mediterranean coast, had been denied to the enemy when the forces of the German-Italian Axis had advanced from Tripolitania into Libya early in 1941. For the greater part of its epic siege of eight months it was garrisoned by 9th Australian Division and several units from Britain, under Major-General Leslie Morshead, unfailingly supported through thick and thin by the Royal Navy and the Royal Air Force. Right at the beginning of the siege there took place a critical action which was crowned by Australia's first VC of the war and the first of many VCs in the long Desert campaign.

On 13 April a strong concentration of German tanks, infantry, artillery and engineers assembled for an assault on the Tobruk defences. That night a small enemy party of some 30 infantrymen, with two small guns, eight machine-guns and a mortar, was sent in to clear a way through the perimeter for the tanks. Covered by the darkness, they infiltrated between two Australian posts, dug themselves in and opened a searing fire on a strongpoint 100 yards away, the liquidation of which was necessary to their plans. This post was held by a platoon of 2/17 Battalion under the spirited young Lieutenant Mackell.

With him was a section led by Corporal Jack Edmondson, a farmer from Liverpool, NSW, aged 27.

Mackell immediately set about turning the enemy out. Taking Edmondson and only five other men with him, he stole out in the dark by an indirect route, ordering the remainder of the platoon to keep the enemy under fire. As soon as he was ready, Mackell, having given a prearranged signal, charged the enemy post with shouts and a shower of grenades. The Germans quickly turned their weapons on them and Edmondson was badly wounded in the stomach and the neck in a rain of machine-gun fire.

Ignoring his hurts, he dashed on in the gloom. In a minute the Australians were right in among the enemy. A deadly rough-house ensued. Edmondson, in Mackell's words later, 'was magnificent'. Mastering his faintness, he killed at least two Germans. His officer, however, was soon in deadly peril, wrestling with a German on the ground while another was coming for him with a pistol. Mackell called out 'Jack!' Edmondson, a few yards away, turned, dashed in and killed both Germans with the bayonet. He then went on and killed at least one more before collapsing. Very soon afterwards he died.

His Victoria Cross was granted not only for his personal valour but also for the fighting spirit by which he inspired the men of his section. The enemy post was cleared, considerably compromising the start of the German assault, which withered away next day under the resistance of the Australians and the aggressive blows of the Royal Horse Artillery.

The Rival Armies

This incident, though little related to *Crusader*, serves to illustrate the spirit that animated the garrison of Tobruk. By

November 1941 the situation was that the main British army was holding a defensive position on the eastern side of the Egyptian-Libyan frontier, 60 miles to the east of the beleaguered Tobruk. Libya was an Italian colony and along this frontier ran a double-apron fence of barbed wire, known to the British as 'the Wire'. Westward of the Wire, from Solium on the Mediterranean coast as far south as a group of strong defences known as the Omars, the German and Italian armies stood arrayed. Several hundred miles still farther west lay Tripolitania, another Italian colony.

The Commander-in-Chief of the Axis forces was the Italian Marshal Ettore Bastico, but in operational command of most of the Axis forces on the frontier (not all) was the German General Erwin Rommel. Hitler had sent him out some ten months earlier, together with a redoubtable force of German tanks, infantry and aircraft, to help his stricken Italian ally after his humiliating defeat by a very small British army under that audacious little commander, Lt-General Richard O'Connor.

Rommel, rated by his fellow-generals in the German army as *un bon général ordinaire*, had positive shortcomings for high military office, but he was a great personal leader, a tremendous thruster, a quick improviser and, above all, an eager opportunist. He thought and acted very quickly, if not always rightly. Bastico's appreciations of British intentions were often right when Rommel's were wrong, but Rommel took scant notice of him and, indeed, had a low opinion of Italians generally, though many of them fought well. Although a Hitlerite, Rommel had honourable ideas about the conduct of warfare and there were no atrocities in the Desert.

By November 1941 both sides were preparing for offensives. Rommel, preparatory to a drive for the rich prizes of Alexandria and Cairo, was determined first to crush the

Tobruk garrison, which was a very serious thorn in his flesh, and to this end he bent all his thoughts and apportioned the main weight of his forces. The Australian division in that garrison had now been relieved by the British 70th Division and the Polish Carpathian Brigade, with 32 Army Tank Brigade, under Major-General Ronald Scobie.

The British intention in operation *Crusader* was to destroy the Axis forces where they stood by attacking from their positions along the Wire in concert with a sortie by 70th Division from Tobruk.

Both sides had recently made significant changes in their command structures and groupings. On the British side the impressive figure of General Sir Claude Auchinleck had succeeded Wavell as Commander-in-Chief of the Middle East forces. The army in the field had recently changed its name and status from the Western Desert Force to the Eighth Army, of historic memory, and its new commander was the handsome artilleryman, Lt-General Sir Alan Cunningham, wearing the laurels of a brilliant success over the Italians in East Africa. The air forces supporting Eighth Army, which included several squadrons from South Africa, Australia and Rhodesia, besides those of the RAF, were to achieve equal fame as the Western Desert Air Force (or DAF) under the able command of Air Vice-Marshal 'Mary' Coningham, a New Zealander. For the first time, the soldiers were to enjoy strong and understanding support from the air.

Under Alan Cunningham were two army corps — 13 Corps, led by the tall, soldierly Lt-General Reade Godwin-Austen, able, strong, much loved, fresh from his success in the Abyssinian campaign; and 30 Corps, under the cavalryman Lt-General Willoughby Norrie. Of the several divisions under them we shall have special reason to notice two. The first was

7th Armoured Division, the celebrated 'Desert Rats', led by the much admired Major-General 'Strafer' Gott, his nickname being derived from the German slogan of the First World War, *Gott strafe England*. The other was the 2nd New Zealand Division, under Bernard Freyberg, VC, who, with 4th Indian Division, were holding the infantry defences along the Wire. On the Axis side stood Rommel's German-Italian *Panzergruppe Afrika*. For our purpose we need to note only the redoubtable *Deutsche Afrika Korps* (or *DAK*), the tough German infantry of 90th Light Division (known at first as the Afrika Division) and the Italian Ariete Armoured Division, not yet under Rommel's command but soon to be so. The *DAK*, wearing their emblem of a palm tree with the Nazi reversed swastika, was commanded by Lt-General Ludwig Crüwell , able and brave but at constant odds with the impulsive Rommel. His two divisions were the celebrated 15th and 21st Panzer (or Armoured) Divisions, with their associated artillery and infantry.

Numerically, the two sides were about equal, though the British tanks outnumbered the Germans'; but this merely academic superiority was invalidated by the superior quality of the newer marks of the German tanks (but not the Italians') and by their more skilful tactical handling. On the British side the new, sleek Crusader tank (which gave its name to the battle) was mechanically unreliable, the various 'cruisers' out of date, and the fast and light American Stuart (or 'Honey') was designed only for cavalry reconnaissance. Besides these there were two tanks not designed for mobile tank battles but for the close support of infantry — the rather slow Valentine and the painfully slow Matilda. These were the equipment of the 'Army Tank Brigades', which were not in the 'armoured divisions', but often acted the same part.

All these tanks were armed with the small 2-pdr gun, firing solid shot. Between them and the older German tanks there was not much to choose. But the big new German tanks were a different story, especially the Mk III, which fired a 4½ lb shot and could kill tanks at 2,000 yards, against the 2-pdr's 500 yards. Moreover, the enemy guns, unlike the 2-pdr, fired high explosive as well as shot. A similar disparity was seen in the wheeled anti-tank guns. The British anti-tank batteries, of which there were far too few, had the same 2-pdr, firing solid shot only, whereas the enemy anti-tank guns fired HE also, and in the 88-mm the Germans possessed a devastating weapon which no tank in the world could hope to face; Rommel had at that time 23 of them, a single one of which could hold up a whole regiment of tanks. Thus the Germans could pick off the British gunners mercilessly with HE at 2,000 yards, without fear of reply, besides inflicting damage to the tracks and external equipment of the British tank. Oddly, the coming battle was to show that the best British weapon was the 25-pdr of the Field Artillery, which was not designed to engage tanks but which, when firing solid shot, could penetrate German armour at 800 yards. All British anti-tank gunners had therefore to be cool and resolute hands, sitting still under shell and machine-gun fire until the enemy tanks got within killing range.

Since it will play a notable part in our narrative, we must observe especially that the 2-pdr gun, manned by regiments of the Royal Artillery, was *porté* on an open, low-slung Chevrolet lorry with all its top-hamper removed, which became known as a 'portee'. The gun could easily be dismounted to fire from the ground but in the mobile desert war the gunners usually preferred to fire from the portee. Though very conspicuous and devoid of protection, it was handled with skill and daring by such regiments as the 3rd Royal Horse Artillery, the Northumberland Hussars[8] and the gallant Rhodesian battery. The portee was, in fact, the invention of a Rhodesian officer, Lieutenant Gillson.

These shortcomings were accentuated by the superior tactical skill of the Germans. They brought their tanks into battle as one concentrated force, deploying according to a well-practised drill, protected by screens of anti-tank guns and supported by field artillery; whereas the British commanders, influenced by peace-time theorists such as Liddell Hart and Fuller, thought in terms of tank *v.* tank. Both armies regarded the tank as the lord of the Desert, but in tank battles the dominant weapon was in fact the German anti-tank gun. *Crusader* was to show, indeed, that the real battle winners were the infantry and the artillery.

To view the forthcoming battle with a comprehending eye, we must imagine an area about the size of the whole of East Anglia — about 80 miles by 60 miles — rising from the sea by a series of escarpments to a plateau of desolate, dun-coloured terrain. The surface is of rock and sand. Except after heavy rain, this part of the Western Desert is motorable almost anywhere. Both armies being largely mechanized, we see vast fleets of vehicles moving across it in all directions — tanks, armoured cars, guns behind their various tractors, Bren-gun carriers, ambulances, small wireless vehicles and the squadrons of large lorries that supply the fighting troops with fuel, ammunition, water, rations and spares.

These fleets of vehicles move very widely dispersed, yet they throw up enormous clouds of blinding dust, in which navigation is extremely difficult. A column often bumps into an enemy one, when there is a mad scramble for safety or a

---

[8] Officially 102 (NH) Anti-Tank Regt, RA, commanded later by the author.

quick, sharp fight. When battle is joined this dusty obscuration is hugely intensified as shells and bombs burst around and a man's wits become further bemused by the terrible racket and by the tracer-lit darts of solid shot and machine-gun bullets that shoot about his ears.

On the eve of *Crusader* a posthumous Victoria Cross was awarded to Lt-Colonel Geoffrey Keyes in a risky attempt made on Rommel personally. A force was landed from submarines behind the enemy lines, and a party was sent stealthily inland under Keyes to attack a house which was believed (wrongly) to be Rommel's headquarters. The only result was a stiff fire-fight within the house, in which Keyes was mortally wounded. The affair was misconceived but was redeemed by the gallantry of Keyes and his companions.

The Break-in

The British moved first.

Cunningham's plan, in simple outline, was for Norrie's 30th Corps, which contained nearly all the armour, to move round the open southern flank, make a 'left hook' behind the enemy and station 7th Armoured Division in a position where it would invite attack from the enemy armour on ground of its own choosing. Godwin-Austen's infantry corps, now in the frontier defences along the Wire, would then advance to Tobruk, whence Scobie would make a sortie to meet them. Norrie was to protect Godwin-Austen's left flank with the Honeys of 4th Armoured Brigade Group under Alec Gatehouse, one of the desert 'characters', who went into battle in an armchair strapped to the top of his tank and with a rug kilted round his waist.

The weather for the approach march on 17 November was abominable, with a blinding sandstorm followed by squalls of cold, sleety rain. Eighth Army had exchanged its tropical kit for warm battle-dress and its morale was exceedingly high. In the chill dawn of 18 November, Strafer Gott's 7th Armoured Division broke leaguer, crossed the Wire and wheeled to the right 35 miles behind the enemy front, preceded by a reconnaissance screen of 4th South African Armoured Cars, stretched out over a 40-mile frontage.

The sky was overcast with low, sullen clouds, so that enemy reconnaissance aircraft did not take wing. Except for the rumbling of the tanks themselves, a vast stillness brooded over the desert, and nothing broke the monotony of the endless gravelly waste except a few stunted bushes of camel-thorn.

JOCK CAMPBELL

Seventh Armoured Division consisted of 7th and 22nd Armoured Brigades and an unarmoured one. The 7th Brigade, led by Brigadier George Davy, was composed of 7th Hussars and 2nd and 6th Royal Tanks, all equipped with out-of-date cruisers. The 22nd, under Brigadier Scott-Cockburn, was equipped with the new Crusader, manned by eager, high-mettled yeomanrymen from Gloucestershire and London, who had never yet been in action.

The brigade with which we shall be predominantly concerned, however, was that then known as 7th Support Group. It was composed of infantry and gunners and its purpose was to provide support for the armoured brigades at need and to hold ground. It was superbly led, and led from the front, by an artillery officer of quite superlative courage who was always in the thick of the fight and whose impossible contempt for bullets was an inspiration wherever he went. This was the legendary Brigadier 'Jock' Campbell. He already wore the DSO and Bar and the Military Cross, and at Sidi Rezeg was to add the ribbon of the highest honour in the brief remainder of his life.

Aged 48, John Charles Campbell had become 'Jock' to his army messmates as a matter of more-or-less established tradition, but in fact in his earlier years he had been Charlie Campbell... After prep school at St Andrew's, he went as a dayboy to Sedbergh where, as we have noted earlier, Kenneth Campbell and Ward Gunn also were educated later. At Sedbergh, Campbell showed that quality of a gay and high-spirited schoolboy which he was never entirely to lose. Soon after school he joined a Territorial artillery regiment in the ranks, but was commissioned some months after the outbreak of the war in 1914, in which he was twice wounded and won the MC. He married and had two daughters.

Campbell was a man of considerable stature and strength, with an athletic and beautifully built figure, broad in the shoulders and slim in the hips. He was of great personal charm, good-looking, quietly spoken, with a delightfully modulated and persuasive voice, but a personality that was at once magnetic and tremendously forceful. His bearing was buoyant, his enthusiasms large, his impetus compelling, his *panache* such as you might expect from a cavalier of olden days. He was the Rupert of the Desert.

Some senior officers disliked him, for Campbell's persuasiveness could become predatory and he was apt to poach on other men's preserves, but to junior officers and to the rank and file he was the very model of the Happy Warrior, though far from moulded in Wordsworth's sententious pattern. In the words of Major Tom Bird of the Rifle Brigade, who served under him in many a spirited fight, 'he had the rare gift of communicating a sense of the joy in battle to all around him.' A Rhodesian gunner who served under him said: 'Whenever he was near me I felt a brave man.' When calling upon someone to undertake a risky mission, he would lay an enormous hand confidingly on your shoulder and say: 'Now's your chance to win fame'; and if you were a man of spirit you swelled with pride at having been chosen, and felt perfectly certain that you would succeed.

Campbell was a fine heavyweight horseman. He had been an instructor at the Army Equitation School at Weedon, played a forceful game of polo and rode to hounds with the Pytchley. The spirit of the hunting field was always in him. Not an intellectual soldier, he was impatient of conventional orders and before battle preferred to say simply, 'Follow me.' Then he would ride out in an open staff-car, standing straight up, and brandishing a blue flag as though it were a drawn sword. He never took cover from enemy fire, but his habit of wandering all over the battlefield, without a fixed command post, was disconcerting to junior commanders and to his own staff officers, who never knew where to find him.

Like most 'old Desert hands', Jock Campbell dressed unconventionally, wearing corduroy trousers and a coloured scarf round his neck, which he would sometimes take off and tie to a stick, to serve as a battle standard. Displaying these characteristics, he had made his name as the originator of what became known as 'Jockcols', which were small, audacious, fast-moving columns, composed of artillery and motor-borne infantry units, which sallied out against some enemy post 'to strop 'em up', as he put it, and slip quickly back.

Withal, Jock Campbell was formidable in displeasure, expecting every officer to be right on the ball, to move fast and to close with the enemy. With his horse-artilleryman's strictness, he brooked no laxity and no hesitancy in action. There was an occasion when he ordered a weak squadron of tanks, already much tried, to attack a large column of German armour that appeared some distance away, and the startled squadron-leader exclaimed: 'My God, sir, we shall simply all get killed.'

'That,' replied the insistent Jock, 'is what soldiers are for. Get on.'

We must now very briefly review the troops in Campbell's Support Group, whose heroic exploits we are about to witness.

His infantry element was supplied by two crack rifle regiments, trained in quick movement and quick thinking. The larger was the 1st Battalion King's Royal Rifle Corps, better known by its old name of 60th Rifles, which we shall employ here. This was Strafer Gott's old battalion, now commanded by Sidney de Salis. One of his companies was composed mainly of Rhodesians, the Royal Rhodesian Regiment being affiliated to the 60th. 'We could never do,' said de Salis, 'without our Rhodesians.' With the 60th were two companies of their honoured rivals, 2nd Battalion The Rifle Brigade, under Archie Douglas. Both were very weak in numbers.

The gunners of 7th Support Group comprised some exceptionally fine regiments and batteries and two quite outstanding COs. The senior regiment was 3rd Royal Horse Artillery, equipped with 2-pdr anti-tank guns and commanded by Constantine Wilson. It was an experienced and much decorated regiment with spirited and dashing battery commanders in Bernard Pinney, Brian Stewart and Robert Eden. The Group's field-gunners, equipped with 25-pdrs, were 60th Field Regiment, RA, a Territorial regiment recruited partly in Grimsby and partly in Lincoln and very ably led by 'Tim' Hely, whom we have seen in Crete; he was one of the very few

Territorial gunners who was later to rise to brigadier (and finally acting major-general in Burma). In the prolonged and deadly fighting to come at Sidi Rezeg he was to show himself a magnificent leader, brave, cool and quick-thinking.

Three other artillery units also came under Campbell's command at Sidi Rezeg, though not normally his own. They included two 25-pdr batteries of 4th RHA, led by the red-haired John Currie, another officer celebrated in the Desert for his exceptional daring, severe in training, gay and inspiring in battle; one may say, indeed, one of the bravest men who never won a VC. Among his batteries was another contingent of Rhodesians. Temporarily added to Currie's command was 203 Field Battery, led by Major Sir Harry Shiffner and borrowed from 51st Field Regiment, a Territorial Army unit from Cumberland and Westmorland, the remainder of whom were in Tobruk. Accompanying these field and anti-tank units was a fighting battery of Bofors gunners from 1st Light Anti-Aircraft Regiment, who defiantly engaged tanks with the same zest as they did enemy aircraft.

TO SIDI REZEG

For the first day of *Crusader* all went well. The great northern wheel of 7th Armoured Division progressed across the barren terrain. They reached their designated ground. Alec Gatehouse's 4th Armoured Brigade Group lay back a little to the right. Several miles behind, at call, was 1st South African Division, a formation still far from fit to fight the Germans.

The British armour took station and waited to be attacked. But nothing happened. The ground chosen was not 'vital ground' to the enemy, who drew the conclusion that the British were merely making a reconnaissance in force. Rommel, engrossed with his cherished design of capturing Tobruk, had pooh-poohed Marshal Bastico's correct interpretation of the signs of a major British offensive; it was, Rommel said, out of the question. Thus the bulk of the German armour still lay at some distance to the north, but the Italian Ariete Armoured Division, which we have seen to be not under Rommel's command, was disposed some 12 miles from the left flank of Strafer Gott's division.

Having failed to draw the enemy armour and finding the enemy in a state of complete dormancy, Gott saw an opportunity for his division to head straight for Tobruk. Cunningham and Norris agreed arid Gott was ordered to march at once on Sidi Rezeg. This was a vital amendment to the *Crusader* plan, which had required the prior defeat of the German armour, and henceforth we shall see a wild battle of opportunism with swiftly fluctuating changes of fortune.

Two actions took place on 19 November, however. One was a fruitless attack by the Crusaders of the new 22nd Brigade against the Ariete on Gott's left flank. The other was an equally fruitless thrust to the south-east by the German armour. Crüwell , commanding the Afrika Korps, saw clearly that a definite British offensive was developing, but Rommel, his eyes focused on Tobruk, would have none of it, and allowed him to send only a strong 'battle group' of about 95 tanks. This group, missing 7th Armoured Division, ran smack into the light Honey tanks of Alec Gatehouse's 4th Brigade at about 4 p.m. There was an inconclusive fight, but it was the German who disengaged and withdrew before dark.

While these engagements were in progress a far more significant event was taking place. George Davy's 7th Armoured Brigade, with two squadrons of South African armoured cars scouting ahead, were on their way to the really vital ground of Sidi Rezeg. This was not only to constitute a direct threat to Rommel's proposed assault on Tobruk but also it would dominate his main line of communication by way of the Trig Capuzzo, or, as we would say, the Capuzzo Track.

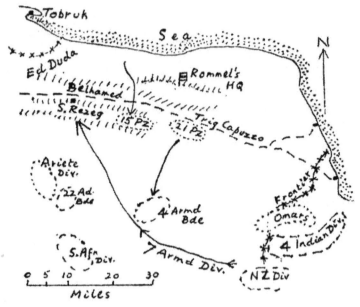

Crusader: dispositions 19 November. Sidi Rezeg seized by 7th Armoured Brigade.

In this part of Libya the desert descended to the sea-level in three giant steps, the risers of which constituted steep or fairly steep escarpments. The area to which Gott's division, now moving across the topmost plateau, was directed was the middle step. It was 2½ miles wide and seven miles long and on its slightly concave surface was an Axis airfield. Immediately below this broad step or shelf, at the foot of the second escarpment, lay the Trig Capuzzo, but it was visible only from the lip of the escarpment, where a rocky ridge ran all the way, rather like the raised crust round the rim of a pie or flan. Towards the western edge of this rocky crust was the square, squat tomb of a Muslim holy man named Sidi Rezeg or, as we should put it, Saint Rezeg, and it was after him that the British (but not the enemy) named the whole of this fateful saucer. The position was overlooked from nearly all sides, particularly by Points 175 and 178 on the east and the south.

Beyond the Trig, that is to say, north of Sidi Rezeg, we must notice another long boulder-strewn shelf of great tactical importance. This locality, the source of much affliction to Gott's division, and afterwards the scene of stiff fighting by the New Zealanders, was known as Belhamed.

Equally significant was a long ridge to the north-west of Sidi Rezeg and clearly visible from it, known as Ed Duda, the importance of which will shortly become apparent, as being the key to Tobruk.

To Sidi Rezeg marched Davy's out-of-date cruisers and part of Currie's 4th RHA. Campbell's Support Group followed. The weather had improved somewhat, the air was crisp, with fitful gleams of sunshine. At 4 o'clock 6th Royal Tanks arrived at the rim of the uppermost escarpment and beheld 22 enemy aircraft on the airfield below. Together with the South African cars, they drove down the escarpment and dashed on to the airfield to seize the rare prize. Three aircraft managed to make good their escape, but the remaining 19 were captured, together with their pilots and all ground staff. The tanks destroyed the aircraft by simply driving over them. Before dark 7th Brigade were in possession and leaguered for the night, with Campbell's Support Group behind them on the plateau above the first escarpment.

But 22nd Brigade were 25 miles away to the south and 4th Brigade 35 miles to the south-east. Not a happy disposition for the intended 'destruction of the enemy armour'.

20 November. Sidi Rezeg Held

And now the 'fog of war' begins densely to envelop the whole battlefield in a material as well as a metaphorical sense. The huge clouds of dust thrown up by the movements of tanks, vehicles and gunfire, the difficulty of distinguishing between friend and foe, the problem of identifying any position on maps that were almost completely blank, the frequent radio failures, the conflict of reports from various sources make *Crusader* one of the most confusing battles ever fought. Columns of tanks or transport were moved hither and thither. British and German formations and units became bewilderingly intermingled. Drivers suddenly found themselves in company with an enemy column. Prisoners were captured and recaptured.

Small wonder, therefore, that the commanders on both sides made tactical mistakes. On 20 November, Cunningham, sparsely informed, believed all to be going well. Rommel, still obsessed with his designs against Tobruk, again misread the portents, believing this time that the British were merely trying to distract him from those designs. He launched Crüwell with nearly the whole of *DAK* on another and badly conducted attack on Gatehouse, which both German generals believed was the main British force, but against Davy's far more dangerous brigade on Sidi Rezeg he sent only infantry and guns.

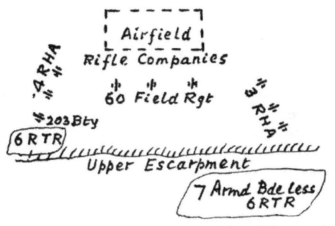

Crusader: Sidi Rezeg; outline deployment of 7th Support Group on 20 November. Diagrammatic, not to scale.

That brigade stood to before the bitterly cold dawn of 20 November. Having only one company of infantry, they had not gone very far beyond the foot of the upper escarpment so that the rocky crest that formed the northern rim of the middle scarp still lay some two miles ahead, beyond the airstrip, now littered with the wreckage of the enemy craft. Unseen beyond that rim the enemy were mustering on Belhamed. Just before first light on the 20th a star-shell burst over the airfield, illuminating the British position, and immediately afterwards an attack was launched from the crest of the second scarp by one Italian and three German battalions, with very heavy artillery support. It failed completely, being broken up by the British guns. So also did other attempts, stopped by resolute and accurate field batteries. But the enemy shelling went on and, indeed, never stopped for the next three days. In preparation for his assault on Tobruk, Rommel had assembled a strong concentration of artillery, including heavy howitzers, on Belhamed, and these guns now turned their muzzles towards Sidi Rezeg.

At about 9.40 a.m. Gott himself came up. Since tanks could not hold ground without infantry help, he ordered Campbell's Support Group to take over on the Sidi Rezeg shelf, which they did smartly in 20 minutes. Davy's brigade headquarters and 2nd Royal Tanks withdrew to the plateau above, but left 6th Royal Tanks on the shelf below, together with the Jerboa and Sphinx Batteries of 4th RHA and Schnifner's 203 Battery. The Group itself, however, though fairly strong in guns, still mustered the equivalent of only half a battalion in its two rifle regiments — far too weak a force for the situation.

The Sidi Rezeg shelf was under almost continuous fire from Belhamed. Campbell was in his small, open staff-car on the bonnet of which flew his brigadier's small triangular pennant. On the wings were the gnomon of a sun-compass, the canvas *chargal* filled with water and the rolled-up sand-mats for extricating vehicles from soft sand. Ignoring the shell bursts, brisk and businesslike, he drove around in his red-banded hat, disposing his regiments to advantage, with the two attenuated rifle regiments along the south edge of the airfield and the guns of 60th Field Regiment behind them, the Sphinx and Jerboa Batteries of 4th RHA and 203 Battery on the left, 6th Royal Tanks in the rear of them and the anti-tank guns of 3rd RHA on the right, mounted on their portees. He was accompanied everywhere by two young Rifle Brigade officers, Ian Whigham and Philip Flower.

Thus, stretched out thinly over some five miles of frontage but of little more than a mile in depth, his group stood fast all day, terribly exposed and constantly harassed by fire and by myriads of flies. To dig trenches or gun-pits in the rocky ground was impossible, but a few shallow scrapes were hacked out. A squadron of Stukas flew in and dive-bombed the armour, but no one was bothered. Otherwise, the enemy made no further attempt to assault, but at nightfall the group stood to in readiness. There was only hard-tack for ration, but an issue of rum gave to the palate an ominous taste.

At the close of that 20 November everyone on the British side was full of confidence. The enemy reactions had been strangely half-hearted and they seemed curiously unwilling to engage in a decisive fight, which was not their custom. Strafer Gott spent the night at Sidi Rezeg, giving orders to Davy and Campbell for the resumption next morning of the advance to Tobruk. Seventh Armoured Division was to fight through to the long ridge of Ed Duda, plainly visible six miles to the north-west, where it would join hands with 70th Division, which was to break out from Tobruk simultaneously. The 7th Support Group was then to be relieved on Sidi Rezeg by the South Africans, and early next morning Gott, accompanied by Wilson, the CO of 3rd RHA, went off to tie up the arrangements with that division.

Rommel, however, had now begun to take serious notice of the British irruption. Late on the night of the 20th he ordered the *DAK* to break off their clumsy attempt to destroy Gatehouse down in the south-east (which Rommel believed had been accomplished) and to make for Sidi Rezeg with all speed. The 15th and 21st Panzers accordingly made an about-turn at dawn the next day and made off northwards, looking to Gatehouse very much as though they were in flight.

21 November: High Tide of Battle

At that same hour on the critical 21 November the Support Group on Sidi Rezeg hastened to their battle positions in the valuable half-hour of semi-darkness before they could be observed by the enemy. Engines started up, guns rumbled into position and infantrymen stood to their arms. The men were chilled, bleary-eyed and silent. A keen wind vexed the face of the desert, driving before it stinging particles of sand. Orders for the advance to Ed Duda had been given out and everyone knew that the first step was for the riflemen to cross the open airfield and attack the rocky pie-crust of the Sidi Rezeg ridge ahead. Sixth Royal Tanks were then to drive down the second escarpment and make straight for Ed Duda. No sooner had Campbell's units taken post than the enemy artillery opened up, firing concentrations. The preparations went ahead notwithstanding. Campbell drove about the field briskly, his vigilant eye alert, radiating an offensive spirit wherever he went.

At 7.45 three companies of the 60th Rifles, with a company of the Rifle Brigade under command on the extreme left, formed up under fire on the southern edge of the airfield to assault the pie-crust ridge. Sidney de Salis, their CO, went round the companies, wishing them luck. Before them, broken only by the wreckage of the German aircraft, stretched 2,000 yards of horribly exposed ground, which they knew would be raked by every weapon the enemy possessed. Though they mustered scarcely 400 swords (the Riflemen's term for bayonets), they were called upon to capture the ridge for a stretch of two miles, against an enemy far superior in numbers and concealed among rocky crags and fissures. In doing so they were to carry out one of the finest infantry actions of the Desert war, in which an inspired courage was matched with fine infantry skill.

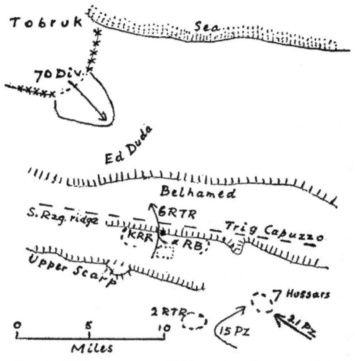

Crusader. Sidi Rezeg a.m. on 21 November. Capture of Ridge by Riflemen, break-out from Tobruk, advance of 6th Royal Tanks, destruction of 7th Hussars.

At 8.30 the guns put down a brief bombardment followed by a smoke screen. The riflemen got up from the ground and strode forward, preceded by their Bren-gun carriers and followed by artillery observation officers. Opposing them, the German-Italian force enjoyed a magnificent field of fire over the stark, open ground. After the first few hundred yards the riflemen and their carriers began to suffer severely under fire from mortars, artillery, the nerve-testing Spandau machine-gun and the explosive bullets of the Italian Breda. At times one or other platoon was checked, but what was left of them pressed their attack with determination and skill, readily supported by their gunners. Most of the carriers fell easy victims to anti-tank guns, but the men on foot pushed on little by little.

The ordeal lasted for 3½ hours as the riflemen darted forward in short bursts under covering fire and the battle became one of the junior officer and NCO, whose example and initiative alone carried it forward. The right-and left-hand companies were on their objectives first, but Captain Hugh Hope's centre company was dangerously pinned to the ground some 80 yards from the enemy, whose orders they could hear being shouted in the pauses of the din. It was then that the first of the Sidi Rezeg VCs was won.

Rifleman John Beeley, of the 60th Rifles, was a clean-limbed, good-looking young soldier of slight build. Born one of twins in Lower Openshaw, Manchester, he was 23 years old and had worked as a stonemason before enlisting in the Regular Army in 1938. He was married and lived in Winchester. In the ranks of his comrades he was not particularly distinguished but, in the words of Hugh Hope, his company commander, he was 'a thoroughly good rifleman'. Normally of a happy disposition, he was under strain now from unhappy domestic news from home. On this morning, armed with a Bren-gun, he was a little ahead of the rest of his platoon, lying close to the rocky ground. Two-thirds of his comrades, including all his officers except Hope, lay dead or wounded. A blistering fire swept the company from front and flank. Yet he was not dismayed and, humble rifleman though he was, not charged with any duty of leadership, he proceeded to execute one of those acts of self-sacrificial heroism which can turn the course of a battle. Was it, as has been suggested, a reaction to feelings of despair caused by the bad news from home? Or did it spring naturally from his training as 'a thoroughly good rifleman'?

All we know is that, searching the craggy ridge ahead, Beeley saw that the worst impediment to progress was a strong-point in which he discerned an anti-tank gun and two machine-guns, manned by seven Germans. Although he must have known that it meant almost certain death, Beeley, in a moment of exaltation, leapt to his feet and ran straight for the strongpoint, firing bursts from the hip. He was hit but did not stop until he was 20 yards from the guns, now concentrating their fire at him. There he coolly halted and, with deliberate aim, opened fire with devastating effect, wiping out the whole of the enemy detachment before he himself, riddled with bullets, fell dead on top of his gun.

His bravery was the turning point in the action at a moment of crisis, as such exploits often are. His comrades, infected with his example, rose behind him and took their objective. At about the same time, Major Geoffrey Peel, of 60th Field, went forward in response to a call for help, met Hope in the fire-swept field and brought down such highly effective fire that the remainder of the enemy all along the ridge also surrendered, but he himself was severely wounded.

The whole of the objective had been taken in that very gallant and exemplary action, illuminated by the heroic initiative of Rifleman Beeley, who was posthumously awarded the Victoria Cross. The riflemen captured 800 prisoners —

twice their own number — together with quantities of weapons, and found the enemy positions choked with dead.

Two squadrons of 6th Tanks, led by Martin Lister and aiming for Ed Duda, then drove boldly down the second escarpment, past the tomb of Sidi Rezeg. debouched on to the Trig below and knocked out six enemy tanks of old types. As they breasted the slope of Belhamed beyond, however, they ran into a devastating fire from a semi-circular screen of anti-tank guns, including four of the deadly 88-mm, hastily brought by Rommel in person. Obsolete, under-gunned and without artillery support, the British tanks stood no chance. Although a few penetrated deeply with great gallantry, all, to the number of some 30, were destroyed in a fearful holocaust of flames and blood. It was the first of a series of crippling tank losses. All that remained of the regiment were 17 tanks still on the ridge.

Nor was this all. Coincidently with the assault by the rifle regiments, another calamitous tank battle was being fought to the east. In obedience to Rommel's overnight order, the full available strength of both Panzer divisions of the Afrika Korps was already on the scene. Even before the riflemen made their assault, George Davy, on the plateau above, had news of the Panzers, to the number of nearly 200, coming up from the south-east. He was obliged to turn to face them, but he now had only 7th Hussars and 2nd Royal Tanks — both equipped with old cruiser tanks — and only eight field-guns of 4th RHA's Balaclava Battery. He ordered the Hussars to locate and delay the enemy, going with them himself, and stationed 2nd Royal Tanks a few miles to the south at call, expecting that both 4th and 22nd Brigades would soon be hurrying up from the south.

The Afrika Korps came in from the east with 21 Pz on the right and 15th on the left. Battle was joined between the

Hussars and the 21st about 8.30. The 15th had a sharp clash with 2nd Royal Tanks but were roughly handled and turned away to the right to join 21st. Opening fire at 2,000 yards, they swept down together upon the Hussars, who were completely outranged, especially by the German's skilfully handled anti-tank guns.

Gallantly the Hussars accepted the unequal odds, but their case was hopeless. They could not touch the enemy and might as well have been armed with bows and arrows. Nearly every tank burst into flames, usually burning alive the crew within. In little more than half an hour they were almost annihilated and their CO, Freddie Byass, was killed. Only ten tanks escaped the holocaust. The 2nd Royal Tanks tried repeatedly to go to their comrades' help, but were also badly cut up at long range by the bristling screen of anti-tank guns.

The immolation of 7th Hussars, however, had not been in vain. They had held the German armour off from the vital ground and given a valuable respite to the troops who held it. The Germans had shot off nearly all their ammunition and exhausted most of their fuel, so that they were obliged to halt to replenish from their supply vehicles. Rommel sent orders that they were to hurry on to counter-attack the sortie from Tobruk, now in full swing, but that could not be done unless the Support Group on Sidi Rezeg were first eliminated.

While replenishment was going on, 16 German tanks drove over the gentle rise to the east of the Sidi Rezeg saucer to see what was there and at the head of the incline were brought to a surprised halt by the 25-pdrs of 60th Field, which Hely swung round to engage them over open sights, and by the little 2-pdrs, on their portees, of two troops of J Battery, 3rd RHA. These were C Troop under Arthur Hardy and A Troop under Ward Gunn. Four of the Panzers went up in flames and the remainder turned tail. It was a foretaste of what was to follow after a brief lull and it was the prelude to the second Sidi Rezeg VC.

Second-Lieutenant George Ward Gunn was the eldest of the four sons of Dr and Mrs G. Gunn, of Neston, Cheshire. He was 29 years of age, very mature for his junior rank. Educated at Sedbergh (like Jock Campbell and Kenneth Campbell), he had afterwards practised as a chartered accountant. At the outbreak of war he had joined the Royal Artillery in the ranks, winning his commission in August 1940, so was not yet due for promotion to lieutenant. Of slight build, he was a good-looking man, with dark hair and wore a black, turned-up moustache in the fashion of the previous generation. He looked very much the soldier and his messmates in the Desert, to whom he was known as 'Ward', found him a charming and attractive personality, full of a gay spirit but firm of purpose. He had already won the Military Cross in the adventurous business of the Jock columns, in which he had made his mark for dash and determination. He had quickly acquired the *panache* of a horse-gunner, wore a blue scarf and the red, blue and gold regimental mess-cap of the Royal Artillery instead of a khaki one.

Gunn's A Troop was deployed near the foot of the upper escarpment and was one of three troops in J Battery, which had distinguished itself in the siege of Tobruk and was commanded by the no less remarkable Major Bernard Pinney, a very gallant officer of the Regular service. He was a small man with puckered features, very experienced, highly professional and strongly solicitous for his men. When he had deployed C Troop, under the tall Arthur Hardy, in a very exposed position to protect the right flank of 60th Field, he had said: 'Look after these boys, Arthur; remember that they

have never yet faced a mass attack by German armour.'
Pinney's third troop, in mobile reserve, was under Eric Pass.
No fewer than four of the six officers in this very fine battery
of a famous regiment already wore the blue-and-white ribbon
of the Military Cross.

We must visualize these fearless anti-tank gunners as
frequently manoeuvring their highly vulnerable portees, either
in an attempt to get close enough to the enemy to ensure a kill
(400 yards) or else to distract the enemy's aim. Together with
their comrades of the 25-pdr regiments, they were now to
engage in one of the great anti-tank contests of the war.

At about 11.30 of that 21st day of November both regiments
of 21 Pz advanced to the east end of the Sidi Rezeg position,
with a powerful force of 60 tanks in the first wave, while flights
of Stukas dive-bombed the whole position and the heavy guns
from Belhamed bombarded it. It was the first time that the
British gunners had faced an attack by tanks *en masse* coming
straight at them, and a very formidable and daunting spectacle
it was. Campbell's thin forces appeared to them puny indeed.
Pursuing their usual tactics, they halted at about 2,000 yards,
opened up with high explosives, advanced a little with their
machine-guns blazing, then halted again. Though spearheaded
by the big Mark IIIs and IVs, they were again resolutely
engaged by 60th Field and Hardy's and Gunn's troops of 2-
pdrs. The Panzers were brought firmly to a halt as soon as they
neared the killing range of the British guns, much damaged by
the volleys of HE from Hely's batteries, even before they
began to fire the more deadly solid shot, and by long shots
from the skilfully manoeuvred 2-pdrs. Six tanks, indeed, were
quickly knocked out.

The Panzers then stood back and blasted the British batteries
and the adjacent terrain with HE and machine-guns. Their field

artillery joined in with more HE. So did the mortars of their supporting infantry. A conflict of the greatest violence erupted in a deafening clangour of more than 200 guns, enveloped in smoke and dust, streaked with the tracers of shot and bullet, stabbed by the flashes of the guns of both sides, inflamed by burning trucks and stacks of ammunition. Never before had the *DAK* had such a reception from what seemed to be an easy prey. Against all their attempts to smash their way through, the stubborn British guns held their ground, although completely exposed and their casualties mounting rapidly.

At the southern end of the conflict lay J Battery's A Troop under Ward Gunn. He had been firing away hard, but at ranges too long for positive killing by the 2-pdr. With extraordinary daring, he began to manoeuvre his guns right forward into the open to close the range. Immediately the opposing tanks swung round on to him in full ferocity.

Four trucks were on fire just behind him and the tide of battle rose to full flood. Gunn was in a state of tremendous exhilaration, which communicated itself to his detachments crouching on their portees. A watching Rhodesian recorded how the gunners, 'completely composed, completely undaunted', knelt at their pieces, the Nos. 1 shouting their orders above the din, the layers aiming their telescopes through the acrid fog with deliberate calm, the ammunition numbers feeding the guns fast with their diet of brass and steel.

As one by one the gunners fell dead or wounded, the remainder of each detachment contracted in obedience to its casualty drill. Gunn himself, riding in a small open truck, darted from gun to gun, continuing to manoeuvre them to better advantage, directing their fire and communicating to them his exhilaration of battle. First one gun, and then a second, was knocked out by direct hits and the portees were set on fire, but the other two continued to engage, scoring effective hits. Tom Bird, the rifleman, crouching in his hole, watched spellbound, his gaze fastened on his friend Gunn. 'Never,' he said afterwards, 'was there a clearer case of a man possessed with the joy of battle.' A third gun was knocked out and burst into flames. Finally, the whole detachment of the last gun were killed outright, except the sergeant, who, quite reasonably, began to drive the portee away.

At that moment Bernard Pinney himself came hurrying up in his truck and shouted to Gunn: 'Stop that blighter.'

Gunn dashed across at once and did so. He and Pinney then jumped up on to the portee, dragged away the dead bodies and manned the gun themselves. Two more enemy tanks were set on fire, but the lone gun became the target for concentrated attack. The portee was hit twice, the second hit setting the ammunition on fire three feet behind the two officers. The flames threatened to engulf them and destroy the portee. Pinney jumped back and began to apply the fire-extinguisher, while Gunn served the piece single-handed, the flames scorching him behind, the shells and bullets streaming at him in front.

The end came quickly. Shot through the forehead, the gallant subaltern fell dead across the gun. Pinney threw away his extinguisher, dragged Gunn's body aside and jumped back to the gun, which he continued to serve alone until it also was put out of action. Miraculously unscathed, he then drove the portee away as the enemy threat here diminished.

Pinney, feeling black and angry, then hurried away northwards to Hardy's C Troop, which he saw to be now the point of crisis, for the Panzers were pressing to get in behind 60th Field, the right flank of which C Troop was protecting. Pinney arrived to find himself in the vortex of another violent whirlpool, the ground littered with the dead and wounded of both regiments. Hely's 25-pdrs, firing over the heads of Hardy's 2-pdrs, were blazing off as fast as the shot could be rammed home in that order of fire known as 'gun control', in which the officers virtually handed over the battle to the sergeants and bombardiers who commanded each gun.

Hardy's 2-pdrs, nearest to the enemy and utterly exposed on their portees, were having the worst of it but the guns were being most gallantly served under their fine NCOs. Both guns of a section under Sergeant Brooks were set on fire, with heavy casualties. The other section, however, under Sergeant Finagin, continued to engage with tremendous spirit, while withdrawing slowly, skilfully and in good order on to the flank guns of 60th Field. From there, seeing that some Panzers were working round their flank, they concentrated their fire on the leaders, knocking out the two leading tanks and obliging the remainder to withdraw.

The gallant Pinney stayed with Hardy's Troop and saw them through their ordeal. He was stricken to the heart by the terrible casualties that J Battery had endured and at the spectacle of their guns caked with the flesh and blood of the men who had served them so faithfully. Early next morning he drove out a single gun to replace one of Hardy's that had been knocked out. Soon after his arrival he was lost sight of, until Hardy went out to look for him and found his dead body, with a shell splinter embedded at the base of the skull.

He and Ward Gunn were both recommended for the Victoria Cross. Gunn was awarded it; Pinney was not.[9]

---

[9] This account of J Battery's action is based primarily on the battery's fortunately very extensive War Diary, the WD of 3rd RHA, Gunn's citation, the very detailed South African official history, Colonel Hastings's history of the Rifle Brigade and the personal narratives to the author by Brigadier Hardy, Brigadier Hely and Major Tom Bird

Thus was fought a ferocious battle between the mixed batteries of British guns and 150 tanks of the Afrika Korps. It was one of the many great epics of the Royal Artillery. The infantry, crouching in their shallow holes, could do nothing but suffer, a terrified little dog running among them in the terrific racket. The British guns fought at considerable disadvantage. Completely exposed, they were fearfully vulnerable to every weapon in the enemy armoury, suffering heavy casualties, yet could not themselves be certain of a positive kill until the tanks came very close, though they could damage and deter at longer range. But they stuck to their guns and fought it out 'eyeball to eyeball' as in the days of old.

The heart of the conflict was where 60th Field and Hardy's 2-pdrs were deployed, and thither Campbell sent a Troop of 4th RHA to help them out. Hely, personally fearless and alert to every emergency, showed himself a superlative and inspiring leader in a tense situation, and the officers and men of all three units rose to the occasion as their forefathers had done on many a field. Everywhere trucks and artillery limbers were on fire, the ammunition blazing fiercely. Guns were wrecked by direct hits and men lay dead around them. Officer casualties were high, but NCOs took over their parts magnificently. Around the smoking guns the spillage of empty brass cartridge cases spread wider and wider. The German bomber aircraft came over again and the Panzers brought up a battalion of motor-cycle machine-guns to add to the din and fury.

It was all of no avail. The ferocity of the defence shook the Panzers. They turned about and withdrew out of sight, heavily bruised. Their attack, admits one of their War Diaries, 'was

---

(one of the witnesses for the VC recommendations of both Gunn and Pinney).

brought to a halt by the weight of the enemy tank and shell-fire'; though what was left of the British tanks, in fact, played a minor role that fiery morning. Five cruisers sent by Campbell to help were soon ablaze. The South African official historian records 'that the guns of the Royal Artillery held off the Panzers at all was due primarily to the courage and devotion of the men who served them'.[10]

Campbell was close at hand, of course, in buoyant spirits, thoroughly delighted at the exploits of his brother gunners. This was that he liked to see: great-hearted troops led by brave officers. He had visited Ward Gunn early and went on to see Hardy, taking back one of his wounded sergeants in his own car.

A little picture painted by Pat McSwiney, whose Bofors light AA guns had been briskly engaging the enemy tanks, aptly epitomizes the gunners' spirit that day. His CO, Lt-Colonel B. L. de Robeck, came up and stood watching Gunn's action, waving his fly-whisk before his face as though to brush away the bullets. When all but one of his guns had been knocked out McSwiney asked him for permission to withdraw and was told: 'No, it is not a case for withdrawal.'[11]

THE AFTERNOON BATTLE

The Support Group knew well enough that this was not the end of their trials. They disposed of their dead and wounded, serviced their weapons, looked round dispassionately at the smoking hulks of tanks, the wrecked and riddled trucks, the litter of twisted steel and equipment, admired the calm devotion of the doctors and stretcher-bearers, took a quick meal and braced themselves for another attack.

---

[10] Agar-Hamilton and Turner: *The Sidi Rezeg Battles 1941*.
[11] *Royal Artillery Commemoration Book*.

It duly came at 3.15 in the afternoon, again from the east but in a different form. This time it was made by two battalions of German infantry, preceded by a smoke screen. Again the enemy was hit by a stinging fire and was soon in trouble, calling urgently for support from the *DAK*. The 2nd Royal Tanks came down from the upper plateau and thrust between the combatants, but the German armour, answering the call of their infantry, launched 50 tanks against them. The British cruisers were able to destroy several of the enemy by skilful manoeuvring but, outgunned as usual by anti-tank weapons, were very roughly handled and had to withdraw.

The German infantry then renewed their attack, backed this time by 8th Pz Brigade. On the sector held by one company of the Rifle Brigade they found little in front of them beyond the smoke and dust of their approach but dead men and wrecked guns and vehicles. It was, in fact, only the dust that enabled them to penetrate here unseen, capture about 30 prisoners and advance to within 1,000 yards of Campbell's command post. Campbell's reaction was swift. Driving over with Philip Flower to the remnants of 6th Royal Tanks, and finding them under fire and with their turrets shut down, he went along them rapping on their hulls with his stick to arouse their attention and ordered them to counter-attack.

Then, with his usual call of 'Follow me', he led them in, ignoring the shell-fire, standing up in his open car, conspicuous in his red-banded hat and holding aloft his blue flag. Within five minutes, seven of the fourteen tanks were on fire, but the Germans lost also and the fervour and audacity of the attack took them by surprise. They believed, their diary states, that beyond the dust-clouds must be yet more British tanks. At the moment of crisis when, by pressing on, they might have won the battle, they once again halted and withdrew. In fact, only a dozen British tanks were now left at Sidi Rezeg.

Indeed, on that one day, nearly the whole of the three regiments of 7th Armoured Brigade had been destroyed and very soon afterwards they disappeared from the Desert scene.[12]

Only the guns and infantry of Campbell's Support Group still remained intact and masters of their field. They were joined that evening by the third wing of 7th Armoured Division — the new Crusaders of 22nd Armoured Brigade — who, slightly scarred by their brush with the Ariete, took station on the left; but the Honeys of Gatehouse's 4th Brigade were still miles away to the south.

The Tobruk Sortie

Meanwhile, a few miles to the north-west, General Scobie's 70th Division had been making its sortie from Tobruk with great spirit. The objective, Ed Duda, lay some seven miles from the south-easterly perimeter of the Tobruk defences. Under the code name *Pop*, the sortie was launched at dawn on 21 November by two infantry brigades and 32nd Army Tank Brigade. The enemy defences, manned by Germans and Italians, were very strong indeed and several miles deep.

Nonetheless, the Tobruk garrison 'popped' to considerable effect. The main enemy defences were captured after hard fighting, with a bonus of 1,100 prisoners, under Rommel's very eyes. The day was made memorable by one of the most heroic achievements in the long history of the Black Watch, when, led by Lt-Colonel Rusk and piped into battle by the celebrated Pipe-Major Roy and Pipe-Sergeant McNicol, their 2nd Battalion stormed the redoubtable strongpoint known as

---

[12] The brigade later re-formed and won fresh laurels in the Burma campaign.

'Tiger', notwithstanding 464 casualties out of the 632 officers and men who had gone in.

'Tiger' was halfway to the final objective at Ed Duda, but Phase 2 had to be called off when Scobie learned that 7th Armoured Division could not get through from Sidi Rezeg; yet Scobie had much for which to be thankful, for Gott's artillery and tanks, to Rommel's annoyance, had effectively prevented the *DAK* from coming in to counter-attack.

'Tiger' was the setting for the next *Crusader* VC. This was to be a rescue operation, of the sort that has often earned the VC for a doctor. The remarkable quality of it was the calm, matter-of-fact deliberation with which all its movements were carried out in disdain of close, concentrated, aimed fire.

Captain Philip (or 'Pip') Gardner was a Dulwich College old boy who had had peace-time Territorial training in the Westminster Dragoons before being commissioned in the Royal Tank Regiment, from which he had had a six months secondment to 4th Commando. He had already won the Military Cross.

Two days after the capture of 'Tiger' he was mounted in a Matilda of 4th Royal Tanks, watching from a distance a troop of armoured cars of the King's Dragoon Guards on a perilous reconnaissance of the open ground of no-man's-land. Two of the cars came under sharp fire and were seen to halt, 200 yards apart, in close proximity to an enemy position, which was pounding them with fire.

To Gardner, the earphones of his radio clamped to his head, came orders from his squadron-leader, Major Jack Pritchard, to go to their aid, in company with another tank of his squadron, commanded by Lieutenant Paul Gearing.

To the order 'Driver advance', the heavily armoured tanks crawled slowly forward, passed the foremost infantry position and soon came under fire. The ground, a slight forward slope, was completely exposed. With the eyes of two armies on them, the tank crews felt like gladiatorial performers in a huge amphitheatre. As they advanced, the enemy fire intensified, the solid shot of anti-tank guns being mingled with the high explosives and with the hiss of machine-gun bullets. At the same time they could see that the two armoured cars were being gradually smashed to pieces at very close range.

Gardner was fortunate to have a very stout-hearted crew, among whom his driver, Trooper Robertson, had already been decorated with the Military Medal. Under Gardner's orders, Robertson manoeuvred the Matilda close to the foremost car, which was now seen to be on the edge of the barbed wire of an enemy-defended locality. Gardner then ordered his gunner, Lance-Corporal McTier, to engage with his Besa machine-gun any post he could observe that was bothering them, and he ordered Paul Gearing to cruise around in the other tank to give covering fire in like manner. Both tanks were being repeatedly hit, but the Matildas' thick armour saved them for a while.

Gardner then dismounted from his tank, under hot fire of all sorts, and with deliberation attached a tow-rope to the armoured car. While doing so, he saw an officer lying beside the car with both legs blown off and covered in blood. This was Lieutenant Peter Beames. Gardner lifted him carefully into the armoured car, returned to his tank and gave Robertson the order to tow.

After a few yards the tow-rope was severed by a shot or shell-splinter. Gardner again dismounted from his tank, walked once more to the car, and decided that its shattered hulk was not worth recovering, but that the stricken officer must be saved. At this moment he was struck by multiple shell splinters all down his left side. Nevertheless, he extracted Beames from the car with great difficulty and put him over his own shoulder. As he turned to carry him to the tank he saw its cupola blown clean off by an anti-tank shot, with the 2-pdr gun split in two and Trooper Richards, his much-valued wireless operator and loader, dead.

Unshaken, Gardner carried Beames over to the headless tank and lifted him up on to the back engine louvres. Then he climbed up alongside him to hold him on, while projectiles of every sort burst or flashed around him, and gave Robertson the order to withdraw.

Meanwhile, Gearing had picked up the crew of the other car and, as both tanks withdrew, they were hotly pursued by the fire of a frustrated enemy. Unhappily Beames did not live, but Gardner was justly awarded the VC for his conspicuous example of cool and selfless courage.

22 November. Day of Crisis

The assessments of the situation by the rival commanders at the end of 21 November were very strange in the light of after-knowledge. The German commanders had begun to be worried. Crüwell believed that the *DAK*, after its repulse by the Support Group, was in danger of being crushed between the anvil of Sidi Rezeg and the hammer of the 'powerful tank forces' of 4th and 22nd Armoured Brigades in the south. Rommel, however, much more concerned about Scobie's break-out, still did not believe that the British intended a major offensive, and saw the situation at Sidi Rezeg as merely intended to deter him from his cherished designs on Tobruk. This he was determined to prevent, to the exclusion of major requirements.

In consequence, at about midnight, Rommel ordered the *DAK* to go over to the defensive, in order to block the relief of

Tobruk, and to be ready to counter-attack, but Crüwell, as he so often did, interpreted this in his own way. He withdrew nearly the whole of *DAK* clean away from Sidi Rezeg, sending 21 Pz to the Belhamed area and 15th several miles away to the east.

Correspondingly on the British side, Cunningham and Norrie, not yet apprised of the severe tank losses, and excusably judging that the Afrika Korps was in retreat from Sidi Rezeg, believed that the battle was already half won. Three times the German armour had disengaged and withdrawn after battle. Cunningham therefore gave leave to Godwin-Austen to launch his 13th Corps infantry from their preoffensive position. By the evening of this 21 November, the eager New Zealanders, under Bernard Freyberg, swinging round by the open south, were already deep in behind the enemy frontier defences on the Wire and had actually crossed the Trig Capuzzo, some seven miles east of Sidi Rezeg, aiming for Tobruk.

RENEWED ASSAULTS ON THE AIRFIELD

At Sidi Rezeg the night of 21/22 November was again cold, with frequent spells of wintry rain, but the blackness was fitfully shot by gun flashes, the streaks of tracer-lit bullets, rockets and Very lights and disturbed by the rumblings of armour. The garrison, now much fatigued, wet, cold, grimy and their numbers much reduced, got what rest they could.

The dawn gave place to a grey and dreary day, the field encumbered with the charred and twisted wreckage of tanks, vehicles and limbers. Sir Harry Shiffner, the admired OC of 203rd Battery, went out on a reconnaissance on the western flank at first light and was killed. The last of the German armour was seen to rumble away northwards, after one of its regiments had had a stiff brush with the yeomanry of 22nd Armoured Brigade, who had arrived on the upper plateau the evening before. On the airfield shelf itself the number of tanks had been made up to 18 and their tired crews had been working all night on repairs. The Support Group was due to be relieved by the South Africans, who were expected to join in the drive to Tobruk, but the South Africans, cautious, half-trained and upset by air attacks, were unconscionably slow.

By midday on the 22nd the Sidi Rezeg area was clear of enemy armour, but the afternoon brought a dramatic and violent change of fortune. Rommel, visiting 21 Pz at Belhamed and impelled by one of his changes of mind, directed Crüwell to quit the defensive that he had ordered only the night before and march at once with the whole strength of Afrika Korps to destroy the British at Sidi Rezeg. To this end he gave Crüwell an additional force of infantry.

Rommel had at last awoken to the truth and now began to show his true form as a swift opportunist. The plan was a skilful one. A brigade of infantry, supported by the Belhamed artillery group, was to make a frontal attack on the escarpment from the north, while the armour of 21 Pz was to make a wide westerly sweep from Belhamed behind concealed ground and surprise the airfield from the west, supported by Axis aircraft. Meanwhile 15 Pz, by a wide encircling movement southwards, were to sweep in to the British rear. But it was the attack from the west that was the most dangerous for the British, as on that flank there was a good deal of dead and broken ground.

The attack of 21 Pz developed just before 2.30. A violent and concentrated fire from all arms crashed down, supplemented by bombardment from the air. A convoy of ambulances, about to evacuate the wounded, fell victims to the bombers and went up in flames and agony. A few minutes later an iron avalanche of 100 German tanks and their infantry brigade burst upon the scene from two directions. Though surprised, the British gunners and infantry reacted at once with an ardour that astonished the enemy. The 4th RHA and 60th Field Regiment opened what the Germans called 'a terrific fire'. Half-naked, unshaven, grimy with dust and sweat, wearied in body, heavily shelled, bombed from the air, machine-gunned by the infantry, they stuck stoutly to their guns, firing at the threatening mass of tanks that rolled towards them.

Campbell was quickly on the scene. Radiating confidence, he watched 4th RHA firing their penetrative 'HE cap on' so effectively that the enemy tanks never closed.[13] Then he went to 203 Battery, where he found Captain John Oswald temporarily in command and himself serving a gun that had been stricken with casualties. As he stood there he saw the recently-arrived Crusaders of 22nd Armoured Brigade, a seemingly powerful force of 79 tanks, sweep in to counter-attack. With yeomanry fervour, they launched themselves against the Panzers in a storm of smoke and dust. The exhausted gunners, unable to distinguish friend from foe in the maelstrom, relaxed — but not for long. With horrified eyes they saw the tracered shot of the little 2-pdrs bouncing vainly off the German armour and watched the Crusaders, hopelessly outranged, go up in flames one after another and their unhappy crews consumed in a horrible death. In a very short time 22nd Brigade lost no fewer than 35 tanks, many of them picked off by the untouchable 88-mms at 2,000 yards.

Alistair Banks, a subaltern in 4th RHA, was filled with rage at those who had designed the British tanks. How magnificent the Crusaders had looked when they first marched out into the

---

[13] In 'HE cap on', the protective safety cap of the fuse, normally removed before loading, was left on, giving a slight delay effect.

desert, how ardently they had attacked, how impotent they had proved against the German guns!

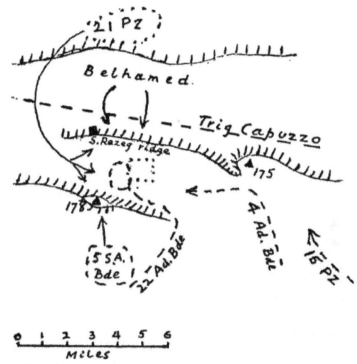

Crusader: enemy attack on Sidi Rezeg, p.m. 22 November.

'Sadly,' wrote Hely afterwards in *The Royal Artillery Commemoration Book*, 'but with grim determination, the gunners took up the battle again, while the tanks re-formed under their protection. Bravely our tanks went in to the unequal contest again, and for a while armour fought armour. But the end was inevitable, and when the remnant of our tanks limped out of battle, the field was left once more to the gunners.'

Meanwhile, with no less spirit, the thin ranks of the riflemen holding the rocky ridge of the escarpment under Sidney de

Salis had clung tenaciously to their post and had quite remarkably repulsed all attempts to dislodge them by the greatly superior enemy assaulting them from the north; but, as the outgunned British tanks disengaged, the Panzers' motor-cycle machine-guns broke in on their flank and rear and gave them no chance.

Cut off and with all their ammunition expended, many of them, including de Salis himself, were captured. By 3.45 the ridge of the escarpment was in enemy hands again. Captain Barrow, however, the forward observation officer of 4th RHA, contrived to stick defiantly to his hazardous post on the ridge, more or less surrounded by the Germans but continuously engaging them until dark, when with remarkable skill he brought his party of signallers safely back.

For even now the gunners and what was left of the tanks contrived to resist so stubbornly that the German tanks were brought to a halt as they manoeuvred afresh in front of the cool and steady men of 4th RHA. In 60th Field, Tim Hely moved round a whole 25-pdr battery (of eight guns) to meet the new thrust, going with them himself. The German tanks were on to them at once with HE and machine-guns and men began to fall at nearly every gun. Happening to turn to his right at the moment when a gust of wind blew away the dust-cloud, Hely saw two German tanks sneaking round to a flank. Only just in time he switched two guns round on to them and knocked both of them out.

While he was absent his E Troop became committed to a desperate little action which resolved itself into another minor epic of that Homeric field, and one in which the qualities of Jock Campbell were typically displayed.

To Hely's annoyance and without his knowledge, Campbell had personally ordered the Troop forward to a very exposed and isolated position. The four-wheel-drive 'quads' that towed the four 25-pdrs had driven up from their place in the rear and executed the dangerous manoeuvre in full sight of the enemy. As the battle smouldered, Hely's adjutant, Captain Charles Bingham, became more and more anxious about E Troop's ammunition state. He therefore dashed out in his truck to find out for himself, and found the guns engaging to the north-east.

He had scarcely dismounted when Campbell tore up in his car, jumped out, shouted 'Tanks!' and pointed to the southwest. The guns swung round in the reverse direction instantly, to see bearing down upon them a force of enemy tanks that would have taken them in the rear. Campbell then shouted to Bingham: 'Adjutant, take No. 3 gun. I'll take No. 1.' Then, pointing in turn to Major James Galloway and Lieutenant Thomas: 'You take No. 2 and you No. 4.'

With the officers doing the jobs of sergeants, the guns fought the tanks for no less than an hour and a half. Almost at once Thomas had a leg shot off and casualties among the men became very high. But again the gunners had the better of the duel, for at length the tanks drew back, stood off and shelled, from a distance. Campbell then hurried off to some other part of the battlefield, but before very long came racing back. As he stepped out of his car a tracered gunshot flashed across his chest, missing it by a millimetre, but taking off a sliver of flesh from his upper arm. The shock of its passage felled him to the ground, badly stunned. Galloway, close alongside, piled his great frame into his truck and he was driven away, but before long he was about his business again, his arm bandaged with a field dressing, in more discomfort than he would allow to appear.

E Troop was now in a perilous position. Miraculously, all the four guns were still in action, but casualties among the men had been severe and attempts to replenish their ammunition had not succeeded. German machine-guns were raking them in enfilade from the right flank, and the enemy infantry, after the reverse to 60th Rifles, were now advancing against them from the same quarter, held off only by machine-gun fire from a few of our ranks. Withdrawal was essential. The quads were ordered up but immediately drew fire. Two were knocked out when 50 yards from the guns. The two others were driven up very gallantly and got hooked into their guns, but the petrol tank of one was then struck by a shell and burst into flames, and the back axle of the other was smashed by a solid shot.

The whole place was now being viciously swept by fire of every sort. The gun detachments were accordingly forced to go to ground. Any attempt at movement by a single man brought instant intensification. Hely felt great anxiety for the many wounded and feared also that the guns might fall into enemy hands without being first disabled. Later in the afternoon he ordered one of his other batteries to put down a smoke-screen, which enabled the wounded to be got out, but the smoke soon drifted away and it was finally not until dusk that the last men were evacuated.

At the critical moment of E Troop's ordeal, when a momentary hush fell on the battlefield and all seemed lost, a Troop of three Honeys appeared over the gentle rise on the east. They were led by Bob Crisp, the South African Test cricketer, on a reconnaissance for 3rd Royal Tanks, the leading unit of Gatehouse's long-awaited 4th Armoured Brigade. Crisp halted, stunned by the fearful scene of carnage and desolation and uncertain what to do. Then he saw a little car racing towards him. It was Jock Campbell, who, on reaching him, stood up and said: 'Come along. We need you. Follow me.'

He shot off in a cloud of dust, himself driving, one hand on the wheel, the other holding up his flag. The enemy reacted with a stiff barrage, but Jock drove straight through the cloud of shell-bursts, black and yellow, weaving round derelict tanks and trucks, the arm that held his flag aloft never wavering. Emerging through the worst of the smother, he waved his arm to the west and raced back.

What Crisp, now alone, saw was the great mass of enemy tanks 1,000 yards away. They at once opened fire and advanced on him. He knew that somehow he must impose delay until his regiment rode up. His Honey was repeatedly hit but miraculously unharmed, and at 800 yards his gunner sent an enemy up in flames.[14]

The little stratagem worked. The Panzers, seeing a cloud of dust approach, and believing themselves to have been attacked by what their diary described as 'a powerful force five times as large as ours', withdrew from battle yet once again, and, indeed, sent out a call to 15 Pz to come to their aid. The Honeys, not realizing how near they were to toppling the enemy completely, broke action almost simultaneously.

So, vastly outnumbered and heavily outgunned by a force that kept them continuously under fire, the Support Group, whom the enemy acknowledged to have fought 'stubbornly and bitterly', still held most of the field. They had, however, endured severe losses. Less than 200 of the gallant riflemen were left. Some 20 guns had been knocked out. The 7th Armoured Brigade was reduced to a mere ten tanks, 22nd to 34. Officers and men were fatigued, red-eyed, caked with dust and sweat, in a fearful scene of death and destruction.

---

[14] Accounts of this incident vary; I have used Crisp's own in *Brazen Chariots*.

Gott decided that the airfield was no longer tenable with the forces available to him, for the South Africans, one of whose battalions had been repulsed with heavy losses in their attempt to capture some high ground to the south-west, were in no shape to take over. He therefore ordered the withdrawal of the Support Group to the plateau above.

Accordingly, the remnants of the infantry withdrew under cover of the guns, but for the artillery themselves the hour was one of great peril. It was not yet dark and every movement was clearly and closely observed by the enemy now holding the crest of the lower escarpment and closing cautiously in on the British batteries.

The gunners, however, true to their training, withdrew as coolly as on a drill order. On the order 'Prepare to withdraw', the quads of the 25-pdrs drove up, the guns were hooked up to their limbers and the limbers to the quads, which moved off to the order 'Drive on'. The portees of the anti-tank guns started up their engines. Thus, Troop by Troop, under covering fire from the remainder, the guns moved out in good order. As dusk began to fall, the last Troop of 60th Field, together with Hardy's Troop of 3rd RHA, faced the advancing German infantry alone, enduring salvos of shell-bursts and a rain of machine-gun bullets. According to gunner tradition, Hely himself, whose truck had been shot under him, stayed with the last Troop, with Hardy in company. To all appearances they were doomed men, but they still fought their guns indomitably, slamming home the ammunition as fast as possible and firing at point-blank range as they crouched behind their flimsy shields, on which the bullets were rattling viciously. Only the four 25-pdrs could fire HE. Hely watched with admiration the 'magnificent bearing' of his NCOs, but watched also the step-by-step advance of the enemy infantry, cautious but seemingly

140

inexorable. He could see no way to extricate and was ready 'to fight to the muzzle'. All hope of survival seemed to be lost, when suddenly a troop of Honeys 'roared out of the gathering gloom, charged straight into the German infantry and, firing with every weapon that they had, halted the enemy attack long enough for the gunners to hook in and pull out'.[15]

In the November gloom that last scene, as the rear-guard guns slipped out of action, was one to inspire awe in all beholders, as indeed its relics were to do for years to come. The hundreds of dead bodies, the flames of burning vehicles and ammunition, the twisted wreckage of guns, the still smouldering ambulances bombed by the German aircraft, the bullet-riddled trucks, the crushed German aircraft, the blackened hulks of British and enemy tanks, with their turrets, tracks and guns ripped off in scrap-heaps of mangled steel, and the roasted corpses hanging out of their turrets gave to that harsh desert the air of desolation upon desolation, yet, to those who had eyes to see, it told also of innumerable acts of unrecorded heroism. Significantly, it told also of the destruction already of some 85 German tanks.

Two brief comments on this hard-fought action deserve recording. Alistair Banks, of 4th RHA, declared: 'The courage of many of the tank crews, going in to almost certain death, was fantastic. The same goes for the 2-pdrs of 3rd RHA; Ward Gunn's driving out to get into close range was magnificent. We in the 25-pdr regiments, however, came out gratified with the knowledge that we had established complete dominance over the Pzs. We could outshoot them easily.'

Hely, who served in the thick of many other battles — in Burma, Crete and Greece as well as those in the Desert — wrote: 'I have always considered Sidi Rezeg to be the most

---

[15] Brigadier Hely in *The Royal Artillery Commemoration Book*.

exciting and inspiring experience of the whole war. Every man of every arm performed his duty to the full and the confidence which this gave to us all made this a truly memorable battle.'

To all who served on that airfield amid the 'reeking tube and iron shard' the grand inspiration had been the daring and example of Jock Campbell, who was most justly awarded the Victoria Cross. Alistair Banks had never really believed the historians who spoke of generals being 'heroes to their men'. Today, however, as he listened to the conversations of his gunners, he found out that it was a true saying. Campbell was indeed a hero to them and when he passed by with his blue flag up, they cheered and waved — phenomenon indeed among British troops — and when he came back from the ridge, holding his side and clearly in pain, there was consternation among them.

But Jock had not yet finished his exploits.

Black Sunday

So ended what might be called the First Battle of Sidi Rezeg. It was but one of many battles in the *Crusader* complex, several of which were to rage on the same scarred ground a few days later. The great expanse of the whole *Crusader* battlefield now became a scene of wild confusion, in which only Godwin-Austen's corps and the Tobruk garrison behaved with any sort of tactical decorum. Dense and bewildering was the fog of war. On the very night that Sidi Rezeg was vacated 15 Pz (on their way to answer 21st's call for help) gate-crashed the leaguer of 4th Armoured Brigade's headquarters by mere chance, completely disorganizing the brigade for 36 hours, but early next morning the New Zealanders similarly crashed those of the *DAK* itself. For our purposes, however, we shall merely adumbrate with a light hand the more easily distinguishable features of this military entanglement, confining ourselves to the broad avenue of events, in which a fifth VC was still to be won.

On Sunday, the 22nd, Rommel, deeming that the British attempt to relieve Tobruk had been foiled and that the armour of 30th Corps was in disarray (as it indeed it was), ordered Crüwell to march the whole of *DAK* southwards, unite with the Ariete Division (now under his command) and wipe out the remainder of the British forces on the main plateau south of Sidi Rezeg. This meant Norrie's 30th Corps, which consisted of 1st South African Division, the dismembered remnants of 7th Armoured Division, the Guards Brigade, and Gatehouse's 4th Armoured Brigade, temporarily shaken by the beating-up of their headquarters but still a strong force.

The Support Group, on quitting Sidi Rezeg, was ordered to withdraw some four miles to the south and join hands with 5th South African Brigade, who were assembled in a rectangular formation, with a huge fleet of their supply vehicles in their rear. Campbell's Group was anything but coherent, and on the misty dawn of the 23rd lay scattered in small parcels, with their own supply echelon alongside the Springboks', thus enlarging the rectangle to about five miles by three. Campbell himself took post on the eastern side. Currie deployed 4th RHA, with 203 Battery under command, on the north-east of the rectangle. Hely put down the trails of the 14 remaining guns of 60th Field in the northern fringe, among the Transvaal Scottish, and the 30-odd Crusaders which remained of 22nd Armoured Brigade, now under Bill Carr, took station on the west.

At about 7 a.m. Crüwell , with a herd of 150 tanks and a lorried brigade of German infantry at his command, took 15 Pz and the infantry on a southerly course to the eastward of

Norrie's forces in pursuance of Rommel's orders. After some
five or six miles the Panzers turned west and crashed first into
the supply echelons like rhinoceroses among a herd of gazelles.
These scattered in wild confusion and a great slaughter seemed
imminent.

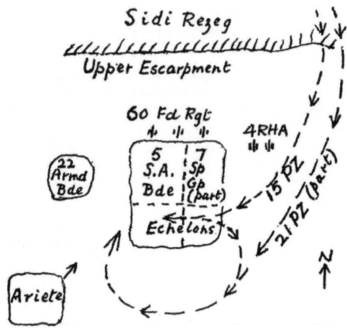

Crusader. 'Black Sunday.' Diagrammatic, not to scale.

The desperate situation (in which no one exercised overall
command) would have been even worse if Jock Campbell had
not been near at hand. 'For the second time,' says the historian
of 11th Hussars, 'he performed one of his prodigious feats.'
After taking into his custody six foot-loose tanks, he mounted
the roof of his Armoured Command Vehicle (a lightly
armoured lorry) and went about calling upon every gun and

armoured vehicle he came across to rally to him. He carried two flags made from his scarves, a red one for 'Stop' and a blue for 'Go'. While everyone else was 'going like hell', he ordered his driver not to exceed eight miles an hour. To all whom he gleaned he cried: 'Expect no orders. Stick to me.'[16]

Among those who had come out with him from Sidi Rezeg, and who stuck close to him all this day, was the Rhodesian Troop of 2-pdrs under Lieutenant Guy Savory, on their portees. One of the little guns was commanded by Bombardier Vere Margesson, who was a brother of the British Secretary of State for War. Out of the welter Margesson saw four German tanks detach themselves from their main column and bear down on Campbell's command vehicle. At once he swung his portee round and moved forward. The Germans spotted him and opened fire with high explosives and machine-guns. Margesson and his detachment, watched by Campbell, remained unmoved and did not open fire until the tanks had closed to killing range. By very cool shooting, he then knocked out three of the four, and the last steered away and made off.

Thus, after a fashion, Campbell managed to form an extempore fighting force, which he took away a little to the south, where he quickly organized them for counter-attack and began shelling the enemy.

Other troops also reacted offensively. Ten Panzers were knocked out by the gallant remnant of J Battery. Hardy's Troop shot up some German lorries, dashed out and captured two staff-cars and their occupants. Bob Crisp, the South African Test cricketer serving in 3rd Royal Tanks, leading a detachment of Honeys that had got separated from his regiment, stumbled upon a battery of German guns, which he took in the rear, overran and captured.

---

[16] *The Eleventh At War*, by Brigadier Dudley Clarke.

Thus, despite the appalling confusion of the fleeing transport, the German armour was surprisingly brought to a halt, uncertain what to do next. The War Diary of 15th Panzers admits unequivocally (though with the Germans' habitual exaggeration): 'Again and again strong enemy battle groups with tanks, anti-tank guns and artillery, came out of the desert and tried to take the Division in flank.'

So sharp was the check to 15 Pz that Crüwell, after extricating his tanks with difficulty, withdrew them away to the south for four hours while he made a new plan for the attack on the South African Brigade, now lying to the north of him. The British resistance had seemed to him so strong that he did not think he could destroy the Springboks without the help of the Ariete and of his own laggard 21 Pz, hard hit at Sidi Rezeg, whom he had ordered to come in from the north. Meanwhile, he kept the Springboks under intermittent shellfire from Belhamed. Then he swung his 120 tanks and his infantry to the south-west and, joined later by the Ariete, bore down again on the South African brigade at about 3 p.m.

That brigade, allergic to advice, was mentally and tactically quite unfit to face a German onslaught. They seemed, said Gott, surveying them from the fringes of the battle, 'to be stuck down with glue'. The infantry were quickly overwhelmed in a collapse long remembered by them as 'Black Sunday'. But the Springbok guns, although badly disposed, gave the enemy a tremendously hot reception, many of them fighting to the end.

The Sidi Rezeg regiments again fought staunchly, knocking out tank after tank, but 3rd RHA, once more in the thick of the fighting, lost heavily. A troop of the much scarred but undaunted J Battery was knocked to pieces by shell-fire at short range. Carr led out his yeomanry Crusaders with undiminished spirit, throwing the enemy on the west side off balance but losing eleven more of his own tanks.

As the Germans drove through the paralysed Springbok brigade and neared its northern perimeter, they came under a very hot fire from the 25-pdrs of 60th Field Regiment. Tim Hely had swung round into 'Action Rear' and again there was a stiff engagement. The gunners endured further casualties but with the utmost zest knocked out several Panzers in swift succession. The War Diary of 8th Panzer Regiment speaks of 'fierce, desperate resistance' and of 'shell-fire without abatement'. Though some of the tanks approached as close as 250 yards, the German penetration was at last stopped.

Currie's guns of 4th RHA and 203rd Battery on the northeast likewise brought the German armour to a halt, but Jerboa Battery, coming under close and intense fire, was badly cut up and nearly overrun until Terence O'Brien-Butler, his driver killed and his signaller wounded, drove over and hazardously extricated them at the last moment.

Meanwhile, at about 4 o'clock, Jock Campbell had led out his small and extempore party of old tanks and guns from the south to harass the Germans in rear and flank. He was still accompanied by Guy Savory's Rhodesian troop of 2-pdrs. On the way the portees got bogged in the soft sand of a saltpan and, at that moment, out of the dust, thirteen Italian tanks of the Ariete Division appeared suddenly on their way to join the Germans. They made straight for the stranded Rhodesian guns, which seemed at their mercy, but, under Campbell's immediate eye, Savory himself instantly leapt into the layer's seat of one of his guns and clean knocked out no fewer than eight of the Italians, most of them in flames. He then surrendered his post to Bombardier 'Rosie' Rosselt, who knocked out four more. It was a brilliant example of quick-thinking offensive action and of the high spirit that animated the Rhodesian anti-tank gunners throughout the Desert war.

By about 5 o'clock the Germans, had completely overrun the Springbok brigade, gathering in some 3,500 prisoners. Nearly all the Support Group and Carr's Crusaders, however, made good their escape, the Crusaders crashing right through the Germans. Hely, whose Intelligence officer had been killed beside him in his car, gave orders to his batteries to withdraw on an easterly compass bearing. Waiting himself to the very end, he found his medical officer, Captain Hugh Stanton, amputating a sergeant's leg and warned him to get away as soon as possible. The doctor replied quietly that his place was with his patient. He completed his amputation under fire and was taken prisoner.

Reluctantly Hely, now alone, mounted his truck and followed the dust of his last guns. Again a shot hit his truck and wrecked it. He got out and began to walk. A truckful of South African officers came by tamely intending to give themselves up. He stopped them, reminded them that the Germans would not let them keep their truck, so would they mind if he had it? They said Yes, and could they go with him? Apparently the idea of getting out on their own had not occurred to them.

When Hely counted the cost afterwards, to 60th Field in those four feverish days, during which his Territorials had fought with rare steadiness and gallantry, he found that it had amounted to 18 officers and 180 men.

Thus the first part of Crüwell's mission had been accomplished, but at very heavy cost, for he had lost another 72 tanks knocked out or disabled and he had also lost severely in manpower, particularly among officers. The erosion of his tanks, begun at Sidi Rezeg, was carried a stage further. Half of his original force had already been eaten away.

Some time during that night Rommel experienced a sort of midsummer madness. At the unpropitious hour of 6 a.m. on the 24th he visited Crüwell and, waving aside all his protests and ignoring the battering that his Korps had endured, ordered him to abandon his plans for completing the destruction of 30th Corps, to about-turn and to embark on a dramatic adventure to which the whole of the Axis armour would be committed. He saw himself suddenly as the master of the battlefield and his opportunist mind saw a chance of executing one of those spectacular *blitzkreig* swoops that always excited his imagination.

Personally leading the Afrika Korps, he set out four hours later, his thundering columns aiming south-eastwards directly towards the main British lines on the frontier. His declared purpose was to bring relief to his own infantry divisions there, now under pressure from the British, but later in the day he changed his mind again and made a new plan by which he proposed no less than the complete destruction of Cunningham's army.

Thus began what Eighth Army was derisively to call 'Rommel's Romp' or 'the Matruh Stakes'. The German column, numbering some 2,000 tanks, guns and vehicles, stretched over some 20 miles of desert and its flanks were harried all the way by some 2-pdrs of the Northumberland Hussars under George Cookson, by Marriott's Guards and by a few tanks. Again the dominant figure was that of Jock Campbell, who, his arm in a bandage, spent the first day and night sitting on the bonnet of his ACV, like a mahout on an elephant, whipping up foot-loose guns, tanks and armoured

cars, bellowing orders and exhortations until his voice sank to
a ghostly whisper.

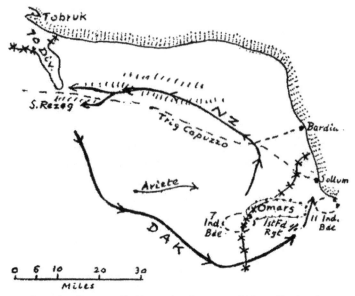

Crusader: 'Rommel's Romp', advance of New Zealand
Division and capture of Ed Duda.

Rommel's counter-offensive, against which Crüwell
continued to remonstrate, was a complete fiasco. Beyond
causing some local embarrassments, pillaging a few petrol
dumps and beating up some tanks under repair in a field
workshop, it achieved nothing at all. Driving to the southern,
open end of the British line facing the Axis fortified positions
at the Omars, the Panzer divisions swung northwards in an
enveloping movement behind the British. It was a typical
Rommel plan, audacious, swift and in full force; but it was
made with a faulty knowledge of the tactical situation and of
the British temper. Rommel's expectations that the British

would panic at this encirclement were completely confounded. Eighth Army stood firm and fought. Their artillery regiments of all sorts again gave the enemy a fierce reception.

Another epic gun *v.* tank battle was fought, behind the British line, on 25 November. At sunrise on that day the 25-pdrs of 1st Field Regiment, commanded by Lt-Colonel T. S. Dobree, were returning from supporting 4th/11th Sikhs in an attack on the Omars when an armoured car brought news that some 25 German tanks were approaching from the south. Dobree's guns immediately deployed in the open to protect the Sikhs and a nearby transport column of the New Zealanders. There was no time to dig in and the guns were in full exposure. Preceded by their dust, the enemy tanks were sighted at 3,000 yards. They were 5th Panzer Regiment on their way to 21st Panzer Division's HQ. Their CO, Lt-Colonel Stephan, had just been mortally wounded in a low-flying attack by the RAF, and the regiment was now led by the portly Major Mildebrath.

The British gunners, lying low, watched the enemy tanks deploy well spaced, according to their drill, and advance to a range of 2,000 yards. There they halted and opened fire with high explosive. Still the gunners made no move. The tanks came on, attacking with their machine-guns while on the move and halting every few hundred yards to open fire again with their main armament. As they came nearer, their fire became more accurate and the gunners took heavy casualties, but stoically lay motionless behind their pieces.

Then, at 800 yards, the gunners leapt to their feet and opened rapid fire, watching the tracer dart towards its target and the solid shot burn red-hot holes in the armour. Under a hail of bullets and high explosives men dropped dead or wounded on every side, but the remainder, pulling aside the bodies of their comrades, stuck to their posts. The tanks moved yet nearer to 500 yards and halted again, and even closer still, till only 300 yards separated the two adversaries. The fight raged in flames and dust for 45 minutes. Sixty-two gunners lay dead or wounded around their pieces. But the guns were served. As one man fell another took on double duty.

Five of Dobree's guns were knocked out. But the Germans had had enough. With nearly every tank hit and seven in flames, they wheeled sharply and turned away. As they did so the 2-pdrs of 2nd South African Anti-Tank Regiment came up on their portees under Major Hudson and knocked out an eighth.

The worst of the fury fell on 52 Battery on the western flank. Upon them the Panzers, making a second attack after withdrawal, concentrated, blasting them at 250 yards. The battery suffered 42 casualties, but the remainder never wavered, giving back shot for shot.

Nor was this all. In the afternoon, Mildebrath having retired some six miles, Rommel came up and, interfering in what was the concern of General von Ravenstein, ordered 5th Panzer Regiment to attack one of the Omars, which he had tardily discovered to be in British hands. Mildebrath, his numbers apparently partly augmented, obeyed, as ignorant as Rommel of what the task involved. Under the gaze of a semicircle of infantry, like spectators in an amphitheatre, he advanced against the Omars, opened fire with HE at 4,000 yards and, receiving no reply, as before, continued to advance in the same manner.

The spectators held their breath as the tanks topped a low rise 800 yards from the nearest guns. At that moment the men of 25th Field Regiment sprang up and the first salvo from their 25-pdrs blew the leading tanks to pieces. To their fire was added that of the heavier guns of 68th Medium Regiment, a troop of Hudson's 2-pdrs and the Bofors guns of 57th Light Anti-Aircraft Regiment. The tanks swung to the west under punishment. Five reeled to a halt and six more were disabled as, to the cheers of the excited audience, the enemy turned and withdrew. That night the diarist of 5th Panzer Regiment recorded that it was reduced to ten tanks, of which only three were fit to fight.[17]

Altogether Rommel lost 30 or more tanks in this ill-considered escapade. Von Ravenstein's division was reduced to 24. The Royal Air Force harried both from on high. Squadron by squadron, the Panzers ran out of fuel and ammunition, as Crüwell had said they would. The hard-driven tank crews, fighting with their customary bravery, were worn out and bemused. Orders and counter-orders poured from Rommel's radio in swift succession. Both he and Crüwell, occupying the same command vehicle, got stuck in some barbed wire and were lucky to escape capture.

Then, on 26 November, after three days of freebooting, came news that sent the 'Desert Fox' racing back. Eighth Army, strengthened now by the reassuring figure of Auchinleck, had refused to be deflected from its purpose by these armoured antics and had continued steadily to do just what Rommel thought he had successfully prevented. For at that moment, far behind him, the New Zealanders were about to join hands with the Tobruk garrison; and that night they did so.

James Jackman

While the Romp was in progress Alan Cunningham, who had been under great strain, was relieved by Lt-General Neil Ritchie, and for the greater part of the time henceforward the

---

[17] *Royal Artillery Commemoration Book* and Agar-Hamilton *op. cit.*

calm and reassuring figure of Auchinleck himself was also close to Eighth Army headquarters, not issuing operational orders like Rommel, but giving overall direction. Rommel, he said, was 'lashing out in all directions' and would bring about his own destruction if Eighth Army kept its head. In the midst of the turbulent and daunting scene 'the Auk' exuded confidence, insisting on the maintenance of the objective, and Bernard Freyberg's eager New Zealanders were briskly getting on with it behind Rommel's back.

Thus two rival and contrary offensives were being conducted simultaneously in opposite directions; by the Panzers on their southern route and by Godwin-Austen's 13th Corps on the opposite course by a northern route, ably conducted throughout. Moving astride the Trig Capuzzo and fighting a battle every day and often at night as well, the Kiwis, accompanied by two regiments of Valentine tanks of 1st Army Tank Brigade, captured Belhamed after a stiff fight and reached the edge of Sidi Rezeg, where there was more very hard fighting, particularly with the Italian Bersaglieri, who fought bravely.

Freyberg's orders were to capture Ed Duda and to join up there with Scobie's 70th Division from Tobruk, but Scobie, hearing that the New Zealanders had been checked at Sidi Rezeg, beat the pistol and captured Ed Duda himself on 26 November. His sparkling success in doing so was memorable for an exploit that led to the fifth Crusader VC.

Ed Duda was a long ridge of high ground. Its importance to both armies was that it dominated the Axis main line of communication. Likewise, it dominated all the ground northwards towards Tobruk, across which 70th Division would have to attack. The distance from the 'Tiger' position, previously captured, was about 3½ miles.

The attack was to be commanded by Brigadier 'Ant' Willison, who would take into battle with him the Matildas of 32nd Army Tank Brigade, together with the machine-gunners of 1st Royal Northumberland Fusiliers and a fine battalion of infantry in the 1st Essex Regiment. It is with the machine-gunners that we shall be chiefly concerned in this narrative.

The Royal Northumberland Fusiliers are a regiment of very old renown, long known in the Army as the Fifth Fusiliers or by their nickname of 'the Fighting Fifth'. The 1st Battalion, commanded by Tubby Martin, was composed mainly of seasoned pre-war Regular soldiers, who had been in more or less continuous action for some 17 months and whose battle drill in deployment and coming into action was quite superb. The battalion's Z Company was led by a handsome young Irishman, Captain James Jackman, himself a Regular soldier of six years' service. The son of a doctor, he had been born in Dublin but lived afterwards at Waterford: then had come Stoneyhurst and Sandhurst before he was gazetted. He was now 26 years old, slim, erect, with a fine face full of character and determination. He walked with an athletic gait and had grown to be a man of great personal charm, deeply religious, but very sensitive and artistic and, as befitted an Irishman, he loved an argument on almost any subject. In his chosen vocation he was ardently professional and was a highly efficient soldier.

To these not particularly remarkable qualities, James Jackman added a more compelling one. 'He was,' said Lieutenant Derek Lloyd, his second-in-command, 'a very much loved man and the soldiers were utterly miserable at his death.' A more junior subaltern, Second-Lieutenant Bill Sanderson, records: 'All of us were devoted to James. Just after I joined the battalion, my platoon sergeant said to me: "Whatever the captain says is right." In action he was always perfectly calm, detached and professional.'

In the previous break-out operation Jackman had already behaved with conspicuous skill and bravery, displaying his rare tactical sense and his gift of leadership. Sanderson relates that 'the way he led 14 Platoon right on to the enemy and then came back for 13 and 15 Platoons, through a shocking amount of enemy defensive fire and in front of a hesitant battalion of infantry, was a mixture of very decisive tactical thinking and pure heroism'.

The attack on Ed Duda went very well. The enemy on the crest were mostly Italians in positions well wired and mined, but Willison (with a woman's silk stocking tied to his mast) met little opposition as his Matildas crawled up the long slope in full view and, though his own tank was knocked out, he ran about angrily to find another. As the Matildas neared the crest, heavy fire burst on them from all sorts of artillery, including the 8-inch howitzers from Belhamed. A blanket of dust from the shell-bursts obliterated everything from view, but as they halted, hull-down, short of the crest, the murk was stabbed with gun flashes. Assuming them to be enemy tanks, the Matildas replied with their 2-pdrs. A gust of wind, however, blew the sand away for a minute and showed Willison that the flashes came not from tanks but from guns on the ground. He radioed to all his own tanks: 'Cease 2-pdr. All Besa.'

Jackman, watching from his position in the rear, sensed that the moment was critical. He had 12 Vickers guns in his three platoons. Each gun, with its detachment, was transported in a small, very old Morris truck, with other trucks for the platoon commanders and sergeants. Z Company moved forward in line-ahead, with Jackman leading, the jovial Company Sergeant-

Major Hughes immediately behind him and Derek Lloyd in the rear of the three platoons.

Following the drill in which he had thoroughly rehearsed his company for the operation, Jackman closed up at speed and sent Hughes forward to a point little short of the crest, where, with complete sang-froid, he dismounted, stood up among the crashes of the 8-inch shells, and waved a large red flag. On this prearranged signal, each platoon broke formation, the drivers stamped on their accelerators and headed fast for the localities of the battlefield that Jackman had previously allotted to them.

With the greatest audacity and with 'very decisive tactical thinking', Jackman, himself leading one of the platoons, took his guns right to the very crest, ahead even of the Matildas, in the thick of the tank *v.* gun battle. As each truck halted, the gun was dismounted and brought into action in a flash, and at once began engaging the enemy guns and other targets. The Trig Capuzzo was in full view below them.

In a memorable demonstration of fearless leadership Jackman then toured the whole of the front, in close proximity to the enemy, standing upright in his truck, visiting each gun to correct its siting and to co-ordinate the fire of all, so that they interlocked. Continuously under shell-fire, he also quickly became the target of aimed bursts from the enemy's own machine-guns. He ignored it all. Beginning on the right flank, he drove right across the front, between the tanks and the enemy guns, and so to his left flank. Seeming to bear a charmed life, he went round again picking out targets and, in the words of his Victoria Cross citation, 'his magnificent bearing was contributory in a large measure to the success of a most difficult and hard-fought action'.

Coming finally to Sanderson's platoon, Jackman dismounted and dropped down beside Corporal Gare's gun, where, kneeling, he began to search the enemy country through his field-glasses. Observing a German truck on the Trig Capuzzo, he ordered quietly: 'Give them a burst.' At that moment a mortar bomb detonated immediately in front. Jackman and Gare were killed instantly and three others wounded.

Jackman's soldierly exploit, for which he was posthumously awarded the Victoria Cross, sealed the success of the operation. By his swift and aggressive deployment, right forward, he ensured protection against immediate counter-attack and provided a shield until the 1st Essex, undaunted by heavy bombing by their own aircraft, were able to come up under the rugged and daring Old Etonian, 'Crasher' Nichols.

Sidi Rezeg Again

Beyond the Trig the New Zealanders that night fought through the devastation of Sidi Rezeg in a hard and bloody battle and joined forces with 70th Division. Godwin-Austen himself went through soon afterwards and signalled: 'Tobruk isn't half as relieved as I am.' Standing out as the most able field commander on either side, he was throughout the confused operations confident and clear-headed and the Kiwis were a magnificent tool for his design.

The whole battle became concentrated in the north on and around Sidi Rezeg and along the Trig, as the *DAK* came hurrying back in the rear of the New Zealanders. The 4th and 22nd Armoured Brigades swung northwards to meet them and a grim battle was fought behind the New Zealanders under a threatening sky for three hours. The enemy were again roughly handled by the British artillery (2nd and 4th RHA and the Northumberland Hussars) and reduced to 43 tanks, but they slipped away during the night and made for Ed Duda, with orders to eject 70 Division from its new-won ground.

Their attempt failed after a long, stiff and fluctuating fight in the face of superlative resistance by Crasher Nichols's Essex, the 2nd/13th Australians and some Matildas of 4th Royal Tanks, the battle ending with a dramatic night charge by the Matildas and the Australians, packed shoulder to shoulder. Meanwhile, by dogged determination the New Zealanders kept the corridor to Tobruk open for five days, capturing 2,500 prisoners. But before long they were under unbearable pressure. Not receiving the relief they expected from the South Africans, overstretched and exhausted after ten days of very hard fighting, one by one their battalions began to be overrun. So was their main dressing station, with 1,000 wounded men. Sidi Rezeg was once more lost. On the night of 1 December, Bernard Freyberg, with permission, withdrew all but one of his brigades out of battle, to reform their valiant and attenuated ranks.

Tobruk was once more sealed off.

As so often happens, however, it was when the battle appeared to many to have been lost that it was in fact beginning to be won. Amid all the mistakes that were made, the one vital thing that Eighth Army did right, under Auchinleck's calm direction, was to maintain their objective. For the enemy's losses had become very heavy indeed. On 1 December, Rommel admitted to Marshal Bastico that the situation was grave, yet he continued fruitlessly to 'lash out in all directions'. The *DAK* was reduced to a mere 40 tanks and was near the end of its tether; 70 Division stood like a rock. Another attempt against the stubborn Crasher Nichols at Ed Duda failed. The New Zealand dressing station was recovered and among those released was Captain Stanton, the gallant medical officer of 60th Field Regiment, who, alongside German doctors, had been attending the wounded of both sides.

On the 7th, in a tempestuous mood, cursing the Italians but blind to his own faults, Rommel was at last forced to admit defeat and began a retreat of 400 miles right back to the Tripolitanian border. He had lost heavily in every department of his forces, including the commanders of all three of his German divisions: von Ravenstein of 21 Pz, taken prisoner, Neumann-Silkow of 15th, mortally wounded, and Summerman of 90 Light, killed in a RAF raid soon after the retreat began.

In retrospect, *Crusader* had shown that the great battle-winning elements were not the armour, whose reign as lords of the Desert had now been brusquely challenged, but the infantry and the gunners; and a year later El Alamein was to prove that dominion conclusively. *Crusader* had also shown, as many another field has done, that a battle, even when ill-directed, can still be won by the steadiness, guts and devotion of the British soldier and his officers, even against a first-class enemy. For *Crusader*, with five VCs in its 19 tempestuous days, was very much a soldiers' battle. In that bewildering whirlpool of arms, amid all the sulphurous smoke, the flames, the blood and swirling dust, among the tangled wreckage of tanks and shattered vehicles, while columns and convoys of both sides struck and weaved in all directions under a lowering sky, Thomas Atkins and his regimental officers had overcome an equally brave enemy in fair-and-square combat.[18]

---

[18] No account *of Crusader* can be written without acknowledging indebtedness, as I now do, to the meticulous South African official history entitled *The Battles of Sidi Rezeg 1941*, by Agar-Hamilton and Turner (OUP), and *The Royal Artillery Commemoration Book* (R.A. Charitable Fund). Other valuable sources are given in Appendix C.

5: GAZALA

After *Crusader* the fortunes of both warring sides in the enormous wastes of the Western Desert resumed again their pattern of ebb and flow. The Nazi-Fascist army under Rommel, driven back to the borders of Tripolitania in December 1941, paused, re-formed and was strongly reinforced, particularly in tanks and aircraft.

The British troops opposing them, however, became much weakened and dispersed, just as they had been a year before on the same frontier, following O'Connor's victory over the Italians. Nor had they any good defensive position. The resilient Rommel, having mounted what was intended as only a limited spoiling attack on 21 January, scattered the dispersed elements of Eighth Army as a fox does chickens, and, tartly brushing aside a restraining order from Mussolini, developed a full-blooded offensive. Early in February, Eighth Army withdrew to a mid-desert position known as the Gazala Line.

Here its right flank rested on the sea some 35 miles west of Tobruk and from there it ran for about the same distance southwards across a particularly arid, waterless, lifeless desert, hot as a furnace in summer and swept by searing sandstorms, until it reached the desolate Bir Hakeim, an ancient halt for Bedouin caravans.[19] Along this line, traversed by a series of escarpments running roughly west-and-east, the army constructed a series of 'boxes' or defended localities, like links in a broken chain, connected by 'mine marshes', one of which was 15 miles long. Here for nearly four months the two armies

---

[19] A *bir* is a well or water-hole.

glared at one another, each building up its strength for the next clash.

German and Italian aircraft rose to a strength which considerably exceeded that of the Desert Air Force. The Deutsches Afrika Korps became equipped with a fleet of new tanks with thickened and toughened armour. The anti-tank guns increased, with 48 of the 88-mm. From far distant shores the British also received new strength. The losses of the Desert Air Force were made good, but they still had no answer to the Messerschmitt 109 F. From America, now Britain's active ally, came 165 of the new Lee-Grant tank. It outgunned all but the newest Nazi tanks (though not the 88-mm anti-tank gun) but suffered serious disadvantages by its conspicuousness, its limited arc of fire and the deadly inflammability of its high-octane petrol. The first trickle of the new 6-pdr anti-tank gun, later to prove a battle-winning weapon, also began to arrive.

No outside source, however, could make good the acute shortage of water, severely felt in the burning, dust-filled air.

As the day of battle approached and the desert sun waxed in ferocity, each side saw a few changes in its commanders since *Crusader*. On the enemy side Crüwell had been succeeded as head of the *DAK* by General Nehring. On the British side Sir Claude Auchinleck was still Commander-in-Chief of Middle East Forces, and Eighth Army was still headed by Lt-General Neil Ritchie. He was a handsome, pipe-smoking officer of a charming personality, with an urbane and tranquil disposition, the last man in the world to 'flap'. Later Ritchie was to prove an able corps commander in Europe, but his temperament was not suited to the quick decisions necessary in the swiftly-moving events of the Desert. After some 20 years as a staff-officer he tended to operate by the staff-officer's method of consultation rather than by decisive command. Moreover, his very equanimity led him to be far too sanguine when things were going badly.

Under Ritchie, 13 Corps was now commanded by 'Strafer' Gott. His corps stood on the northern wing and was composed wholly of infantry and infantry-support tanks. On the coast was 1st South African Division, now fit and battle-worthy, under the cagey Dan Pienaar. In the centre, led by the fearless 'Tickler' Ramsden, brandishing his fly-whisk, was 50th (Northumbrian) Division, a fine, fighting Territorial formation from Yorkshire and Durham, wearing its 'Tyne and Tees' badge.

The 30th Corps, still commanded by Willoughby Norrie, lay in the centre and the south, behind the infantry and the mine marshes. Its chief elements now were 1st and 7th Armoured Divisions. The 1st was led by the forthright and soldierly Herbert Lumsden and the 7th, the Desert Rats, by the adventurous Indian cavalryman, Frank Messervy, a man of many hair's-breadth escapes, who was to prove a great success as an infantry leader in Burma but who was not very fortunate in the armoured battles of the Desert.

The division's old Support Group of Jock Campbell's day was now 7th Motor Brigade, on a surveillance mission in the deep south. Still farther south lay the lonely Bir Hakeim box, garrisoned by the gallant Free French under the able Brigadier-General Koenig; they were separated from 50th Division by the mine marsh 15 miles long.

The Battle Begins

The enemy was ready first. His objective was a limited one; he aimed to capture Tobruk and the orders from Rome were that Rommel was to go no farther than the Egyptian frontier, 65 miles farther on, when the main Axis effort would switch to a massive assault on Malta, with the invasion of Egypt to follow later.

It was Rommel's first large-scale deliberate assault. His plan, based on very defective knowledge of the British dispositions, was not so much audacious as foolhardy, for his sense of strategy was much inferior to his tactical flair. In essence, his method was simply a repetition of the 'Romp' of six months before. He counted on destroying Ritchie by a powerful 'right hook' round the southern flank, followed by a sweep up to the coast behind the South Africans. He reckoned to do this in 24 hours and then to seize that prize that had tantalized him so long — Tobruk. On these calculations he deserved to lose the forthcoming battle; that he won it was due to the mistakes of his adversaries, his own speedy opportunism in taking advantage of them and the well co-ordinated battle drill of his divisions.

In the early hours of 27 May, raising huge clouds of dust, Rommel himself led out a force of 500 German and Italian tanks, together with the Panzer Grenadiers of 90th Light Division and 10,000 vehicles. Sweeping down to the south, he rounded Bir Hakeim and then swung in behind Eighth Army. He surprised and scattered *seriatim* most of the elements of 7th Armoured Division that lay just round the corner, captured Messervy's own divisional headquarters and swept on, northwards now.

By noon, on a day of fierce, shimmering heat, Rommel believed that he had already won the main battle, as he had expected, and he sent 90th Light Division pushing deep into the north. Halfway to Tobruk, however, Nehring's *DAK* was brought up very sharply and suffered heavy losses when skilfully attacked by 2nd Armoured Brigade under Raymond Briggs and by the Matildas of 1st Army Tank Brigade. Rommel was now in that desolate stretch of the desert plateau to become notorious as 'the Cauldron', deep in behind the British defences, but he had already lost one-third of his tanks and the remainder of his force lay scattered in Eighth Army's back-yard, very short of fuel, and with the British mine marshes behind him.

With considerable moral courage, Rommel bit in a little deeper still next day with 21 Pz, but before the end of the day found himself in serious difficulties. He had lost 200 tanks and to Briggs he had lost 27 guns. His supplies were in imminent peril. His enemies lay all round him, in some disarray but full of fight. He admitted that 'he was very worried indeed'. A great and decisive British victory seemed to all men to be at hand. Indeed, the sanguine Ritchie is said to have exclaimed, 'Now we've got him!'

So it should have been. Unhappily, at the moment when purposefulness and prompt action were obviously needed, his headquarters was beset with indecision and sluggishness. Before long the whole command structure degenerated to a soviet of generals. Unfair burdens fell on junior commanders, themselves left to act on purely local knowledge. There was no unanimity of effort by tanks and infantry. There was, in short, no vigorous generalship.

The third day of battle saw the 2nd and 22nd Armoured Brigades plunged in a murderous armoured battle fought in the Cauldron in a searing *khamsin*. Coated with dust and sweat, men panted for breath as the scorching wind swirled about them. Both sides fought themselves to a finish and at the end Rommel was forced to abandon his objective and devote himself to saving the *DAK* from destruction.

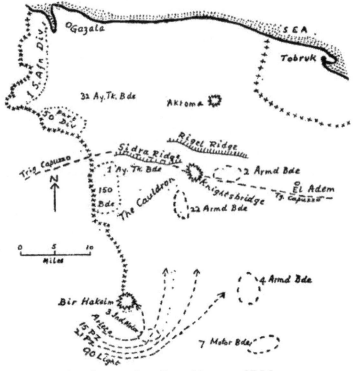

Gazala: opening dispositions on 27 May

In this emergency he showed himself at his best. Taking a firm grip of the deteriorating situation, he recalled all his most forward elements and, in accordance with classic military doctrine, concentrated his forces and stood at bay, pinned back against the British minefields but shielded from attack in front and flanks by a thick screen of anti-tank guns. While the soviet of British generals debated, he put his Italians to clearing two lanes through the unoccupied British minefield on his left rear to ensure his supplies. Then he turned with overwhelming force against the isolated minefield box behind him, held by Haydon's 150 Brigade (50 Division). Here 4th and 5th Green

Howards, 4th East Yorkshires, the guns of 124 Field Regiment, and the residue of 42 and 44 Royal Tanks fought him yard by yard in one of the most memorable defensive battles, for nearly three days till the last round of ammunition was spent, and Haydon himself killed, with no help from outside. Applauding them, Rommel said: 'As usual, the British fought to the end.' With his rear thus secured, he stood ready for the expected British counter-attack.

All this time a fiery heat enveloped the battlefield. Mirages danced on the shimmering horizon. Dust-devils spiralled up from the desert floor, to be followed by blinding sandstorms driven by a hot wind and mingled with the black smoke from burning tanks and vehicles. The severe water rationing accentuated the soldiers' trials. Rommel enjoyed air support as never before or after. But the morale of the British soldier stayed high. He fought with a blind courage which won the enemy's praise but which was vitiated by the fumblings of the higher command.

The 5th of June

For a fortnight the Cauldron seethed with fire, smoke, dust and blood. Not until 5 June did Ritchie at last make a serious effort to smash the *Panzerarmee*'s bridgehead, but it was to end in a disaster that was redeemed only by the valour and discipline of the fighting men who were committed to it. It was aimed at the enemy from two directions simultaneously. The main blow was to be from the east (under divided command) by one brigade only of 7th Armoured Division and two brigades of 5th Indian Infantry Division, while a secondary stroke was to be aimed from the north. We shall examine the latter first in brief terms, seeing there the prelude to what was to be the second Gazala VC.

167

The northern attack fell to the Matildas of 'Ant' Willison's 32nd Army Tank Brigade, which we have seen earlier doing so well at Tobruk and in which Philip Gardner had there won his VC. He was still with them, but acting as Liaison Officer with 50th Division. The brigade was required to capture an escarpment known as the Sidra Ridge, which formed the northern limit of the Cauldron and which was now firmly held by 21 Pz Division. The scarp was not very steep, but from the top the enemy had a commanding view of the approach to it.

Willison's brigade (which on this occasion he did not himself lead) was composed at that time of 7th and 42nd Royal Tanks. They mustered 76 Matildas. Commanding the 7th, on the left flank of the attack, was Lt-Colonel Bob Foote, known to his familiars as 'Fairy' Foote. An officer of the Regular service, he had already won the DSO. He was 37 years old, had been educated at Bedford School, and was of short and stocky build, fair complexioned, with a round face and conventional moustache. He had an equable disposition and his voice was quiet and controlled, until he broke into his infectious and rather high-pitched laugh. Obviously, one would say, a man of sound dependability and cheerful temper. On three occasions in the past week or so of fighting he had already shown his qualities of leadership and tactical skill and in two minor engagements had seen off superior enemy tank forces, despite the handicap of his weaker guns.

With a battalion of infantry standing by to follow them up, the brigade moved off at the first flush of light. Battle was joined just before 6 a.m. Emerging from a smoke-screen after their long, slow crawl over the open plain, the Matildas were struck by a violent storm of fire at a range of 400 yards from the flank screen of massed anti-tank guns at the top of the scarp, and were terribly mauled. The leading squadrons went up in flames at once. Foote, as was his custom, led in his regiment sitting on the outside of his tank. It was quickly knocked out. He jumped off and mounted another. As he was doing so he was wounded in the neck by a machine-gun bullet, not severely. His second tank was also knocked out and thereafter he led his regiment on foot under intense fire. There was little he could do except go from tank to tank, giving directions and encouragement and help in the grim business of extricating the wounded, but what mattered most was that his personal example and steady bearing maintained calm and order when many men would have wrung their hands under the cloudburst of disorder that broke over them.

He observed that the enemy's guns were well dug in and that they were supplemented by tanks, also dug in. The proposition was hopeless without powerful artillery support. So violent was the enemy fire that in a very short time no fewer than 64 of the brigade's 76 tanks were knocked out, Captain Craig's squadron fighting until every one was lost.

Foote observed to his adjutant, Captain Maclean: 'This is just damned silly. There's nothing to do but go.' Orders came from Willison by radio for Foote to take command of the remnants of both units and he therefore, with skill and calm and in good order, pulled them back a little, rallied them and put them in hull-down positions in a fold of the ground, where they stayed put until 8 p.m. defeated but not routed. Foote had advanced a little farther towards his VC.

The mutilation of the Heavy Brigade bore too painful a resemblance to that of Cardigan's Light Brigade, but was of far less serious importance than the calamity which befell the main attack by 7th Armoured and 5th Indian Divisions, against the enemy bridgehead from the east. It began promisingly in the chill darkness of 3 a.m., when the moon had gone, but had not been directed against the enemy's vitals, came under concentrated artillery fire and was driven back in confusion, the tanks failing to support the infantry through ambiguity in their orders.

The enemy saw his chance and in the afternoon, with the sun beating down like a hammer and with dust-devils dancing excitedly, launched a shattering counter-attack against the scattered and disorganized brigades. The headquarters of both divisions were overrun. The command structure broke down. Each unit fought its separate battle against the tanks, with the inevitable results. Unaided by their armour or airforce, shelled, dive-bombed, crushed by tanks, the infantry and gunners were badly cut up, dispersed and broken, yet many gallantly stood their ground.

The next morning the remnants of the two infantry brigades and their regiments of artillery tried on their own to hold a line, but, attacked on three sides by the tanks of 15 Pz and the Ariete, they stood no chance. Raymond Briggs started to go to their help with 2nd Armoured Brigade by a route of his own choosing, but was ordered to change course, and ran into trouble. The unaided infantry were overwhelmed and most of the gunners, fighting their ordnance to the last man, died at their posts; 96 field guns were lost, a crippling blow.

An Italian observer relates admiringly how, before the tanks finally closed in, a troop of British guns was kept in action to the end by a single gunner, who was seen running along the line of guns, firing each in turn. Six months later, when the Eighth Army returned in triumph after the victory of Alamein, the 25-pdrs of the South Notts Hussars were found still in position, the gunners still lying where they had fallen, the dead layers still crouched over their sights and all around them a devastation of their own burnt-out vehicles and of wrecked enemy tanks.

No VCs were awarded for any of the remarkable deeds of heroism in desperate situations on these two days. The valour of Lt-Colonel Ted des Gras, of the Royal Northumberland Fusiliers, who died manning a 2-pdr abandoned by another unit after a day of shining leadership; the epic of the South Notts Hussars under Colonel Seeley, who were ordered to fight 'to the last man' and virtually did so, with Seeley mortally wounded; the stubborn stand of a battery of the Northumberland Hussars — these and many other heroic actions in the smoke of conflict remain recorded only in regimental annals.

Springbok VC

A brighter picture was to be seen in the South African boxes in the north, where the first positive Gazala VC was won in a small and less deadly action. In response to the *DAK*'s urgent appeal for help when first locked up in the Cauldron, the Italians had made an ill-mounted attempt to break through the Springbok lines and had been decisively seen off. Then had begun a series of spirited raids against the enemy's lines, one of the most successful of which was a small raid by three platoons of the Royal Natal Carbineers, made at the same time as the British and Indians were beginning their ill-fated assault on the enemy's Cauldron position.

In the platoon commanded by Lieutenant K. H. Douglas was a sergeant named Quentin Smythe. He was a slight but well set-up figure, light in weight, modest in height, with well-chiselled features and a happy temperament. He was 25 years of age and was one of eleven children of a family in the rolling uplands of Natal. He had a passion for cricket and was a great lover of animals. With pre-war training as a volunteer in the Natal Carbineers, Smythe had seen service under Alan Cunningham in the campaigns of East Africa and Abyssinia, and came to Gazala a seasoned soldier, a very good marksman and an expert grenadier.

In the bitter cold of 3 a.m. on 5 June, as the partial moon gave way to the immense canopy of stars, the three platoons of the Carbineers filtered noiselessly forward through the minefield protecting their Alem Hamza box. From over their left shoulders they could hear the distant rumble of the busy artillery on the rim of the Cauldron, but in the entrenchments ahead of them, manned by the Italian Trento Division and stiffened by German machine-gunners, all was quiet. Their objective, enveloped by the night, was a stretch of elevated ground 3,000 yards away.

Emerging from the minefield, the Carbineers moved across the dark waste of no-man's-land towards their objective. Douglas's platoon was on the left flank. Direction and distance were controlled by the platoon leaders, each holding a compass and counting the paces. At 2,400 yards they halted and went to ground. At 5.20, while it was still dark, the South African artillery opened their barrage. The Carbineers still lay low, all eyes on their watches. At 5.30 Douglas gave his platoon that thrilling order 'Fix bayonets!' The 30 dark shapes rose and closed up to the barrage, with Sergeant Smythe at his post in their rear.

As the Springboks topped the slight incline the barrage stopped, but no enemy was immediately encountered. Then came the cry 'Enemy half-right!' Douglas swung the platoon round. With their bayonets high, they charged down the slight slope, shouting their Zulu war-cry, and fell upon the enemy.

At that moment Smythe saw his officer fall. He sprinted forward, found him to be wounded and unable to rise, and himself at once took command. A vicious close-quarter fight ensued, amid shots, grenade-bursts, the crackle of automatics, shouts and curses. Smythe himself, armed only with rifle and bayonet, slew four of the enemy. The first he shot dead at a range of ten yards. The second was a German emerging from a dug-out a few yards away and preparing to throw a grenade. Smythe leapt upon him and drove his bayonet deep into his chest; the German convulsively clutched the hilt of the bayonet with both hands, releasing the catch that secured it to the rifle, so that Smythe's rifle came away without bayonet.

This strongpoint having been overrun, Smythe led the platoon on to the next. As they approached it an enemy sprang up and flung a grenade. It burst close to Smythe, a splinter from it lodging in his skull just above the right eye, suffusing his vision with blood. Either then or soon afterwards he was also hit three times in the feet.

Scarcely had he recovered his faculties than the platoon came under fire from a machine-gun some 50 yards away. Smythe at once ordered his men to ground, resolving, in spite of his wounds, to attack the machine-gun alone. Wiping off the blood that kept running down into his eyes, he armed himself with grenades and crawled forward in the half-light, with the streams of machine-gun bullets darting just overhead, till he was within grenade range. Then he sprang up and threw a grenade with a cricketer's accuracy, wiping out the whole detachment.

The sergeant then hastened back to his platoon, to find it dispersed in three or four groups, each engaged defensively. He rallied them quickly and led them on again to the final objective. As they approached it they were dangerously attacked at point-blank range by a 47-mm anti-tank gun. Its flash and blast were near enough to dazzle them and its tracered shot darted among them in the semi-dark. Once more Smythe went forward alone and, in a remarkable feat of skill and nerve, shot two of the crew and took the remainder prisoners. The final objective was thus carried.

Smythe at once set about consolidating the captured position, ready for the expected counter-attack. It did not come, but, as the sun rose, the platoon came under heavy fire from artillery, mortars and machine-guns. Smythe, though now much affected by his wounds, disdained them all and set a shining example of leadership in the difficult situation that arose.

Full daylight showed him that he stood in a salient and separate from the other platoons on his right. As he looked out over the shell-swept scene, alert for emergencies, with the blood from his head wound still trickling down into his eye, he saw the men in the platoon to his right begin to move back. He did not know that the order to withdraw had been given; so he stood fast.

As the other platoons pulled out, the enemy, following up, began to close in on Smythe's post and to concentrate their force on to it. His heart, he confessed afterwards, was in his mouth. 'The bullets were coming in thick and fast', and the enemy, like the hosts of Midian, were creeping round and threatening encirclement.

For half an hour longer he clung on, until it was obvious that the situation was untenable. The South African artillery were putting down good defensive fire, and accordingly, taking advantage of it, Smythe very properly ordered a withdrawal on his own initiative and carried it out in soldierly order. In an hour and a half of stiff fighting the platoon had lost only one killed and seven wounded and the object of the raid had been fulfilled, with a useful bag of prisoners.

'Fairy' Foote

Having defeated the British counter-attack on 5 and 6 June, the *Panzerarmee* turned southwards in strength to subdue Hakeim, where Koenig's valiant Free French, ensconced in a maze of minefields, had been defying one assault after another. They continued their defiance against the vastly superior numbers now hurled against them until almost at the end of their tether, when Ritchie ordered their withdrawal after ten heroic days.

The loss of Hakeim, which was not vital ground, was followed by a far more grievous reverse. While the German armour was down south, Willoughby Norrie sent 2nd and 4th Armoured Brigades against them, and the two forces clashed in a savage, bewildering and exhausting fight in a shimmering heat haze and amid dense clouds of black smoke billowing from the burning tanks. The British armour was sorely stricken, mainly by the boldly handled German anti-tank guns. About 150 tanks were lost that gruesome day, the saddest and heaviest in the whole history of British armour. The Battle of Gazala was virtually lost that day.

There was nothing that the British armour could do but withdraw northwards, with the enemy biting hard at their heels. On 13 June, the eighteenth day of the battle, a critical action was fought which was to influence events and at which 'Fairy' Foote was to complete the series of achievements that won him the Victoria Cross.

Standing at the north-east corner of the Cauldron was a strong backstop box known as Knightsbridge. Sited on a small, rocky plateau, which gave good command over much of the surrounding desert, it was used throughout the battle as a pivot of manoeuvre for the British armour and was staunchly manned by part of 201st Guards Brigade, 2nd RHA under Lyndon Bolton and Dick Taylor's battery of the Northumberland Hussars. The enemy had made no serious attempt to assault the place. Lying directly in the path to Tobruk, Knightsbridge constituted the main obstacle to the enemy advance and it became the key point in the critical fighting on 13 June as the *Panzerarmee* followed hotly on the heels of the British armour. The left flank of Eighth Army was now facing, not to the west but to the south, dangerously parallel to its L of C.

On the morning of the 13th the residues of Raymond Briggs's 2nd and Bill Carr's 22nd Armoured Brigades stood at bay a little to the east of Knightsbridge, ready to fight the *DAK* once more. The evening before, the Germans had forced two sharp prongs up northwards on either side of Knightsbridge, so that the box now formed the tip of a pronounced salient. At its left rear (to its north-east) lay 15 Pz and to its right rear 21st. Everyone knew that it was the last chance of saving the Gazala position. The British armour, although a shadow of its former self and in spite of the hard knocks it had taken, faced the day with unbroken spirit. The troops on both sides, however, were tired out and they now had to face a gruelling day of frequent and violent sandstorms, which on occasions put a stop to fighting.

The enemy's intention on the 13th was for 15 and 21 Pz to turn inwards towards each other and so envelop the troublesome Knightsbridge and then to get in behind 50th Division and the South Africans and bottle them up. To that intent, 21st bore down at 2 p.m. on the isolated 2nd Scots Guards, 2½ miles from Knightsbridge, with 37 tanks, 2,000 or more infantry, backed by field artillery and mortars. After resisting this overpowering attack for nearly five hours, the battalion was obliged to withdraw at dusk, its movement bravely and sacrificially covered by 6th South African Field Battery, under Major J. H. Newman.

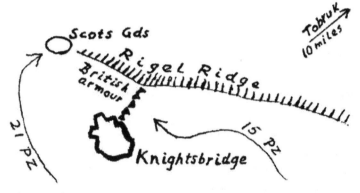

Gazala: the action at Knightsbridge, in outline, on 13 June.

To the east of Knightsbridge, meanwhile, a bitter battle was being fought in the whirling sand by 2nd and 22nd Armoured Brigades against von Vaerst's 15 Pz, under the eyes of Rommel and Nehring. Gradually both British brigades were forced by superior gun-power to give ground as the Panzers pressed hard to turn the left flank of Briggs's brigade near the edge of the Rigel Ridge, where The Queen's Bays, reduced to 12 tanks, doggedly held their ground. Disaster seemed inescapable when the Bays ran out of ammunition at about 10 a.m., but mercifully, just when Knightsbridge and the two armoured brigades seemed doomed to encirclement, 'Fairy' Foote came

177

slowly grinding in with 7th Royal Tanks and slipped into the Bays' shoes in the nick of time. 'Before we knew where we were,' he said afterwards, 'we were in the thick of it.'

By this time Foote's name had become a by-word for gallant and skilful leadership against odds, and he was now to give further proof of those qualities. Since Sidra Ridge his battalion had been made up to about 25 Matildas. The situation that he saw was that of a typical tank *v.* tank battle, with the two sides hammering at each other at 800 yards, the red tracer flickering to and fro, sometimes ricocheting high in the air as a shot hit a tank but did not penetrate, or burning a red-hot hole in the armour as it struck home. He was grateful to see, at his left rear, a stout-hearted little troop of 6-pdrs doing splendid service by helping to keep the enemy at arm's length. The range was too much for the Matildas' own puny 2-pdrs to kill, but they might still cripple.

Moving up into the battle, with his adjutant, Maclean, manning the gun, Foote and his crew felt the tell-tale jar that meant that the tank was hit. Under very hot fire Foote himself dismounted and walked quietly from one tank to another giving the crews instructions and confidence. He knew that the situation was critical, that he was up against superior weight of metal, but that somehow he must contrive to hold the enemy off on that dangerous flank along the ridge for the rest of that day. He was very tired, having in the last two weeks had only an occasional hour's sleep in his car.

At that moment the elements unexpectedly came to the aid of the hard-pressed brigades by raising a sandstorm so dense and violent that, although a torture to the parched tank crews, it blanketed the whole battlefield for nearly three hours. When it ceased, Foote called for his supporting artillery to put down a smoke-screen, which effectively provided another blanket, but which ceased when the gunners had shot off all their smoke-shell.

As soon as the smoke drifted away the duel was resumed with increased violence and under a remorseless sun that caked the red-eyed crews in sweat and sand. Only about one and a half hours of daylight remained. Nehring's Panzers, now reinforced by additional 88s, were determined to capture the Knightsbridge box and push on before dark. The British armour was just as determined to stop them. The ground was dead flat, giving the British tanks no chance to protect themselves in a hull-down posture. Upon Foote's Matildas the Germans rained down showers of high explosives as well as armour-piercing projectiles as they strove to turn that stubborn flank along the ridge. Foote himself, a man given to moderate statement, said afterwards: 'We were subject to a concentrated fire from all the weapons the enemy could bring to bear.'

Almost at once the leading squadron went up in flames and most of their crews were cremated alive. At once Foote himself then went to the front in his own tank and deployed the two remaining squadrons on either side of him. Standing erect in his turret so that he should be plainly visible, he ordered his tanks simply to 'Conform to my movements'.

He then set his wits to cancel out the Matildas' shortcomings. Using the Matildas' own smoke projectors, he put down a smoke-screen ahead and moved a few hundred yards *nearer* the enemy. This threw out the enemy's range, while he himself re-engaged them. As soon as the enemy found the new range and began to hit his Matildas again he put down another smoke-screen and retired, with the same intent. His own tank was hit repeatedly and badly damaged. His 2-pdr, hit directly in the muzzle, split longitudinally and peeled back like the skin of a banana. His Besa machine-gun was also destroyed. He could no longer fight, but he could still lead. By repeatedly edging his small squadrons forward and backward he confused the enemy and succeeded in at least diminishing the rate of his own casualties, though they were still very severe. Observing a tank silent and not conforming to his movements, he dismounted again, walked over to it and found everyone inside dead, killed by the fragments of armour-plating violently flung about by a hit from an 88.

The bitter duel went on. In the 90 minutes of daylight left, the 25 Matildas were reduced to seven. As Foote said afterwards, 'It was touch-and-go whether we would not be written off before night came.' But when that blessed hour arrived they had won their fight. They stood on the same ground as they had held all day. They had won by the inspiring example, the cool wits and the professional skill of their leader and by the gallantry of the exhausted tank crews. The regiments on their right had likewise held their ground. The garrison of Knightsbridge was saved and withdrew quietly that night, with the Valentines of 8th Royal Tanks guarding their rear amid a blaze of coloured lights and Very flares as the enemy patrols closed cautiously in.

This was the culmination of the episodes by which Bob Foote won the Victoria Cross, but we have not yet seen the last of him.

Tobruk Lost

It was very nearly the end. The British armour had shrunk to a mere 70 tanks. The next day the *DAK* received some sharp and spirited rebuffs in their attempt to bottle up the South African and Northumbrian Divisions and, while a life-line was still open, Ritchie ordered a general withdrawal that night (14 June). The Springboks drove out boldly past the exhausted and sleeping Germans, but 50th Division, their rear blocked and their doom apparently sealed, made an audacious and spectacular escape under Ramsden, by smashing their way out *westward* through the Italian defended positions and swinging south and then east behind the enemy's back at Hakeim. Thus began the long, rapid retreat across the heat-stricken desert, vigorously pressed by the enemy, known to old Eighth Army hands as the 'Gazala Stakes'.

It began calamitously with the loss of Tobruk, where the garrison was commanded by a young and inexperienced South African general. Attacking with the concentrated strength of all arms, under massive air support, the enemy penetrated the derelict outer defences on 20 June and became engaged in a series of piecemeal actions against weak, hastily collected and uncoordinated forces, which they heavily outweighed and in which 4th and 7th Royal Tanks and several British and South African batteries, whose resistance Rommel described as 'extraordinarily tenacious', were virtually wiped out. The young garrison commander lost his head and the next day abjectly surrendered the remaining half of the fortress, to the consternation and disbelief of the 32,000 men who still remained to him. Among the prisoners taken were the two VCs of the Royal Tank Regiment. Philip Gardner escaped with Willison, but both were captured after walking in the desert for three days. Bob Foote, who had again led his few Matildas with exemplary personal courage, also made a getaway, but tore an Achilles tendon when jumping from a wall and was inevitably picked up.[20]

---

[20] Fifteen months later Foote escaped from a POW camp and rejoined Eighth Army.

The Gazala Stakes went on at high momentum. Hitler and Mussolini, impressed and elated, were now easily persuaded to forgo the assault on Malta and authorized Rommel to do what he ardently wanted: to invade Egypt and capture the glittering prizes of Cairo and Alexandria, into which Mussolini began to prepare for his own triumphal entry. Rommel, driving his tired troops with commands to be 'ruthless', was eager to complete Ritchie's destruction and to rush on. Ritchie tried to halt him at a line that hinged on the small, fortified Egyptian town of Mersa Matru on the coast, 200 miles back from Tobruk, and at this moment Auchinleck relieved him and took personal command of Eighth Army.

That was on 25 June. The South Africans had been sent right back to Alamein, but the Army had just received some useful reinforcements. On the northern flank General Holmes had arrived with the headquarters of 10th Corps, and under him were 10th Indian Division, rushed over from Iraq and deployed round Matru, and 50th Division, lying inland a little to the south-east. Farther off in the Desert lay some unwisely scattered Indian battalions and behind them the New Zealand Division returned to add their experience and high spirit. Deep in the Desert, 30 miles from Matru, was Lumsden's 1st Armoured Division, hastily made up to some 155 tanks of assorted types.

Late in the day after Auchinleck had assumed command, Rommel mounted his attack on the flimsy new position. It took the form of a 'typical Rommel' right hook, swinging in from the south and hinged on 90th Light Division in the centre, and the dawn of the following day rose to illuminate one of the most shining deeds in the annals of the Victoria Cross.

The 151st Brigade of 50th Division was composed wholly of men of the Durham Light Infantry, a regiment of the Line long renowned for its valour on many fields. They were the 6th, 8th and 9th Battalions. The 9th had made a particularly bold and resourceful escape when 50th Division had broken out westward from their Gazala boxes and was now commanded by John Slight. In his ranks was a young private soldier who was apparently in no way remarkable and in appearance was a very ordinary young man of middle height, whom no one imagined would qualify for the Victoria Cross, that he was to win in death.

Adam Herbert Wakenshaw was one of a family of thirteen souls living in a very poor neighbourhood in industrial Gateshead, on Tyneside. He grew up in very tough social conditions, which served not to depress his spirit but to stiffen it. A former company commander, Harry Sell, describes him as having 'that seemingly helpless mystification that grew out of distressed areas constantly harassed by well-meaning officials'. What he really wanted to do was to become a soldier and he tried to enlist at the age of 16 but his mother heard about it and promptly brought him home. He did not get his wish until the war had been in progress for more than a year and until then he had been in many humble employments — as a newsboy, in a tripe factory, in the coal-mines and as a builder's labourer. The 'mystification' gradually dissipated after he joined the Durham Light Infantry and he found in the army a definite purpose and good comradeship. His open, boyish face laughed at life. He married and had a son. In time he found himself in 9th Battalion's anti-tank platoon, in which, without shining, he became a good, reliable gun-number. The platoon, excelling in brigade competitions, had an exceptionally high morale and was often picked to accompany the Jock columns.

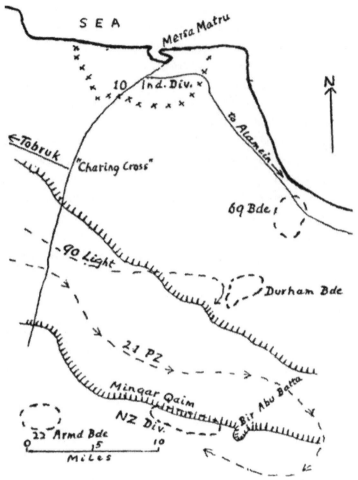

Withdrawal from Gazala. Actions by Durhams and New
Zealanders near Mersa Matru.

At dusk on the night of 26 June the battalion arrived
hurriedly at its allotted post on some slightly elevated ground,
16 miles south-east of Matru. It was the extreme left-hand unit

of the division and on its own left was nothing. To the north were the other two battalions of 151st Brigade. Slight deployed his companies as best he could in the swiftly falling darkness, allotting one anti-tank gun per company. He knew that the enemy was on the move somewhere in front of him against the scattered Indian units. The ground was hard rock, in which it was impossible to dig proper defences. The moon, again at the full, mounted the heavens majestically, immense and brilliant. The men lay down to sleep on the rocky floor, with double sentries posted.

The night was an uneasy one. Vague sounds disturbed the ear. Distantly to the westward could be heard the crackle and crash of an action between the enemy and the Indians. From overhead come the deep-throated purr of aircraft, followed by the dull roar of distant bombs. A huge Albacore flare burst in front of the battalion and hung motionless from its parachute, illuminating the desert with an eerie brilliance that challenged the moon. After it had subsided, the dark shapes of tanks and vehicles appeared and halted to the right front of the Durhams, and a number of men dismounted, but after an anxious time they moved away. The immense and lonely silence of the desert enveloped the night.

An hour before dawn the battalion stood to arms. Almost at once the darkness was punctuated by gun flashes as the enemy began shelling. As the blackness changed to grey, a few tanks and self-propelled guns on tank chassis, detached from 21 Pz to support the Panzer Grenadiers of 90th Light Division, crawled up. They halted at a distance and began to engage the 25-pdrs of a battery of 74th Field Regiment in a very isolated position to the north of Slight's battalion. Before it was yet light, the enemy advanced and overran the battery. The DLI anti-tank gunners, thinly spread out among the companies, crouched at their little 2-pdrs. They watched the black shapes of the tanks or self-propelled guns begin cautiously to close in on them in a half-circle, accompanied by the Panzer Grenadiers. Spotting the four 2-pdrs, the enemy guns, standing off, began to plaster them with high explosives in their usual method. The well-trained gunners made no reply, holding their fire until the enemy closed to killing range. They began to take casualties as the splinters burst among them, but stood fast, immobile. Very slowly and cautiously the Panzers closed in nearer still. At 400 yards the four little guns burst into life and immediately scored. Several armoured vehicles went up in flames and smoke.

Wakenshaw's gun had been the first into action and had knocked out a German gun-tractor, putting a round through the engine. The enemy halted once more and began to blast the position with mortars as well as shells. All the detachment of Wakenshaw's gun were killed or seriously wounded. His own left arm was blown off above the elbow.

As he lay on the rocky ground a sergeant-major in a trench several yards behind saw him struggling to recover himself and shouted, 'Come on, Wakenshaw, it's time to go.' Wakenshaw took no notice, perhaps did not hear, and struggled to his knees. The sergeant-major, seeing no one else alive in his company sector, shouted, 'Look out for that armoured car on the left. Come on, we must go.'

Wakenshaw, however, had risen to his knees. By an extraordinary effort and in spite of the intense fire he crawled back to his place beside the gun and found that the gun-layer was doing likewise. Together they engaged the enemy again, the layer aiming the gun, Wakenshaw moving on his knees to and from the ammunition box and loading the gun awkwardly with one arm. Five more rounds were fired, scoring hits.

Another enemy shell then burst close alongside the gun, killing the layer. Wakenshaw was wounded a second time and hurled several yards away by the blast of the shell.

Dazed, but still undeterred, he slowly dragged himself back to the gun and served it single-handed as best he could. Having placed yet one more round in the breech, he was about to fire when a direct hit on the ammunition killed him and destroyed the gun.

Bit by bit the battalion, which that day took the full brunt of the attack by 90th Light, was then inevitably worn down, but the Durhams fought so doggedly that it took the enemy two hours to isolate and overcome the three forward companies. When it was obvious that the position was irretrievable, Slight ordered such men as were left to withdraw, but many were captured, including Slight himself, who was shot in the shoulder as he clung to the outside of a truck.

Nevertheless, Wakenshaw and his comrades had done better than they could know. Though overcome, they had in fact stopped the enemy advance. The battalion and the divisional artillery had inflicted such very severe casualties that the Panzers halted, abandoned the ground that they had won and withdrew from the battle to lick their wounds some miles back. That evening, when the 8th Battalion went over to collect the private possessions of the dead, they found, among the widespread wreckage, the mutilated and charred body of Private Wakenshaw and the carcass of a tank 200 yards away. The gun that he and his comrades served so faithfully now stands in the forecourt of Brancepeth Castle.

Sell wrote of him (to the author): 'The Army fulfilled his demands and I am sure he was happy. He accepted authority and his training produced the type of man who throughout our history has followed his appointed leaders to the end... To me

Wakenshaw will remain as a person who, having no benefits from fortune or society or even by birth, nevertheless rose to heights of spectacular courage in war, which in peace might well have passed unnoticed in the daily fight against fortune, in which he would to the end have been an uncomplaining loser.'

The Break-out

Elsewhere on the Matru sector the enemy made little progress on the morning of that 27 June. In the extreme south 15 Pz were checked by Lumsden's 1st Armoured Division, but a ticklish situation beset Bernard Freyberg and his New Zealand Division late in the day, when Charles Upham once again showed his fighting qualities and began the second series of exploits that was to lead to the Bar to his Victoria Cross.

The NZ Division (less one brigade) was dug in above a steep *minqar* (or cliff-like escarpment) known as Minqar Qaim. It was not 'vital ground' and the division was in a mobile role, fully motorized and isolated from other formations. In the forenoon of the 27th, while 15 Pz was being held by Lumsden, the 21st, a much weakened force under von Bismarck and accompanied by Rommel himself, pushed through on the south of 90th Light and bumped into some of the New Zealand transport on the plain below the high scarp on their right flank. Rommel halted von Bismarck and ordered him to turn south and destroy the unexpected enemy.

The desert heat was at its worst, the sun glaring down from a white-hot sky. About midday the enemy began to shell the New Zealanders and continued to do so for the rest of the day. At about 2 p.m. the tanks of 21 Pz began an encircling movement round Freyberg's eastern flank and came right round to his rear. The Panzer infantry, lorry-borne, followed quickly, de-bussed and launched a series of attacks on all quarters during that sweating afternoon until nearly dusk. All were vigorously repulsed.

During the fighting Upham, now a captain in 20 Battalion, had again shone as a battlefield leader. Wearing his Victoria Cross ribbon, he had come to be regarded with some awe as well as affection. As soon as the shells began to fall he became filled with the excitement of battle. His voice rose. His language ripened. Exposing himself conspicuously, he ran continuously among the weapon-pits of his company position, ordering, exhorting, exuding and inspiring robust confidence. Himself a glaring target for the enemy, he rebuked others for exposing themselves. When one of his platoons was harassed by a machine-gun which they could not locate in the trembling heat haze, he motored boldly over in a truck and stood up like a lighthouse on the roof of the cab, searching with his binoculars and deliberately drawing fire so that he could spot the enemy weapon.

Notwithstanding the firm repulse of the Panzer attacks, it became clear to Freyberg that, with his supply route cut and his ammunition running dangerously low, he could not maintain his isolated position for long. The whole of Eighth Army was under provisional orders to cut back to Alamein, and Freyberg had been given discretion to act on his own initiative. He therefore decided to break out from the ring of his enemy that night.

At 5 o'clock, just after he had given out his withdrawal orders, he sustained his tenth or eleventh wound, while watching the repulse of the enemy's attack on his rear. He was sharply hit in the neck by a shell splinter, and command of the division was taken over by Brigadier Lindsay Inglis of 4th Brigade, who carried out Freyberg's plan with impressive resolution and skill.

Of the courses open to him, Inglis decided to make his break-out to the east. He would blow a hole in the ring by shock tactics and pass the whole of the division through. He gave the task of striking the blow to his own 4th Brigade, led now in his stead by Jim Burrows, CO of 20 Battalion. The attack was to be a silent one, without benefit of artillery, but forced through by bayonet, rifle and grenade alone. No reconnaissance, no 'probing'.

The sun set behind a huge crimson curtain and was succeeded by the steel-blue moon. Both armies were goaded into intense activity. On every side but the west the New Zealanders saw flares and signal rockets of every colour shoot up from the encircling Germans. By a complicated series of manoeuvres they mustered for the break-out in their prescribed order of march for each brigade — the infantry, withdrawn gradually from their battle positions, in the lead, followed by the massed fleets of transport, tightly packed together in the manner of desert movement by night, and their flanks guarded by the artillery.

The three infantry battalions of 4th Brigade formed up in the moonlight in arrow-head formation, facing east. At the point of the arrow was 19 Battalion, with whom marched a gallant company of the Essex Regiment under Major D. J. M. Smith, who had strayed into the Kiwis' flock and been taken under their wing. The left barb of the arrow-head was formed by 20 Battalion, in which Upham marched behind his new CO, Major Ian Manson. Dettmer's Maoris formed the right barb. The whole brigade was from the very start inspired by that same, unexplainable spontaneity that we have seen in Greece and Crete. An hour and a half late in assembling, they did not move off until 2 a.m., but they then did so instinctively, without any order, as though, in the words of the New Zealand historian, 'a familiar spirit had whispered' the order to them.

As silently as possible the shadowy forms melted away into the night under the sinking moon. After about 1,000 yards they bumped the enemy, as they had expected, in the vicinity of a well known as Bir Abu Batta. They were the 104th Panzer Grenadiers. They had spotted the New Zealanders just in time and, waiting until they were at close range, opened a heavy volume of fire from machine-guns, rifles and anti-tank weapons.

For a moment it seemed to Burrows to be impossible to get forward without heavy casualties, but the reaction of the New Zealanders and their Essex comrades was extraordinary. Again, no orders were given, but again, as the streams of coloured tracer darted towards them, they spontaneously broke into a charge in the old manner, with cheers, shouts and the battle-cries of the Maoris. It was, said Burrows, 'a most amazing and thrilling thing'. They fell upon the enemy in their weapon-pits with ferocity, shooting, bayoneting, bombing. The slaughter was considerable. The New Zealanders burst clean through the defences like bulldozers in a matter of minutes.

Beyond the slight, rocky eminence of the *bir* however, and in the path of 20 Battalion, was a hidden gully crowded with transport and with German grenadiers hastily turning out to meet the avalanche. Many were practically undressed, without trousers or boots, but dropped into their slit trenches and prepared to fight back. The battalion gave them no chance to organize. With a yell Upham and his comrades swooped down on them like tigers, followed by 19 Battalion. A savage and riotous fight followed among the vehicles. The night was filled with shouts, screams, explosives and the crackle of machine-guns. Upham was armed with a revolver and with a haversack full of the grenades that he favoured so much. In a fighting ecstasy, his voice rising high and shrill, he called upon C Company to follow him. Leaving the business of bayoneting to others, he broke through and made for the vehicles, in which he saw many of the enemy trying to escape. Into these he tossed his grenades one after another with deadly effect, leaping up on to them as they began to move. From the back of one vehicle, already under way, a German opened fire on him with an automatic. Upham raced up to it and threw in his grenade, killing all in the truck and setting it on fire. He leapt at a crowded staff-car as it tried to pass him, pulled open the door, tossed in a grenade and shut the door again. Meanwhile, his left hand was busy with his revolver also. He was wounded in both arms and running with blood but, in his customary manner, took no heed.

The Germans fought back as best they could but, being unprepared, had no chance against the fury of their assailants. By now the gully was full of blazing vehicles and dead grenadiers. Few escaped. The brigade passed over them like the Angel of Death, gained the open desert beyond and halted as quiet fell, sweating, trembling and exhilarated. Upham, his tension still unrelaxed and his wounds still unheeded, reassembled his company. Burrows sent up the success signal. The brigade's transport, with its protective gunners, drove forward over the scene of carnage and halted in close order for the infantry to mount. Then at a slow, disciplined speed, the brigade began its long march eastwards to the lines of Alamein. Not till then did Upham bother to have his wounds dressed. But he had not yet won his bar.

The next night it was the turn of the troops in the Matru area in the north to make a similar and spectacular break-out. These were the Northumbrian and the 10th Indian Divisions, together with 10th Corps troops. They had no initial hole to punch, but the audacity of the operation, in which something like 30,000 troops on wheels drove right through the Germans at night, with plenty of scuffles on the way, is still difficult to apprehend, even by those who took part in it, among whom was the author's regiment.[21]

---

[21] 121st Field Regiment, RA, under Lt-Colonel Edmund Stansfield.

6: RUWEISAT

By 30 June, Eighth Army had completed its scramble back to the Alamein 'line', which was then little more than a line drawn on the Desert map. It was the last ditch before the vital Nile Delta, with Alexandria only 75 miles behind.

By this time the soldiers of both sides were exhausted, except for the South Africans, who had had a long respite and who occupied the Alamein 'box' on the coast, virtually the only prepared defences. Conditions for all men were trying. The sun beat down with hammer blows. Vast swarms of silent, soft-winged flies tormented them by day and mosquitoes by night. A plague of distressing desert sores afflicted the body. The water ration was still very limited.

For the first time in the Desert war there was no open flank by which armoured forces could manoeuvre. On the north was the sea, on the south the vast marshy Qattara Depression, virtually impassable to vehicles. The distance between the two flanks was only 38 miles. We must notice in particular the very important Ruweisat Ridge, a bare, rocky outcrop that lay in an almost dead-straight line east and west, athwart the front, ten miles long and eight miles from the sea. Like the spine of some enormous and fabulous monster, this bony outcrop, though nowhere more than 35 feet high, commanded the desert for some miles around and was to be the altar on which whole regiments of men were to be sacrificed as the shells detonated viciously on its crustaceous surface during the months of bitter fighting ahead.

Reaching the Alamein position on 30 June, Rommel attempted to rush it by cutting in south of the box, but he was very firmly held off by the South African artillery and a scratch force of Indian infantry, British Territorial gunners and half a dozen Matildas (an action at which the author was present).

Auchinleck immediately went over to the offensive and there began what even the staid Official Historian of the Cabinet Office describes as 'the violent and bloody battles of July', which lasted for the whole of that month and which are known properly as the First and Second Battles of Ruweisat.[22] He brought back from Syria Leslie Morshead's 9th Australian Division, posted them on the coastal sector and set them a number of objectives, some of which they won in a series of bitter encounters.

Rommel was thus forced back on to the defensive, and the Desert Air Force, its strength built up again, began once more to play an effective and impressive part. As soon as the Australian operations were over, Auchinleck gave the order for the instant capture of Ruweisat Ridge, the greater part of which was in enemy hands. The task fell to the New Zealander Division, still under the temporary command of Lindsay Inglis, and to 5th Indian Brigade, with 1st Armoured Division under orders to give tank support at first light next morning. On 14 July the troops were ordered to attack 'tonight'.

The notice was minimal, the proposition formidable. The assault on the ridge was to be from the south-east and was to be made at an angle to the objective. The Indians, on the right of the battle, would have to penetrate for an average of two miles, but for the New Zealanders on the other flank the distance was no less than six miles. Across this wide plain their leaders would have to count their paces over broken ground in the dark, fighting the enemy on their way. That enemy was known to be the Italian Brescia Division, well 'corseted' with

---

[22] Incorrectly called by some writers the 'First Battle of Alamein'.

Germans, but it was believed that there was only a thin crust to penetrate before reaching the ridge. In the event the situation proved to be far otherwise.

In the New Zealand sector Howard Kippenberger's 5th Brigade was on the right and Jim Burrow's 4th on the left, directed against the western (and critical) extremity of the objective. The attack was to be a silent one. They knew that they would arrive on the ridge out of range of the defensive fire of their own artillery until the guns could move up, which could not be done until the intervening ground was cleared of enemy.

The two NZ brigades, both much below strength, formed up on their start-line and moved off at 11 p.m. on 14 July. Each had two battalions up, with the third following half an hour later. The night was cold and quiet. There was no moon, but the massed legions of stars gave dim illumination for a few yards. After 2½ miles mines and barbed wire were encountered and almost immediately the leading battalions were assailed by a fire of quite unexpected vigour. Gun flashes, signal rockets of many colours, Very flares and the red darts of machine-gun bullets broke the blackness of the night.

The leading sections of the New Zealanders deployed from file into line and pressed on. They went for the enemy strong-points at the double, overcame most of them quickly and passed on to find yet more strongpoints, which were distributed in depth throughout the whole zone of attack. Here was no mere 'outer crust', as had been expected, but a fully reticulated defensive system. Those that could not be quickly overcome were by-passed to be dealt with by the second wave.

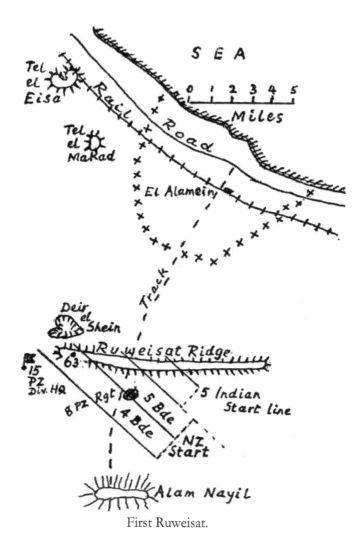

First Ruweisat.

More surprising still was the ominous appearance of the dark shapes of German tanks, but even these did not interrupt the tremendously spirited advance. Three tanks appeared in the path of Kippenberger's brigade and all were quickly disposed of. One was set on fire by a sticky bomb. The others were audaciously attacked by Sergeant Lord, who shot the tank commanders as they stood up in their open turrets, then leapt up on the hulls and killed the drivers and gunners within with grenades and tommy-gun. Well before dawn all or nearly all the New Zealand objectives had been won and some companies had even passed beyond the ridge, to create near-panic in the Pavia Division. Quantities of prisoners were taken, together with a large stock of warlike booty. It was an exceptionally fine infantry achievement, deep into the enemy's guts. On the right the Indians had so far been only partially successful.

Upham Again

It was in the reserve battalions of both NZ brigades, however, that the most dramatic incidents occurred and in each of them a Victoria Cross was to be won. We shall look first at the dazzling achievements of 20 Battalion, still commanded by Ian Manson, as it had been at Minqar Qaim, and with Charles Upham still leading C Company.

The battalion was the reserve unit of 4 Brigade, moving half an hour after the two leading battalions. Burrows, normally their own CO, was with them, and he had also brought forward four troops of anti-tank guns on their portees. When the leading units bumped into the enemy front positions 20 Battalion began instinctively to break into a run to join their comrades in the battle ahead, as they had done at Minqar Qaim. Burrows stopped them promptly and held them back for about half an hour. Mortar bombs began to fall and some 15 casualties were incurred.

Burrows, disturbed at the surprising weight of fire in front and apprehensive lest his leading units might be getting 'carved up', told Manson to send a good officer forward in a jeep to discover the situation, and Manson in turn told Upham. It was characteristic of Upham that, as so often before, he went himself. As always before battle, he was in an emotionally aggressive mood.

He moved off into the night slowly into what he described afterwards as 'a very colourful show of flares going up, tanks firing and red tracer bullets'. Very soon he found himself among shadowy weapon-pits and unseen strands of barbed wire that wound themselves round his wheels, and began to encounter pockets of confused Germans and Italians. Occasionally unseen German tanks on his left swept the ground with fire.

Feeling insufficiently armed, Upham took the first opportunity of seizing a German machine-gun. With this he cleared his path. As he got farther forward he found the Germans badly cut up and the Italians surrendering in hundreds. He picked up a lone gunner officer named Douglas Green and continued to range the shadowy battlefield. On several occasions the jeep ran into a trench but the two officers had no difficulty in getting the Italians themselves to lift it out. Upham's reconnaissance over this extraordinary scene lasted for an hour, when, having discovered the state of the forward battalions, he returned unscathed, with his jeep trailing a tangle of barbed wire, and reported to Burrows.

The battalion, with Upham's company on the sensitive extreme left, pushed on into the night, scrapping on the way. It was not until shortly before dawn that really stiff fighting took place and then it was very stiff indeed. Burrows, having gone forward himself, had ordered Manson to attack and occupy the extreme western end of Ruweisat Ridge, where a rocky protuberance, known as Point 63, stood out as a challenge over the declivities on three sides of it. It was a position of extreme exposure, but Burrows expected the British tanks to arrive soon after first light.

As the night began to fade into day, Manson's battalion was approaching the ridge in good order when, quite suddenly, it was attacked by extremely heavy fire from the open left. Manson ordered Captain Maxwell's company to make straight for Point 63, then dashed over to Upham and ordered him to wheel to the left and attack the assailants, whoever they might be. C Company obeyed at once and moved up to a slight ridge in that direction. From there Upham found himself looking down into a shallow depression. In it, at a distance of some 400 yards, were about a hundred trucks, a quantity of infantry and a number of German guns and machine-guns firing at speed on the other companies attacking the ridge.

Most men would have considered a frontal attack by a weak company on such a target over open ground, without artillery support, to be an act of madness. But Upham, filled with exaltation and giving no thought to niceties of flank movement, stood up at once and shouted: 'Come on, C Company, come on!' As one man, they rose and swept down the incline after him, in another full-blooded, old-fashioned charge. A terrific fire met them, but nothing could stop the inspired impetus of those who escaped the hail. High and compelling, Upham's voice was heard above the din by all, calling them on as he raced forward, head down.

Fearful gaps were torn in his ranks. Almost in the first minute he lost all three of his platoon commanders — two killed and the third blown up by a shell-burst. Not long afterwards he himself crashed to the ground, his left elbow smashed by machine-gun bullets. Few men could have carried on with so severe a hurt, but Upham staggered up and went on blindly, overtaken now by some of his own men, but still shouting: 'Come on, C Company.' In another minute they were right in among the guns and the entrenched machine-guns with grenade and bayonet and the deadly business of close-quarters fighting amid shots, explosions and screams. Upham, dazed with pain, was shouting and cursing, but still managing somehow to throw a grenade and still be able to lead a rush against the last machine-gun.

Past the guns sped the slender remnants of C Company to chase the flying infantry and to swarm in among the trucks as they tried to get away. Past them, too, and on to the far end of the depression, stopping only when they were assailed by fire from half-concealed tanks. Though they did not know it, they were scarcely a mile from the headquarters of 15 Pz Division itself. Then suddenly all was still.

Upham, unable to go on, had handed over his company to Company Sergeant-Major Bob May. He looked around and in the red haze that descended on him found himself in undisputed possession of the field. Every gun and every vehicle had been destroyed or captured. Every enemy was either dead or a prisoner. Forty-two Germans and more than 100 Italians stood captives of C Company, who themselves numbered less than 50.

Looking behind him in the quickening dawn, Upham could see that the rest of 20 Battalion was now well established all around Point 63. His charge had succeeded in its purpose. Captain John Sullivan, the Intelligence officer, hurried down to see him and took command of the company. Upham was driven back in a small truck to the Regimental Aid Post on the lower slopes of the ridge, where his wound was dressed by a young medical officer, Captain R. J. Feltham. He refused morphia, knowing that it would impair his faculties, but he agreed to rest for a while and lit up his pipe. The RAP, crowded with a constant flow of wounded, was itself under severe fire, but Feltham improvised a Geneva flag by painting a white towel with a cross marked in blood, to which the enemy gave due respect.

Learning that his company had been slightly withdrawn to a less exposed position, Upham got up, overcoming his intense pain, and walked over to them, coming again under fire. Their casualties had been so crippling that the remainder had now been absorbed by Washbourn's A Company. With his right hand, assisted by May, Upham set about disabling one of the captured 88s, watched by three wounded German gunners who lay alongside. Then he stepped over to the hated Huns and gave them a drink from his water-bottle.[23]

Sergeant Keith Elliott

Meanwhile, on the plain behind the assault battalions, an extraordinary scene had been disclosed as the new day had dawned. Far from having been cleared of the enemy, it was dappled with groups of them, some still fighting, some trying to get away, others merely waiting to be taken prisoner. Stretcher-bearers were collecting the wounded of both sides. New Zealand vehicles were trying to get forward. Strings of prisoners were trailing back. Many of the enemy strongpoints that had been missed in the dark came to life and continued to resist strongly for several hours, particularly Stronghold No. 2, which stood almost on the Division's centre-line and could not be brought to surrender until the New Zealand artillery, bringing down fire behind their own infantry, had pumped 1,000 shells into it. The most serious result of all this confusion was that the New Zealand artillery could not get forward to give defensive fire to their infantry on the ridge when the most

---

[23] *Brigadier J. T. Burrows*

critical moment came.

The confusion of first-light brought also the first serious blow to be suffered by the Kiwis. All unknown to them, about ten tanks of 8th Panzer Regiment had been leaguered for the night right in the division's centre-line. Three that had become detached had been dealt with in the manner that we have noted, but in the half-light before dawn the remainder quickly seized the opportunity of attacking the unprotected infantry right under their noses. 'Spitting flames like dragons', in the words of the watching Kippenberger, they made a devastating attack on 22 Battalion, the reserve unit of his brigade under Major Sidney Hanton a little short of the ridge. Nothing could tackle them but a few anti-tank guns, which were quickly knocked out. The German tanks then bore down on the helpless infantry with their machine-guns blazing, and some 350 officers and men had no option but to surrender.

The calamity that befell 22 Battalion, however, was mitigated by the inspired valour and enterprise of a stocky, sturdily built sergeant, with well-moulded features, named Keith Elliott. A tough rugger forward, he was 26 years old, resolute, perceptive, full of moral courage and destined for Holy Orders. He had been wounded and taken prisoner in *Crusader*, but released by the British forces when they chased Rommel back to the frontier of Tripolitania.

Elliott, on that grey morning of 15 July, was commanding No. 11 platoon, which was down to 19 men and posted on the battalion's extreme right. As soon as he saw the enemy tanks attacking the company to his left rear he took independent action and, with admirable presence of mind, ordered the platoon to go *forward*, by section rushes, to a low ridge that he saw 300 yards away. The movement at once drew fire from the tank machine-guns and a bullet scored a streak across Elliott's chest, having been fortunately diverted by the pay-book in his breast-pocket. The platoon 'ran the hell of a gauntlet' without loss and gained the shelter beyond the little ridge, whence they were the agonized witnesses of the capture of their comrades behind them. Judging himself to be still in danger, Elliott moved his platoon on another 400 yards, which took them beyond the top of Ruweisat Ridge itself, where they joined others of the division and where the sergeant's wound was dressed.

Here they were in fact on a section of the ridge where 23 Battalion had penetrated deep into the territory north of it held by the Pavia Division. Very shortly a distressed lance-corporal from the other battalion appeared and told Sergeant Elliott that his officer and batman were lying wounded out in front, the officer with his eye shot out and bleeding badly. This was the starting-pistol, as it were, of a whole series of scarcely credible exploits by the little sergeant.

He at once went forward with eight men, but soon came under fire from a post some 500 yards ahead. Shortly afterwards another post opened up on their right. Ordering Corporal Garmonsway to take four men and press home an attack in the latter direction, Elliott himself went ahead with Privates Lancaster, Jones and the Canadian-born Smith. They went straight for the first post and on their close approach the eleven Italian defenders surrendered. Elliott's party started to disable their anti-tank gun and machine-guns, but while doing so were fired on by two more enemy posts — one another 100 yards ahead and the other still farther on and to the right.

Elliott sent Smith back for reinforcements but, without waiting for them, he, Lancaster and Jones, *taking their prisoners with them*, went on to capture the other two positions 'fairly easily'. They now had some 50 prisoners and had penetrated deep into enemy country. While they were disabling the weapons in the third post, a fourth opened fire from their left front, 100 yards away. Still trailing their prisoners with them, the indomitable three advanced against the new enemy and were well on their way when streams of bullets were rained upon them from yet a fifth post, this time from their left rear and about 200 yards away.

Leaving Lancaster and Jones to deal with No. 4 (while still shepherding the flock of prisoners), Elliott himself turned back against No. 5 single-handed. Something told him that this was different. He ran across the dead-flat ground, but the bullets were close and persistent. Seeing an abandoned water-truck, he made for it, took such cover as it offered and began to snipe the enemy. Their return fire punctured the water-truck and the water gushed over him, which he found very refreshing in the intense heat. A burst from the enemy machine-gun, however, wounded him sharply in the thigh. For a moment he was shaken, but was stirred to fresh activity when he saw a sniper from another direction harassing Lancaster and Jones. He rolled over, fired and saw the sniper fall. He turned again to Post No. 5 and decided that the time had come to close. He dashed in, halted at close quarters to throw a grenade, felt a sharp stab in the knee as he was hit again, but charged home. The machine-gunner and some others lay dead and 15 more surrendered to him.

Elliott had now taken three wounds and, although none was separately severe, he was limping and beginning to feel groggy. Nevertheless he did not regard his mission as ended. He could not leave Jones and Lancaster, who were still fighting at Post No. 4, so, herding the new troop of prisoners, he made his way back to them (finding that Jones had also been wounded) and helped them finish the job, while the whole crowd of prisoners looked on.

Their captives here were mainly Germans, including two doctors. The three military shepherds then made their way back to the ridge, where they found that Corporal Garmonsway's section had silenced three machine-gun nests and had captured another 64 prisoners, including a German officer and sergeant. Thus by midday Elliott's attenuated platoon had not only killed or wounded an estimated 30 of the enemy but had also bagged no fewer than 140 prisoners.

The gallant little sergeant was taken away to a dressing station of the Indian brigade on his right, and some nine weeks later learned that he had been awarded the Victoria Cross. Garmonsway received the Distinguished Conduct Medal.

Bar to the VC

The enemy was slow in mounting his counter-attack on Ruweisat Ridge. According to German doctrine this was not a case for an 'immediate' counter-attack by the forward commander but for a major one organized by higher command. Rommel allotted the task to Nehring, giving him his last resources.

Throughout the morning and afternoon the New Zealanders around Point 63 were subjected to an ever-increasing volume of artillery and mortar fire, from which they suffered very heavy casualties in their exposed positions, under direct observation. The slightest movement drew immediate fire. More than half the officers of 20 Battalion were killed or wounded. The hard rock, upon which shells detonated with particular violence, defied all attempts to dig protective trenches. The anti-tank guns, still *en portée*, were extremely vulnerable. The men suffered severely also from the withering heat, from thirst and from the appalling clouds of flies that infested the insanitary positions left by the Italians. The wounded were in acute discomfort.

The counter-attack came in with great impetus and skill at about 5 o'clock. The declining sun dazzled the vision of the defences and huge clouds of dust were raised by the enemy's tanks, armoured cars and shell-fire as they advanced. No targets presented themselves to the defence until the iron avalanche was within 250 yards. No defensive fire from their own artillery could reach them. The exposed anti-tank guns claimed a few victims but were quickly knocked out one by one. The armoured vehicles rolled in among the infantry unimpeded. Hundreds were taken prisoner. In less than an hour 4 Brigade was overcome and the western extremity of the ridge was lost. As the sun began to make contact with the horizon in a great cloud of blood-red dust, the long-overdue British tanks at last appeared and at their approach the enemy withdrew.

Among those taken prisoner was Charles Upham. As soon as the enemy counter-attack took form he made his painful way over to C Company, in order to be 'with my boys' at the moment of crisis. A mortar bomb burst close to him and wounded him severely yet again. This time it was a crippling wound in the leg. He collapsed and was taken by the enemy.

He spent the next three years in a prison camp, making unsuccessful attempts to escape. When the war was all over and Upham released, he was invested with the Victoria Cross by King George VI. A few weeks afterwards the King sent for Kippenberger, who was in London, a major-general now and minus both feet, which he had lost in the Italian campaign. The King told him that a recommendation had been submitted to him for the award of a Bar to the Victoria Cross for Upham and that he had gone into the papers very carefully. He said that it was a very, very unusual thing: in 90 years there had been only two cases. He wanted to know more about it and asked Kippenberger for his opinion. 'Kip', Brigadier Burrows tells us, replied: 'Sir, in my opinion Captain Upham won the Victoria Cross many times over.'

Private Gurney of Australia

Auchinleck kept on hammering the enemy, but with no tactical success, other than keeping Rommel on the defensive. All the enterprises that he launched during July began well through the valour of his troops but finished badly from some error in battle management by the higher commanders and their staffs. What Clausewitz called 'the friction of war', a frequent occurrence among German generals (including Rommel's), broke out among the British generals also. None was more brusquely critical of plans than Leslie Morshead, the swarthy, strong-willed, civilian soldier who so ably led 9th Australian Division.

That division, wearing its emblem of a platypus and boomerang, was composed almost entirely of civilian soldiers. They had a free and easy discipline of their own and the 'democratic' image loomed large. They were exceptionally good human material, with high morale and stubborn fighting qualities, but were reluctant to learn the mechanism of military operations from professional soldiers and so had to discover it the hard way, which they were now in the process of doing.

They had all this time been battering away in their own fashion on the coastal sector immediately to the west of the Alamein box. Here the black ribbon of the coastal road was flanked on the north by dreary salt marshes that bordered the glaring white sand of the seashore. Parallel to it on the landward side, at a distance of about three-quarters of a mile, ran the narrow military railway. All along the coastal strip, on both sides of road and rail, there stretched a series of rocky knobs, mounds and pimples, like giant molehills, tactically important for giving or denying observation. The most significant of these were the twin humps of a *tel* or mound known as Tel el Eisa ('the Hill of Jesus'). A mile apart, both stood at a height of 24 metres and were known as 24 East and 24 West. The capture of the Tel and another attempt on Ruweisat were the objects of Auchinleck's next offensive, which he ordered quickly for the night of 21/22 July.

This was the Second Battle of Ruweisat, another badly designed and expensive failure, in which two regiments of the virgin 23rd Armoured Brigade, freshly out from England under Brigadier Misa and eager for action, were sacrificed in an heroic but useless Balaclava charge deep into enemy country, losing some 87 out of 100 tanks that had gone into battle. On their left the New Zealanders again gained their objective with their usual *élan* but were once more let down by the armour. All along the line the valour, dash and determination of the troops were set at nought by faulty thinking and battle management.

The Australians' part in Second Ruweisat was to be marked by the last Victoria Cross before the Battle of Alamein. They were required to attack in two directions — northwards along the coast and southwards by two stages to capture the twin humps of Tel el Eisa and the Miteiriya Ridge. The affair with which we shall be concerned in this series of hard-fought and sanguinary conflicts is the assault upon the Tel. For this task two battalions were detailed.

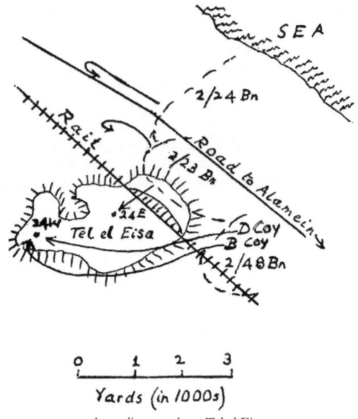

Australian attack on Tel el Eisa.

Weir's 2nd/23rd Battalion was ordered to capture Point 24 East (as well as another feature to the north-west), and Hammer's 2nd/48th was to win 24 West. Both were battalions of fine mettle, but were already tired after some 12 days of hard fighting in fierce heat, constant night activities, little sleep and persecution by swarms of flies. Dick Hammer was one of the 'characters' of the division, a magnetic commander whose motto was 'Hard as nails' and who was known to his soldiers as 'Tack Hammer'. His battalion was to have a phenomenal war record, winning no fewer than four VCs, of which we are about to witness the first.[24]

The attack on the Tel, supported by artillery concentrations, went in at dawn on the 22nd, starting from about the line of the railway. Weir's battalion went at 24 East head-on with only two companies, yet his success signal went up within 30 minutes out of the dust and smoke. This was the signal for Hammer, on Weir's left, to move off for the farther objective of 24 West. Again only two companies were used, one going straight for the objective, the other swinging round on the far left. The distance was two miles.

Almost at once both companies came under scourging artillery and mortar fire, but they continued to advance in good formation, leaving a trail of dead and wounded men among the camel-thorn. After a mile they encountered close fire from the enemy's forward position and the right company lost all its officers. When within about 100 yards of the objective it was halted and pinned down prone to the unyielding rock by concentrated defensive fire from machine-guns as well as high explosive. The whole scene was blurred by spouts and clouds of sand and particularly damaging were some machine-guns on the left flank. It seemed that human flesh had no hope of penetrating that storm of steel. A glimpse of the scene is given in an account by a soldier of the company, who wrote: 'The noise was terrific. German machine-guns were spreading their fire right across our front. The continuous call for stretcher-bearers told of our casualties. My section had just cleaned out a pocket of Germans when I saw another section cut down.

---

[24] The other three were Private P. E. Gratwick and Sergeant W. H. Kibby at El Alamein posthumously, and Sergeant T. E. Derrick in the South-West Pacific.

Wally Shane fell and did not move. Then, a little forward, sergeant Lin Evans was hit twice…'

It was in this officerless crisis, when the assault seemed bound to fail, that an inspired soldier appeared out of the dust and smoke and by the example of his daring cleared the way forward. He was Private Arthur Stanley Gurney, an electrician from Western Australia, aged 36. In the heart of the maelstrom he suddenly jumped up and charged full-tilt at the nearest enemy machine-gun pit, followed by Private Ivan Hanel. When within a few yards of the post, Gurney threw a grenade. As he did so a German leapt out at him with a string of oaths, but Gurney, turning quickly, finished him off with the bayonet.

The two then dashed into the enemy weapon-pit and dispatched two more Germans with the bayonet. Gurney then, alone, jumped out of the trench and raced forward towards another machine-gun about 30 yards away, reached it through a rain of fire, bayoneted two more Germans and sent a third back as prisoner. He then made for yet another enemy post, but a grenade detonated at his feet, its blast throwing him to the ground but not wounding him. He rose, grabbed his rifle, reached the third post, where he was seen by his watching comrades to be again wielding the bayonet 'with great vigour'. That, however, was the last to be seen of him until his dead body was found in the enemy pit very soon afterwards.

For the reaction of Gurney's comrades to this inspired example was dramatic. Fired with a new ardour, what was left of D Company rose from the rocky ground and pressed home to their goal. Their mission was accomplished. The exploit, like that of Private Beeley at Sidi Rezeg and many another, serves convincingly to show how the bravery of the humblest soldier in a critical moment can influence the battlefield. Gurney's citation for the Victoria Cross in the *London Gazette* ends appropriately: 'The successful outcome of this action was almost entirely due to Private Gurney's heroism at the moment when it was most needed.'

On their left the similarly officerless B Company, led with great gallantry and skill by Sergeant Wally Prior, was also able to come forward. They joined hands and the two held on grimly for 14 long hours, exposed to violent fire and the heat of a vicious sun and parched with thirst, with the wounded lying out in great agony. Towards nightfall the two companies, finding that they were now surrounded by the enemy, fought their way out, carrying their wounded. In their long ordeal, marked by many incidents of exceptional heroism, they had lost no fewer than 53 killed and 69 wounded. Hammer now directed his reserve companies to a position forward of 24 East, whence they dominated the lost ground on the farther point, and the enemy did not attempt to occupy it.

The Australians' other operations had mixed fortunes. As so often before, they took their objectives but could not hold them. Auchinleck made one more attempt in July to break through the stubborn enemy front but could not do so. The two armies, having fought each other to a standstill, settled down to construct vast defended minefields, and no more fighting took place until the historic arrival of Generals Alexander and Montgomery.

7: WADI AKARIT

After his defeat by Eighth Army under General Montgomery at the battle of El Alamein in October 1942, Rommel began his long long retreat of nearly 2,000 miles. It was conducted with speed but in good order, and wherever there was a good defensive position he stood and fought. Montgomery defeated him every time, but on each occasion Rommel slipped away skilfully just at the moment when he seemed to be 'in the bag'. The Allied Air Force were now dominant and did much as they liked.

Longer and longer, more and more tenuous, became Eighth Army's line of communication. The Desert in which they had had their birth was left far behind, though much of the terrain was still barren. In four months they advanced some 1,300 miles, right through the whole of Libya and Tripolitania, bringing to an end all Italian rule in North Africa and emerging into the French colony of Tunisia. To reduce the severe administrative strain, Montgomery had dropped off five divisions after Alamein; and at Medenine, on the Tunisian border, Rommel in turn thought that he had Monty in the bag. On 6 March 1943 he launched a confident but ill-designed attack on Eighth Army, hoping to bite off the head of its thin, serpentine body, but suffered a severe defeat at the hands of the steady British infantry and artillery in what Montgomery described afterwards as a 'model one-day battle'. The infantry, now highly skilled in battle behaviour and knowing just what to expect, waited quietly and, with their own 6-pdr anti-tank guns, slaughtered the most modern marks of German armour at ranges down to 40 yards.

Medenine, indeed, was a singularly easy victory. Eighth Army, now world-famous for its long series of victories under Montgomery, had become a magnificent force of seasoned, great-hearted troops in the highest state of morale, superbly supported by their ardent comrades-in-arms of the Desert Air Force. Good generalship had at last been matched with first-class soldiership.

Medenine was Rommel's last battle in Africa. Dejected and at odds with his fellow-generals, he retired to Germany and his place in command of what now became known as *AOK1* was taken by the competent Italian General Giovanni Messe, with Fritz Bayerlein as his able chief-of-staff. Soon afterwards came the stiff week-long Battle of Mareth, where the enemy held a very strongly fortified position, with concrete emplacements with deep trenches built by the French. Of critical importance to the Axis, it was cracked open by the Durham Light Infantry of 50th Division and outflanked over very difficult terrain by the New Zealanders and 1st Armoured Division (now commanded by Raymond Briggs).

In the opening phases of this battle on the night of 20/21 March an assault had to be made on a very tough hill-bastion to secure the Durhams' left flank. In this assault Lt-Colonel Derek Anthony Seagrim, commanding the 7th Battalion of the Green Howards, won the Victoria Cross for quite superlative bravery in the old-fashioned manner, rallying a confused company caught in a deep anti-tank ditch under murderous fire, personally setting up the scaling ladders, going first over the top, calling out 'Come on, Green Howards' and then going straight for the enemy machine-guns with pistol and grenade. He never knew that he had won the VC, for he was killed a fortnight later in the Battle of Wadi Akarit.[25]

---

[25] His brother, Major Hugh Seagrim, DSO, MC, was posthumously

Six days after Seagrim's fine feat of arms the first Maori VC was won by Second-Lieutenant Moana-Nui-a-Kiwa Ngarimu in the New Zealander's left hook behind the Mareth line. In a very tough fight over rugged ground he led his platoon to capture a hill against determined Germans and, although wounded in shoulder and leg, held it all night and next morning against repeated counter-attacks, meeting the Germans standing up face to face. Reduced to three men, he still clung on until reinforcements arrived and then, tommy-gun at hip, he fell dead on top of one of his adversaries.

Lalbahadur Thapa

Quickly following upon Mareth came one of the most remarkable one-day battles in modern military annals, curiously neglected by historians, and one in which audacity in conception was marked with brilliance of execution. For the Highland Division, indeed, it was the most difficult and, except for Alamein, the most severe of all their battles, and so highly did it rank that it won recognition as a battle honour in the colours of several regiments. As Bernard Fergusson has said, 'it was a proper soldier's battle'. Only first-class troops could have won it and three Victoria Crosses were to be awarded for that day's work.

The AOK1 had pulled back to a lofty position of great natural strength overlooking a water-course known as Wadi Akarit, a position that Rommel considered superior to the Mareth Line. Here a complex of rugged hills erupted sharply from the Tunisian plain, overlooking its dead flatness for several miles. One would have thought it impossible for troops even to get anywhere near those commanding ramparts, which

---

awarded the George Cross for his sacrificial courage in operations behind the Japanese lines in Burma, where he was brutally executed.

dominated every blade of grass which at that season clothed the plain. It was the last enemy position that Montgomery would have to overcome before joining hands with General Alexander, commanding Eisenhower's Allied divisions now gradually edging towards Tunis, and the enemy knew well that, if Akarit fell, his fate in the whole of Africa was virtually sealed.

Topographically, this fortress-like barrier, its western flank denied by salt marshes, was laid out by nature in four distinct sections, very important to our narrative. On the eastern flank, next to the Mediterranean Sea, was a five-mile stretch of flat ground traversed by the wadi, now dry but some 300 yards wide and a severe obstacle. Then the hill barrier reared abruptly out of the plain. At this eastern end, nearest to the coastal flats, was a *jebel* (a hill or hill range) called Roumana, a long, bare, steep, stony and undulating ridge, 500 feet high, impassable to vehicles.

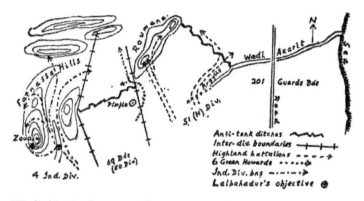

Wadi Akarit. Contours diagrammatic. Approximate position of Lalbahadur's objective shown by a black circle.

Nearly three miles to the west of Roumana there towered the Jebel Fatnassa, a cluster of tangled hills aptly described by the official historian as 'a horrible-looking labyrinth of pinnacles, chimneys, gullies and escarpments'. Dominating this Fatnassa massif, and standing sentinel over the plain below, was a fierce conical hill, shooting up steeply to 900 feet, which formed the most southerly peak of a freakish jumble of crests and crags collectively called Zouai. Beyond lay other lofty pinnacles and crests and between all these craggy heights of Fatnassa mazy corridors twisted in and out.[26]

Between Fatnassa and Roumana, forming the centre of the enemy position, was a stretch of rolling downland, which provided an easy enough passage for armies except for the fact that it was dominated by the hills on either side. To these natural hill barriers the enemy engineers had added stiff artificial ones in the form of deep anti-tank ditches, making jagged scars across the foothills, the approaches to which were peppered with mines. They were extremely unpleasant traps for infantry as well as for tanks. One of these zigzagged along the foot of the central downland, and the other stretched from the eastern end of Roumana to a point on the Wadi Akarit. We may regard this second ditch as an extension of the Roumana defences, the two forming one unit when it became the concern of the Highland Division.

The enemy defences were manned by 12 German and 26 Italian infantry battalions. Their numbers are not known but undoubtedly some were weak. Most of the frontal defences were manned by Italians, with the Germans held ready for immediate counter-attack. What was left of the tanks of 15th Panzer Division lay in readiness a little in the rear. Montgomery mounted 27 battalions, but employed only 18. In artillery the enemy guns, numerically, considerably exceeded

---

[26] I have abbreviated the full Arabic names of these features. Zouai appears on the maps as a *rass*, or headland.

those of the British, with results that will appear. They included no fewer than 63 of the powerful 88-mm, of which 28 were deployed in an anti-tank role. The infantry had large quantities of automatic weapons and light guns. The Germans also employed their new multiple rockets, somewhat frightening but not very accurate.

Montgomery, having decided to hold the coastal strip defensively with 201st Guards Brigade, gave the attack to Oliver Leese's 30 Corps and the follow-through to the New Zealanders and armour of Horrocks's 10 Corps. Leese in turn allocated the infantry assault to 51st (Highland) Division, a brigade of 50th (Northumbrian) Division and 4th Indian Division. The Highlanders, commanded by the tall, lean, pertinacious Douglas Wimberley, had been in the van of the chase ever since Alamein. The Indians, under 'Gertie' Tuker, an intellectual soldier, highly experienced in mountain warfare, had been in the Desert even longer, known to all by their emblem of a red eagle about to strike.

Tuker, in fact, after consultation with Wimberley, was responsible for the daring plan of attack as finally evolved. With his quick brain and his eye for a mountain situation, he saw that the forbidding Fatnassa massif was the key to the enemy fortress, for it overlooked not only the plain but also the flank and rear of the other features and, once taken, would turn the enemy's centre. Though it looked to most men (including the enemy) to be impregnable, Tuker undertook to capture it himself by a night attack. He saw also that the enemy would discount the likelihood of a serious attack here, so would not man it strongly. Roumana was allotted to 51st Division, and the centre sector to the Yorkshiremen of 69th Brigade under Brigadier Cooke-Collis, an able and alert young commander who congratulated himself on his hardness of hearing in the midst of shell-fire, because, he said, 'I can't hear the damned things burst.' The whole plan demanded from the troops the highest degree of boldness, stamina and training and, with its preliminary storming of the heights of Fatnassa by night, inevitably reminded one of Wolfe's historic assault upon Quebec.

The 5th of April was an agreeably warm day. The little African winter was over and the sun was waxing in strength. In the long, open, sandy plain the grass and the wild flowers were beginning to wither to a dusty grey-green. The silence that so often precedes a big battle was enlivened by little more than a shrill chorus of the cicadas. Eighth Army was in tropical kit, but carried their pullovers in their knapsacks, for the nights were cool. That day, under the eyes of the enemy, they began to filter across the plain and edge quietly up to the frowning hills.

The battle opened that night with a spectacle of high martial drama, as the Indian division, guided in their approach by small parties of signallers who crept out at dusk and set up pinpoint lamps showing to the rear, made for their craggy objectives on the left. It was very dark, but the flashes, shots and detonations that soon punctuated the night enabled the British regiments lying in the plain to watch the sensational assault upon Zouai's high cone by the 2nd Gurkha Rifles, formerly Tuker's own and now led by James Showers.

Wearing rubber-soled boots, they went for the 'horrible' objective in silence, without benefit of artillery. The author, sitting entranced beside Cooke-Collis at the advanced command post of 69th Brigade, and unaware that, beyond the curtain of the night, a VC was being won, watched and heard the sudden outbursts of fire, the long flashes of the Italian Bredas stabbing the night, the streams of tracered shot, the crackle of grenades, the chatter of Bren and tommy-gun as the Gurkhas, cat-footed and cat-eyed, rapidly fought their way up the steep uprising of the hill. What could not be observed was the gleam of the swinging Gurkha kukri. Higher and higher rose the flashes and the streaks of coloured tracers, till at last the pinnacle was reached and, for a moment, all was silent.

In this stirring feat of arms the dominant factor had been the native mountain craft of the Gurkhas, and by none was it demonstrated more impressively than by two sections of Captain Nicholl's company led by Subedar Lalbahadur Thapa, who opened the gate to the fortress and so won the first VC of Wadi Akarit.[27]

Lalbahadur was a short, stockily built man with a black moustache. Aged 35, he had had 17 years' service, was a fine shot with rifle and pistol, was always immaculately turned out and had a delightful sense of humour. With his very small force of only about 14 men, he was now expected to crack open a preliminary ridge which gave access to the main approaches to Fatnassa. The ridge was traversed by a path passing through a narrow, winding cleft in the rock, thence emerging into a small arena encircled by steep slopes and perpendicular cliffs, 200 feet high. The approach was covered all the way by the enemy's heavy machine-guns, sited in built-up stone *sangars* on the forward slope, enfilading the approach on fixed lines of fire. If ever there was a death-trap, this was certainly one. Silently Lalbahadur, pistol and kukri in either hand, led his men up the boulder-strewn slope in the enfolding night. Just as silently they pounced upon the first enemy post, leaping down into it from behind, and finished it off with kukri and bayonet.

The cries from their victims brought to life the enemy posts higher up, who very soon poured down fire. The machine-guns

---

[27] See 'Note on the Indian Army', Appendix F.

awoke first, then came volleys of hand-grenades and soon afterwards the concealed mortars farther back flung down their high explosives. The Gurkhas broke into a run and, with the subedar always in the van, overcame all the enemy, but themselves suffered casualties. With great skill, Lalbahadur led them by a route which enabled them to attack each post from the rear. He himself leapt into one machine-gun nest and killed four Italians single-handed, two with the pistol and two with the kukri.

Emerging from the cleft into the enclosed arena, the Gurkhas ran into murderous fire, suffering heavily, but the subedar still led them onwards and upwards with rare dash and gusto. Before he reached the crest of his objective his force was reduced to two men. Undeterred, the three triumphantly gained the crest, where they stumbled on the last enemy post and went for it. Lalbahadur killed two with the kukri, his riflemen killed two more, and the remainder fled. He had thus secured the ridge that dominated the main corridor beyond. The gate into the massif was open. Though clearly illuminated by flares dropped from enemy aircraft, the remaining companies of 2nd Gurkhas poured through to assail the steep sides of Zouai, while the Royal Sussex, the 6th Rajputana Rifles and the 9th Gurkhas made for their own craggy objectives, the battalions passing through one another and changing direction in the rugged terrain and the dark in a brilliant exhibition of the soldier's craft. On the right the 4th Essex, its assault company led by an artillery officer, drove through to a high point threatening the enemy's rear. Throughout the next day the battalions, ably supported by the divisional artillery, shook off one counterattack after another dangerously launched by German troops.

All acknowledged the magnitude of their debt to the 'surpassing bravery' of Lalbahadur Thapa. Colonel Showers recommended him for no more than the Military Cross, but General Montgomery himself upgraded it to the VC.

Private Anderson

On the right of the Indians the Yorkshiremen of 69th Brigade stood to arms in the dark on their exposed plain. Beyond the curtain of night stretched the rolling downland which was their objective, barred by a particularly fierce anti-tank ditch 8 to 10 feet deep. Standing sentinel to the enemy main defence and in front of them was a steep pimple, bursting straight up out of the plain to a height of 300 feet. It dominated both the right flank of the brigade and the left flank of 51st Division, so that its early capture was essential to both before the main assault.

A company of 7th Green Howards went for it in the flank at 3.30 a.m. under Captain Mansell, and won it with great spirit after a stiff uphill fight. The main assault was then put in, in unison with the Highlanders, under an artillery barrage in the chill of 4.15 a.m. It was launched with what General Messe described as 'an apocalyptic hurricane of steel and fire'. At first all did not go well with the Yorkshiremen. The 7th Green Howards and 5th East Yorkshires deployed and advanced to the anti-tank ditch, which lay deceptively beyond the dead ground of a reverse slope prickly with mines. Here the two battalions were caught in severe fire but pressed on down into the ditch, where they found their feet clogged by deep mud and where they were trapped by a concentration of pre-planned defensive fire from all weapons, the most damaging of which was enfilade fire from the Roumana hills. Here Derek Seagrim, again leading his battalion into the ditch, was mortally wounded. A few scaling ladders were set up by the courageous

Sergeant C. Craddock and others, and Corporal J. O'Rourke led a gallant and successful attack on an enfilading machine-gun, but all was in vain. The two battalions withdrew some 200 yards, behind the crest, and went to ground, still under fire, bringing many of their wounded with them but inevitably leaving others behind.

In the ranks of 5th East Yorkshire Regiment was a private soldier named Eric Anderson. In person slim, fairly tall and dark, he was 27 years old, a married man, a practising Churchman and came from the suburbs of Bradford, where he was a motor mechanic. He was a man of a quiet, modest disposition, described by the medical officer (Captain R. F. Clark) as 'of upstanding character, with lofty ideals' who won his admiration 'for the way in which he conducted himself both in and out of battle'.

Anderson was one of the battalion stretcher-bearers and as such was under the orders of the doctor. It was his dangerous business, as one of a team of four, to seek out the wounded in battle and carry them back to the medical officer at the Regimental Aid Post. They were devoted men who saved many a soldier's life, regardless of their own, by getting him back quickly to the doctor, whose Aid Post was set up on the edge of the conflict and often within it. Throughout the action Anderson had shown impressive composure and, as the rifle companies withdrew, he saw many of his friends lying out between the crest and the ditch, helpless and pinned down by fire.

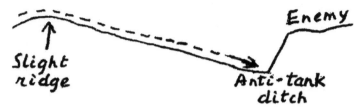

Private Anderson's exploit.

It was now daylight. Lying on top of the ridge itself was Sergeant Jack Freeman, observing for his mortar platoon, and close to his left was an artillery observation officer and his signallers. As the sun dispersed the early morning mist they were astonished to see the lone figure of Private Anderson crawling down the deadly, fire-swept slope ahead of them. They watched him right down into the deep tank-trap, 150 yards away, under full observation by the enemy. There he picked up a wounded soldier, administered morphia from one of the small capsules that he carried, heaved the man over his shoulder and, while the bullets ripped up the ground round about, laboriously crawled back to the relatively safe side of the ridge. Thence the wounded man was taken back to Captain Clark's Aid Post.

This was but the beginning. The observers on the ridge held their breath when they saw Anderson go out a second time and bring back another wounded man in the same manner. Yet a third time he went out, without thought for himself and seeming to bear a charmed life as the enemy's mortars and machine-guns opened on him on each occasion. A lone and gallant figure, he ventured forward a fourth time, almost recklessly it seemed, for 'the reeking tube and iron shard' cannot be defied for ever. The physical effort alone was remarkable. But as he had started back on each of his missions of rescue some man still lying helpless had cried, 'Can you come back for me, Andy?' and he would not refuse. Thus he gathered up his fourth comrade and was in the act of carrying him back to safety when he himself was mortally wounded.

For this sacrificial act of valour Anderson was posthumously awarded the Victoria Cross, Sergeant Freeman being one of the signatories to the recommendation.

In those localities where he lived and worshipped, his memory is still kept very much alive by tributes that testify to both his character and his gallantry. Plaques have been set up at Thornbury Boys School (new Thornbury Middle School), where he was educated, at St John's United Reformed Church, where his wife worshipped, and in Beverley Minster. At his old school there is also an 'Eric Anderson Prize', awarded to the outstanding pupil of the year, and a service is held on the anniversary of his death, when his Victoria Cross citation is read out.

Very soon after Anderson's act of sacrifice the Yorkshire brigade was enabled to win its objective by a skilful manoeuvre. Cooke-Collis, having received permission to encroach on the Highland Division's territory on his right, sent 6th Green Howards round the pimple in a neat right hook that took them through a gully in the foothills and so behind the ditch, which the Italians rapidly abandoned. It was a fine example of 'restoring the momentum of the attack'. The Germans began to plaster the new approach with their multiple rockets, which screamed and roared through the air with eldritch tones and detonated noisily in scattered showers, but the whole of the brigade's objective was taken and firmly held thereafter. A squadron of Sherman tanks of 4th County of London Yeomanry and the anti-tank guns of the Northumberland Hussars followed through the bursting rockets but, on topping the ridge, the tanks were quickly knocked out one after the other (under the author's eyes) by the deadly and skilfully sited 88-mms.

Lorne Campbell

Meanwhile 51st Division's attack on the right had gone like clockwork.

On that open plain all the great names of the old Highland Brigade were arrayed in the African night — Black Watch, Seaforth, Gordon, Cameron, Argyll and Sutherland. With them were their machine-gunners of 7th Middlesex Regiment and parties of Royal Engineers, to clear routes for the tanks and the anti-tank gunners. Ready to come forward were Ricky Richard's Valentines of 23rd Armoured Brigade and some 'Scorpion' tanks fitted with heavy chain flails to thrash a way through the mines.

Douglas Wimberley, their divisional commander, had a problem of peculiar difficulty. He had to assault a dog-leg objective over difficult terrain and thus to make two separate and divergent attacks at right-angles to each other. His divisional artillery (under Brigadier George Elliott) was restricted for ammunition and could support only three battalions, whereas Wimberley would need five. He solved the problem by directing two battalions against the western extremity of his objective in the Roumana hills and one battalion against the eastern extremity of the big antitank ditch, following these up with two other battalions who would then turn inwards to meet each other in the angle of the dog-leg. The artillery barrage would support the first three battalions and then be diverted for the other two. It was a scheme that demanded skilful planning by Roy Urquhart, Wimberley's chief staff officer, and a high level of training in his troops.

The Jocks were in great form that day. The lilt of the bagpipes lent impetus to their hearts as they stormed over wadi, hill and ditch, wearing on their backs the white cross of St Andrew to distinguish them in the dark. All their objectives were reached before 7 a.m. Quantities of prisoners, guns and other booty fell to them. The sappers blew their gaps immediately behind them. Wimberley was fortunate enough to have a command post in the plain below, from which, like a general of other days, he could watch for himself the progress of his battalions. He saw the western end of Roumana fall quickly to 5th Seaforths and 5th Camerons and the eastern end of the ditch to 7th Argylls. He saw 2nd Seaforths and 7th Black Watch follow up for their inward-turning manoeuvres. It was not long, however, before he was able to observe the enemy's inevitable counter-attacks on Roumana and on his extreme right he could discern the outlines of an action in which the third VC of the day was soon to be won.

The 7th Battalion Argyll and Sutherland Highlanders, to whom this extreme right-hand task had been entrusted, was commanded by Lt-Colonel Lorne MacLaine Campbell. Aged 41, he was tall, slender, good-looking, with black hair and moustache: a typical Campbell, one might say. He had already won the DSO in France in 1940 and a Bar to it at Alamein, and was the nephew of Admiral Gordon Campbell, the celebrated Q-ships VC of the First World War. He had been educated at Dulwich College (like Pip Gardner), was a Master of Arts of Merton College, Oxford, and in civilian life was a wine-shipper in London, whence he journeyed frequently to Scotland for his Territorial training.

Campbell's task now involved the capture of enemy positions covering the Wadi Akarit (here 24 feet deep), consisting of several well-sited positions in depth, before the ultimate objective 600 yards beyond the big ditch. To do this, he had to start his attack at an angle to the divisional axis. The battalion, with their machine-gunners and other elements, after an approach march of seven miles, reached their start-line at 7 p.m. on the 5th, dug themselves in, breakfasted at 1.30 a.m. and had two hours' sleep before rising to a silent reveille.

The barrage came down at 4.15 a.m. on the 6th and the Argylls went forward, carrying all before them. The enemy infantry put up a poor show in face of the spirited onslaught of the Argylls' 'bonnie fechters'. The ditch was scaled by rope ladders and even by clambering on the shoulders of the captive Italians, who made no objection, and the Argylls passed on another 600 yards to form a bridgehead. The shelling and mortaring encountered, however, was severe and increased in violence after the capture of the ditch, when indeed it became the heaviest that the battalion had ever endured in any of its battles. At 7 o'clock in the morning 7th Black Watch, under James Oliver, came up according to design and swung left-handed, under cover of a smoke-screen, to secure the western part of the ditch, a tough assignment which they fulfilled with skill and guts at heavy cost.

The Argylls, on their new-won ground, stood ready to meet the counter-attack. It came in soon enough and was made by German Panzer Grenadiers of 90th Light Division, but was broken up by the division's gunners, as were two more launched in the morning. Yet another, supported by eight tanks, was seen off in the afternoon, but all the time the battalion continued to be battered by heavy shelling and mortaring. Casualties mounted seriously and the troops were under great strain. Just behind them tanks, ambulances and vehicles were on fire as they came through the gaps hazardously made in the minefield and the ditch by the Royal

Engineers. The gaps and the whole bridgehead were under direct observation by the Germans, so that the British tanks had great difficulty in getting forward.

At 6 o'clock in the evening a more formidable counterattack developed under a dense curtain of fire. One of Campbell's companies was forced to give ground a little but the battalion still clung on to their bridgehead. Enemy infantry penetrated in one or two places and fierce close-quarter fighting took place in the dusk before they were thrown out. Another penetration was made between the Argylls and the Black Watch, but as night fell both still stood masters of the field. For the Argylls, having lost ten officers and 150 men, it had been the most vicious one-day battle that they had yet had to endure.

That they had been able to hang on was due primarily to the inspiration and example of Lorne Campbell. He dominated the battle, indifferent to danger, and was always in the forefront, wherever danger threatened. When his forward company was imperilled by the last German counter-attack he went forward personally under heavy fire, brought them back and stayed with them until the attack was held. He was wounded in the neck by a mortar-bomb splinter but still moved about, erect and composed, as an example for all to see of steadiness under intense pressure.

Campbell had made his command post in a series of shell-holes and small trenches in as hot a spot as any a little beyond the ditch. David Russell, adjutant of 7th Black Watch, gives a vivid picture of him as Oliver's battalion came up for their swing to the left. Campbell was, he said to the author, lounging about as though on a picnic, although bleeding from the neck. 'The effect of talking to him was quite electric and gave an enormous boost to my own morale. It was clear that all his soldiers were looking at him almost in awe of a man who had quite clearly inspired them. They were all buoyed up and carried along by his presence. Indeed, extraordinary though it may sound, there was a sort of aura of peace whenever he went in that most unpleasant place.'

Likewise, Noel Roper-Caldbeck, when he came up at the end of the day with 1st Black Watch, saw Campbell 'standing in the open and directing the fight under the close-range fire of enemy infantry'. It was Roper-Caldbeck, in fact, whose account formed the basis of Campbell's citation for 'magnificent leadership when his now tired men were charging the enemy with the bayonet and were fighting them at hand-grenade range'.

The Argylls were not the only battalion of the Highland Division to be fiercely engaged all that day. In the angle of the enemy's dog-leg position some ground was lost, but it proved to be of little importance, for during the night the enemy cleared out all along Eighth Army's front. A month later, bottled up in Tunis by the combined forces of Eighth and First Armies, under General Alexander, the Axis forces, some 450,000 strong, surrendered. All Africa was clear of Nazis and Fascists.

8: DAVID AND GOLIATH

Nine Victoria Crosses were awarded during the war to officers and ratings in the submarine service. Three of them went to the famous 10th Submarine Flotilla in the Mediterranean, where John Linton, David Wanklyn and Tony Miers harried the German and Italian shipping in long-sustained underwater odysseys which have become naval legends, but in which Linton and Wanklyn themselves and their gallant ships' companies perished. A quite unique pair of VCs was gained in the same dangerous waters by Peter Roberts and Petty Officer Gould who, in a scarcely credible act of nerve, removed two live aircraft bombs from HMS *Thrasher* in the enemy-infested waters near Crete.

What we shall be concerned with in this chapter, however, are the extraordinary exploits of those daring young men who sailed in what became known as the midget submarines and, like little Davids, attacked the Goliaths of the sea.

Before the end of the summer of 1943 the tide of the World War had begun to flow freely in favour of the Allies. The Allies had overrun Sicily and were about to invade Italy. In Russia the Germans were being rolled back by the Red Army. In the Far East the Japanese had been forced to a costly defensive among the far-flung islands of the Pacific.

At sea, as we have noticed in Chapter 3, the Navy and the RAF had at last begun to get the upper hand of the submarine 'wolf-packs'. There still remained, however, the menace presented by the Germans' big surface warships. The *Scheer*, the *Hipper*, the *Scharnhorst*, the *Gneisenau* and the *Graf Spee*, shrewdly handled, had already shown what damage they could do when loosed into the open seas. The great *Bismarck* had been brought to book only just in time, but there remained her giant sister, the new *Tirpitz*, the most modern and most powerful warship of the world's navies. This magnificent ship displaced 45,000 tons and carried a main armament of eight 15-inch guns, with 28 other guns. Beneath the crust of her upper decks she was armoured with a secondary steel deck, eight inches thick, proof against the heaviest bombs then in existence. Like *Bismarck*, she was believed to be virtually unsinkable, and the death *oi Bismarck* had certainly shown that an enormous amount of high explosive was necessary to destroy her.

In Chapter 3 we noted how Hitler ordered his big ships to avoid a fleet action with the Royal Navy and to be locked up until an opportunity should occur for their employment as mere marauders of Allied shipping. In this policy he was enormously helped by his seizure of Norway in April 1940. The saw-edged coast of that country, deeply indented by fiords and masked by innumerable islands, provided ideal lairs for pirates, and gave to the German ships two great advantages: they were provided with remote and secure anchorages and they were exceptionally well placed to sally out either into the Atlantic to prey upon Allied ships or to attack the British convoys carrying war stores through Arctic waters to the help of the Russians. The Royal Navy was thus faced with one of the oldest problems of sea warfare: how to get at enemy ships skulking in inaccessible and heavily defended anchorages.

The Midgets Emerge

For some forty years the Navy had been experimenting with various types of miniature underwater craft, but with little encouragement from Whitehall, and it was not until some daring Italian naval officers sneaked under water into

Alexandria harbour in December 1941 and inflicted considerable damage to two of our big warships that midget craft were given serious attention. Mr Churchill wrote a terse note which said, in effect: 'If the Italians can do it, we can.' The Japanese had also used midget craft, and in the last year of the war the Germans themselves were to build them by hundreds.

From Britain some remarkable successes, including the sinking of two Italian warships in harbour, were soon scored by what was known as the 'Chariot', or 'human torpedo', in which two men in diving suits sat astride a very small, open, underwater chassis, like tandem cyclists, behind a large detachable war-head, a task that needed considerable nerve and stamina. More or less parallel with them, the midget submarine was also at last being actively developed. This was the conception of Commander Cromwell Varley, a long-retired submarine veteran. Unable to get Admiralty approval, he had built a prototype (*X3*) himself on the Hamble River. Her trials in 1942 were a conspicuous success and the Admiralty then ordered six to be built by Vickers-Armstrong. They were named *X* craft.

Except that it did not carry torpedoes, the *X* craft embodied in miniature all the essentials of a conventional submarine. It was barely 51 feet long with a pressure hull only 5 feet 6 inches in diameter and an overall beam when carrying its explosives of 8 feet 6 inches. Above the pressure hull was the 'casing', a narrow platform serving as an upper deck. The boat's bottom consisted of a cluster of tanks of all sorts — for ballast, trimming, compensating, fuel, fresh water and so on.

Internally, the craft was so crammed with machinery and other gadgets that there was only one spot where a man could stand erect, and then only if he did not exceed 5 feet 6 inches in height. This was a low dome beneath which the captain stood at the controls of the pencil-thin periscope. The other three of the crew had to sit at their controls, hedged about by a clutter of pipes, levers, gauges and valves, and could move about only in a crouching attitude, or even, in some places, by wriggling on their bellies. There was no conning-tower and the submarine rode only a few inches above the water when surfaced.

The forward compartment was filled by a large battery for the electric motor that propelled the boat when dived, and provided power for the pumps, lights and control equipment generally. The midships compartment formed the control room, housing the periscope and the controls for propulsion, navigation, diving, trimming, releasing her explosives, and all other of the boat's operations.

Farther aft was the engine room, crammed almost to the brim with the small diesel engine (for propulsion when surfaced), the electric motor, pumps, compressor, oxygen cylinders, etc. Into this compartment a man could only just squeeze himself.

An ingenious feature of the X craft was the 'Wet-and-Dry' (or 'W-and-D') compartment, situated between the control room and the batteries. Here was the water-closet (or 'heads' in naval parlance) and above it was the forward hatch. When it was necessary for a man (in diving suit) to get out under water he entered the 'W-and-D', shut the watertight doors behind him, waited until the compartment was flooded from one of the main ballast tanks, opened the hatch over the WC and climbed out, returning by the reverse process. One of its purposes was to enable a diver to get out and cut a way through underwater nets, and we shall see Leading Seaman Magennis using this hatch at Singapore later on. The W-and-D also served as a normal exit when surfaced, and as an emergency exit when using the Davis Escape Gear.

In addition to the very slim periscope, the midget was fitted with a so-called night periscope, which was merely a pair of periscopic binoculars, set just above the hull and of very limited range. A small overhead port or window of armoured glass, inset in the dome of the hull, showed the captain when he was underneath his prey.

This remarkable miniature submarine had a surface range of 1,500 miles, subject to human endurance, and a submerged range of 80 miles at 2 knots. Her maximum surface speed was 6½ knots, and her submerged one 5 knots. She could dive to 300 feet. Instead of torpedoes she carried two very large underwater bombs or 'charges', each weighing four tons, and filled with two tons of Amatol, equivalent to a full salvo from ten torpedo tubes of a modern submarine. They were fixed to each side of the hull and streamlined to its shape, running almost the whole length of the boat and looking like two halves of a torpedo split lengthwise. The boat made her attack by releasing these underwater bombs beneath the keel of the enemy ship, when they dropped to the bottom and were detonated by a clockwork time fuse. They were released from inboard by a wheel-and-worm mechanism and the fuse was also set from inboard.

The operational crew usually consisted of three young officers and an engine-room artificer. The No. 1 (first-lieutenant) controlled the diving and trimming mechanisms. In front of him sat the helmsman (who might be an officer or a senior rating), whose main task, seated at a steering wheel, was to keep the boat strictly on the course ordered by the captain, whose normal post was at the periscope, at which, unless himself a midget, he had to stoop sharply or to kneel. At least one man in each crew was a trained diver, recruited from the Chariot teams. The only sleeping quarters were two very cramped bunks, into which it was only just possible to wriggle. A tiny electric cooker allowed hot meals to be prepared.

Thus life in a midget submarine, when submerged for any length of time, was decidedly uncomfortable. The inability to stand erect after many hours of crouching was a considerable trial. A short, folding induction pipe admitted a little air when on or near the surface, and oxygen could at need be switched on from large 'bottles' when submerged; but, apart from these reliefs, the crew lived in an atmosphere that, after a time, became very stale and fetid. Excess carbon dioxide could be passed through absorbent material by fans, but after long submersion men still became very drowsy. The discomfort was aggravated by the heavy condensation resulting from the heat of instruments and the human body. Everything sweated and streamed with moisture. Men's clothes got wet through, electric circuits were shorted and small fires broke out.

All these factors and the inherent peril of such craft meant that, as in all submarines, the crew had to be a very close-knit fraternity, bound together in the comradeship of close contiguity and common danger. Constant vigilance and instant obedience were rules of life.

For readers not familiar with submarine terminology there is a short glossary in Appendix D.

'Hazardous Service'

Volunteers for 'special and hazardous service' were called for and there was no lack of them, with a good sprinkling of Australians, New Zealanders and Canadians besides those from the mother country. There were two Frenchmen, under assumed names. All were mad keen, high-spirited young men, full of pith and ardour. Most were from the reserve forces: the Royal Naval Reserve, chiefly men whose peace-time occupation was in the merchant service or other maritime employment, and the Royal Naval Volunteer Reserve, who might be anything. Most of those selected were, appropriately, small men. Indeed, Ian Fraser, one of those later to win the VC, was a mere shrimp of a man, but Bill Whittam, whom death was to rob of a decoration that he deserved, stood 6 feet 5 inches.

The first X craft were delivered in January 1943 and in time became part of 12th Submarine Flotilla, commanded by Captain Willie Banks. Intensive training, with some unhappily fatal accidents, was begun under tight security first at Rothesay and in Loch Striven in Argyllshire and later in the remote and beautiful Loch Cairnbawn, in the extreme northwest of Scotland, 25 miles from Cape Wrath.

The first two experimental craft, $X3$ and $X4$, were commanded by two tough and wiry little men who were to be the first midget submariners to win the Victoria Cross. They were Donald Cameron and Godfrey Place, with whom, and with whose shipmates, this narrative will be chiefly concerned.

Cameron was a quiet little Scot of 26, full of tenacity and initiative and fond of his pipe. He hailed from Carluke, in Lanarkshire. As a boy, his real aim had been to join the Royal Air Force and he had actually passed into Cranwell only to be told that he was too young and would have to wait. Not content to hang about, he entered the merchant service and at the beginning of the war joined the RNR as a midshipman and saw service in an armed merchant cruiser patrolling the Atlantic. A year later he transferred to the submarine service and took part in several patrols in the North Sea before he got 'hooked' on the exciting possibilities of Varley's first X craft in

238

1942, in which he had served in the very first trials and which he was now commanding.

Godfrey Place, on the other hand, was RN and four years younger. Small and slim, he wore a crop of thick black hair and was of that steady, unruffled disposition that so often distinguishes the submariner, but his quiet demeanour was enlivened by a shrewd sense of humour. His deep voice was seemingly inappropriate to his stature. Highly professional and of a quiet and serious demeanour, he was distinguished by a meticulous attention to technical detail, which was to serve him and his crew in good stead. He had joined the submarine service in 1941, served in the famous 10th Submarine Flotilla at Malta and had already won the DSC, together with the Polish Cross of Valour for service in a Polish submarine. He was one of the very earliest Midget volunteers. Both he and Don Cameron had married Wren officers, Place's marriage occurring only a few weeks before the operation now to be recorded, with the gallant, ill-fated Henty-Creer as his best man.

The Lurking Enemy

The very short nights of the Arctic summer forbade any adventures by the midgets during that season of 1943, and up to the end of August the targets that they were to attack had still not been chosen.

Admiral Sir Max Horton, head of the submarine service, aimed to use them for attacking any of the German heavy ships in Norwegian waters that might offer themselves as promising targets. Bergen, Trondheim, Tromso and the Alten Fiord were their most favoured lairs, and a basic, flexible plan was made that could be adopted 'to any of them'. Among the enemy ships known to be on the move in those far northern waters were the great *Tirpitz* herself, the battle-cruiser *Scharnhorst*, of 32,000 tons, and the pocket-battleship *Lützow*, of 10,000 tons.

By September all the signs pointed to the farthermost of all these anchorages as being the most likely place to catch the enemy. This was the complex of small fiords radiating from the Alten Fiord, a remote inlet in the extreme north of Norway, masked from the open sea by a cluster of jagged islands. One thousand miles from the north of Scotland and beyond the range of RAF bombers, it lay approximately at 23° East and 70° North, within the Arctic Circle and just round the corner, so to speak, from North Cape itself. There the Germans set up a complete mobile naval base and thither in due course went the three heavy ships, together with a flotilla of destroyers, a repair ship and numerous auxiliary craft. Clearly the big ships were to be based here for attacks on the convoys to Russia, which passed to the north of North Cape. They were now kept under daily photographic surveillance by the Royal Air Force, using the long-range Spitfires of Coastal Command, which re-fuelled at an airfield that the Russians half-heartedly allowed us to use at Murmansk. They were watched also by Norwegian patriots, among whom was Mr Torstein Raaby, who took rooms overlooking the main anchorage and kept the British Naval Intelligence accurately informed by wireless almost hour by hour. Early in September the Senior British Naval officer in North Russia signalled the exact position where all the heavy ships were now securely locked up and with every sign of permanent residence.

Lützow was in Long Fiord. *Tirpitz* and *Scharnhorst* were in the small, obscure Kaa Fiord, a mere crevice among the bare and inhospitable mountains at the uttermost extremity of the Alten and some 55 miles from the open sea, looking on the map like the bottom of a deep rat-hole. As if this remoteness was not enough, they were protected by every known security device. Each ship was caged within what the air photographs showed to be a double anti-torpedo net, the Kaa Fiord was screened by an anti-submarine net, and the approaches to it were covered by batteries of guns and torpedo tubes. Small anti-submarine boats constantly patrolled all the inlets. Hydrophones were liberally deployed to detect the underwater sound waves that would signal the approach of a hostile craft.

Finally, out in the open sea, a deep minefield shut off all those channels between the islands that gave access to the Alten Fiord. The remoteness, the minefields, the anti-submarine net, the anti-torpedo nets, the patrols and listening devices created collectively a formidable series of obstacles. Other factors to be carefully assessed were the weather and the relative hours of daylight and darkness in those regions.

In view of what was to happen, there is a special interest in the crafty lay-out of the anti-torpedo nets that protected *Tirpitz*, which lay in 17½ fathoms of water (105 feet). The air photographs showed two lines of the buoys from which such nets, made of steel wire, were suspended. Measurement of the buoys on the photographs suggested clearly that the nets could not have been more than 50 feet deep. This inference was to be denied by events and very nearly wrecked Place's attack. It was subsequently assumed that there were in fact three separate nets, reaching right down to the sea-bed, the innermost being anchored there and suspended from an underwater buoy, the middle one hung direct from a surface buoy in the normal way, and the outermost also hung from the surface but suspended by steel wires, to cover the intermediate space between the other two.

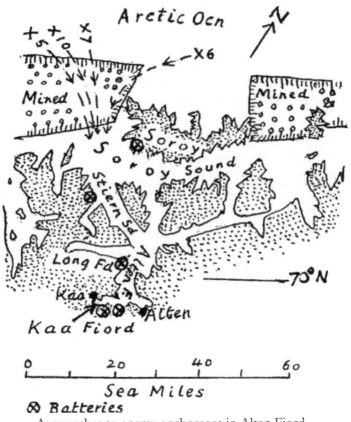

Approaches to enemy anchorages in Alten Fiord.

Despite all these hazards, it was resolved to launch the midgets on an attack against the big ships, and a plan was evolved under the code-name *Source*; though from the audacity of its conception it might well, one may think, have been called *Sauce*. The operation was under the command of Rear-Admiral Claude Barry. The plan was still a flexible one, in case the enemy ships should in the meantime change their anchorage.

The first problem was how the little craft could be enabled to make the approach passage over the 1,000 miles of the North and Arctic Seas. The method resolved upon was to tow them by larger, conventional ocean-going submarines until they neared the minefield. There the chicks were to be loosed by their mothers to begin their run-in of about 100 miles to the targets. After their attacks, they were to return to the open sea, be picked up again by their parents and towed home. Should the midgets be unable to return, their crews were to walk across Norway into the neutrality of Sweden. Because of the danger of handling heavy cables on the very narrow, exposed casings of the midgets, the towing was to be done on nylon ropes (as used for towing gliders), through which telephone lines were run.

A necessary condition for the operation was a period when severe weather was unlikely, with some moonlight, and the hours of daylight not too long. All these factors pointed to 20 September, when the moon was in its last quarter. As in all such operations, a limiting factor was the endurance of the crews of the midgets, and accordingly the practice had been evolved of picking two crews for each — one for the long sea passage and the other for the attack, though both were trained to carry out the full mission. The attack crews would take over from the passage crews when the midgets were slipped from their parents just outside the minefields. This was to be after dark on 20 September, so that the midgets could get underneath their prey soon after daylight on the 22nd.

Quite clearly, therefore, Operation *Source* was to be an exceptionally daring and hazardous mission and one calling for skill, nerve and a severe trial of human fortitude and endurance.

First Misadventures

The expedition sailed from Cairnbawn Loch at dawn on 11 September, each pair independently, passing some 75 miles west of the Shetland Isles. The midgets, on tow, were manned by their passage crews and the attack crews were on board the larger submarines. All, related Peter Philip, the passage commander of *X7* (who was 'Uncle Peter' to the children on South African radio), felt the drama of the moment. After 15 months of training, the tiny craft were at last about to attack the world's largest. Though the attack crews would have the greater honour, the passage crews faced a more severe trial of endurance, for they would have to spend nine days in their cramped quarters in the conditions that we have described, submerged all the way. The little fleet, which carried three future winners of the Victoria Cross, lined up below, where 'ERA' stands for Engine Room Artificer.

> *X5*: ATTACK CREWS: Lt H. Henty-Creer; Sub-Lt T. J. Nelson; Midshipman D. J. Malcolm; ERA R. J. Mortiboys. PASSAGE CREWS: Lt J. V. Terry-Lloyd; Ldg Seaman B. W. Emmet; Stoker N. Garrity. Parent ship: HMS *Thrasher* (Lt A. R. Hezlet).
> *X6*: ATTACK CREWS: Lt D. Cameron; Sub-Lt J. T. Lorrimer; Sub-Lt R. H. Kendall; ERA E. Goddard. PASSAGE CREWS: Lt A. Wilson; Ldg Seaman; J. J. McGregor; Stoker J. W. Oxley. Parent ship: HMS *Truculent* (Lt R. L. Alexander).
> *X7*: ATTACK CREWS: Lt B. G. G. Place; Sub-Lt L. A. C. Whittam; Sub-Lt R. Aitken; ERA W. M. Whitley. PASSAGE CREWS: Lt P. H. Philip; Able Seaman J. Magennis; Leading Stoker F. Luck. Parent ship: HMS *Stubborn* (Lt A. A. Duff).
> *X8*: ATTACK CREWS: Lt B. M. McFarlane; Lt W. J. Marsden; Sub-Lt R. X. Hindmarsh; ERA J. B. Murray.

PASSAGE CREWS: Lt J. Smart; Ldg Seaman W. H. A. Pomeroy; Stoker J. G. Robinson. Parent ship: HMS *Seanymph* (Lt J. P. H. Oakley).

X9: ATTACK CREWS: Lt T. L. Martin; Lt M. Shean; Sub-Lt J. Brooks; ERA V. Coles. PASSAGE CREWS: Sub-Lt E. Kearon; Able Seaman A. H. Harte; Stoker G. H. Hellett. Parent ship: HMS *Syrtis* (Lt M. H. Jupp)

X10: ATTACK CREWS: Lt K. R. Hudspeth; Sub-Lt B. E. Enzer; Midshipman G. G. Harding; ERA L. Tilley. PASSAGE CREWS: Sub-Lt E. V. Page; ERA H.J. Fishleigh; Petty Officer A. Brookes. Parent ship: HMS *Sceptre* (Lt I. S. Macintosh).

Of these, Terry-Lloyd and Philip were South Africans and McFarlane, Marsden, Shean and Hudspeth Australians. We may note that *Thrasher* was the historic boat in which Roberts and Gould had won the VC 18 months earlier.

Making a good nine to ten knots, the little expedition set off on parallel courses, approximately NE by N, 20 miles apart. In order to make the best speed, the midgets were towed submerged, while their tugs rode on the surface till they neared the enemy coast. The weather was fine and for the first four days all went well. The midgets surfaced every six hours for 15 minutes to charge batteries and to ventilate.

On 14 September, Rear-Admiral Barry received further reports of RAF reconnaissances from Russia that the enemy ships were still in Alten Fiord. He therefore now allotted definite targets for the midgets, by signal to their tugs, each of which had a separate re-ciphering code. His orders were:

X5, *X6* and *X7* to attack *Tirpitz*
X8 to attack *Lützow*
X9 and *X10* to attack *Scharnhorst*

The trouble then began. The weather worsened. The submerged midgets were severely bucketed about by the wrathful sea. Proceeding by a series of jerks as the tows alternately slacked and tightened, they plunged deep, reared up, twisted and rolled, like a hooked salmon. When surfaced, they rolled and pitched frantically. The passage crews had a fearfully rough time. Harsh strains were imposed on the nylon cable and the telephone lines they carried. On the night of 14/15 September *X8* broke away from *Seanymph*, was not sighted again for many hours and, after a series of mishaps and a gruelling time for her crew, had to be scuttled two days later to save the expedition from being compromised.

Next afternoon *X7* likewise broke adrift from *Stubborn*. Like a leaping fish, the midget shot up out of the water for half her length and splashed back again with a crashing belly-flop. With considerable difficulty, an auxiliary tow was passed from *Stubborn* by a rubber dinghy in full daylight and both then proceeded on course after a dangerous 90 minutes.

Worse was to follow. *X9*, in tow by *Syrtis*, surfaced for one of her breathing spells. At the end of it both dived and *X9* was never seen again. The assault force was thus reduced by the end of the 17th to four midgets. *Lützow* was to be left to enjoy a suspension of her sentence and only *X10* was left to attack *Scharnhorst*. All three midgets allocated to *Tirpitz*, however, were still fully viable and it is with them, but predominantly with *X6* and *X7*, that our narrative will henceforth be mainly concerned.

On 18 September these four craft resumed passage on tow, and soon after dark that evening, the rough weather having abated somewhat, a rubber dinghy from *Stubborn* successfully transferred Place's attack crew to *X7* and took off Peter Philip's exhausted passage crew. On going ahead, *X7*'s tow parted for the second time, so that *Stubborn* had to extemporize with a heavy 2½-inch wire cable, a prolonged and dangerous operation in which Place and Whittam, his No. 1, had to be secured by ropes for three hours against being washed overboard, both getting very wet, cold and bad-tempered. Course could not be resumed for some five hours, by which time it was 1.30 a.m. on the 19th.[28]

Attack Crews Take Over

That evening the other three attack crews were transferred to their midgets, where they found the passage crews exhausted and shaky, many of them, after nine days without budging, being unable to stand. For *X7* there were some critical minutes while she and *Stubborn* were surfaced. A very large, horned mine that had broken loose from its mooring drifted on to the towing cable, slid along it and was lodged against the bows of *X7*. So much Whittam saw through the night periscope. Place thereupon went out on to the casing, where he fended the mine off gingerly with his foot, loosed its mooring wire from the tow and, with relief, watched it drift slowly astern.

By early dawn on 20 September the towing submarines, having sighted the snow-tipped Norwegian mountains, shaped course for their slipping positions outside the minefield. The weather improved dramatically, the wind dropped to a southeasterly breeze, the sea calmed, visibility was good, but the Arctic breath was bitterly cold. That night, between 6.30 and 8 o'clock, the remaining midgets were slipped and headed off on the surface independently for Soroy Sound, while their mother-craft turned about and took up patrolling stations.

---

[28] The times in this chapter are GMT. Local time was about 1½ hours ahead.

The midgets were now on their own. Within their cramped cylinders the crews sat at their operational stations. All knew the hazards ahead but were confident that they would overcome them. Cameron recorded that he felt like 'a tin god in a tin fish'. They kept watch-and-watch, two at a time. Still riding on the surface they passed safely over the first hazard — the minefield, which would have been fatal to craft of deeper draught. Everything was dead quiet and very cold. They entered Soroy Sound, a wide channel between the off-shore islands, just before midnight, while the small moon pursued its course to the horizon through snow-laden clouds. Black smudges on either hand bore witness to the shapes of the tall, rocky cliffs typical of the Norwegian fiords, austere and barren. From far ahead lights from Norwegian houses sparkled in the keen air. They were now in highly sensitive waters, and before dawn broke soon after 1 a.m. they switched from their diesel engines to their quiet electric motors, turned on the oxygen, dived to 90 feet or so, and shaped for the narrow Stiern Sound, where they knew that batteries of enemy guns and torpedo-tubes were concealed.

All began to experience some difficulty in keeping their boats properly trimmed as the seawater began to be diluted with fresh. *X6* developed defects in her periscope, which it was to take all the wits of Cameron and Goddard to overcome; and in *X7* an internal exhaust pipe from the engine had split, releasing noxious fumes. Every hour or so they came up cautiously to periscope depth to check their positions and beheld themselves in bright sunshine and in clear translucent turquoise water, with towering rock-cliffs on either hand, for by 2 a.m. it was fully light. Along the fringes of the austere coast the cabins of fishermen and hunters and here and there a small farm were to be seen. Cameron was so 'benumbed' with cold that his hands were as though paralysed. Vessels of various kinds were encountered but successfully avoided. Aircraft frequently passed overhead without spotting their sinister torpedo shapes. Indeed, throughout the operation there was plenty of enemy movement.

By the afternoon they were through Stiern Sound and into Alten Fiord proper. Here the landscape softened somewhat, with little green valleys and many little houses. A few hours later Place saw the threatening shape of a large warship, which he judged (rightly) to be the *Scharnhorst*, for the great battle-cruiser had left her anchorage in Kaa Fiord for gunnery practice. It looked, thought Place, as though *X10* was going to be robbed of her prey.

The long day brought Cameron and Place, according to plan, to a group of small islands four miles from the mouth of Kaa Fiord just before 7 p.m. of a misty evening. Here, separately, they surfaced after dark in reasonably good concealment among rocks and islets, to charge their batteries, get some fresh air and a hot meal, and make good defects. In *X7* Whitley patched up the broken exhaust pipe. The crews did not see one another, nor any other *X* craft, though Henty-Creer must also have been thereabouts. The moon glimmered through filmy clouds and draped the scene with a veil of silver. All began to feel the tension that precedes great events, for tomorrow was 'the day'. In the still air voices from a fisherman's hut, breaking the icy silence, came drifting to them over the narrow waters. The headlights of a car flashed and disappeared round the bends of the twisting coast road. The throb of ships' engines from the direction of Kaa Fiord reminded them that the enemy was awake and about. Then, one by one, the lights of the little town of Alta, to the east, began to fade, leaving the world to darkness and the little submarines. Each in his little steel shell, separated from all his kind, felt very lonely, but, like Nelson at Copenhagen, 'would not be elsewhere for thousands'. To Cameron the feeling of pride that he was sitting in the middle of an enemy fleet was mingled with that of a 'very, very small and lonely boy'.

At 45 minutes past midnight on 22 September *X7* put out again and submerged, shaping about south-west for Kaa Fiord to make her attack. Ten perilous miles lay ahead and little of darkness was left. *X6* followed an hour later. The weather for their desperate venture was ideal, though very cold. A milky light suffused sea and mountains, but the sky was overcast and a fresh breeze whipped up white horses that would help conceal their underwater approach and their slim periscopes. A threat of snow was in the air.

The next hazard was the double anti-submarine net across the mouth of the Kaa. They knew from Intelligence reports that the wide gate at the southern end was likely to be open, but that it was guarded by depth-charge throwers and a hydrophonic listening post and that an examination vessel was posted outside to stop and check all traffic. Fortune favoured them. There was no need for the divers to get out and cut a way through the net. They crept through into Kaa Fiord unnoticed, an outward-bound German minesweeper conveniently showing *X7* the way. They escaped detection by the hydrophones and by magnetic detectors, having recently been degaussed.

Only three miles to go now. But three very perilous miles. Many known and unknown dangers lay in the final fiord. Craft of all sorts were either on the move or at anchor. A big repair ship was anchored within a protective net. Some destroyers were secured alongside a tanker. Another tanker lay close inshore. Right in the middle of the fiord was an empty cage of anti-torpedo nets believed to have been previously occupied by the *Lützow*. *X7*, proceeding now with all due caution, came up to periscope depth to check position but had to duck again immediately as a German motor-launch was seen coming at her head-on.

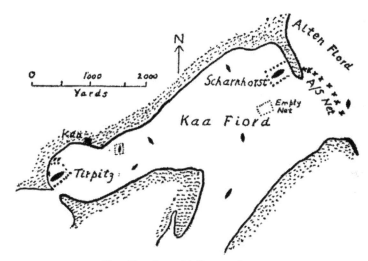

Kaa Fiord on 21 September.

Almost at once she got tangled in *Lützow*'s old torpedo net. She wriggled and huffed and puffed, employing all the dodges that she had practised repeatedly, going ahead, reversing sharply and manipulating her tanks, but was held fast for a full hour, fearful of agitating the surface buoys that sustained the net. The trimming pump for transferring water ballast from one tank to another was out of action and the gyro compass went crazy after so much shaking.

Getting clear at last, *X7* dropped like a stone to the bottom, with a dangerous froth of bubbles. Place, hoping her bubbles had not been observed, kept her there for another 20 minutes while the gyro steadied, the oxygen hissed quietly from its bottles and the chronometer ticked away its unforgiving minutes. Not until 6 a.m. was she able to proceed, precariously trimmed at periscope depth, and at last beheld the great, towering bulk of her target in the bright morning light, imperious, forbidding and challenging, her superstructure towering aloft like a castle, her bows daringly flared, her decks bristling with artillery. Place, calm and unemotional at the periscope, merely remarked: 'Well, she's there.'

Tirpitz in her lair. Adapted from the sketch made by Donald Cameron, by permission of his widow, now Mrs E. Compton-Hall.

The delay to *X7* enabled *X6* to overtake her, but Don Cameron was having increasing difficulty with his periscope, which constantly clouded over. He could see nothing but a green film. After dodging a small ferry-boat and an antisubmarine patrol in Alten Fiord, he did not pass through the gateway in Kaa Fiord until just after 5 a.m. He then took *X6* down to 60 feet, where he and Ernie Goddard stripped and cleaned the periscope, while proceeding very slowly by dead reckoning, all hands silent and tensed. On coming up to periscope depth again, he was disconcerted to find himself so close to the big repair ship that he had to alter course suddenly.

Thenceforward he followed the northern shore. The periscope clouded over and the brake of its hoisting motor burnt out. From then onwards the periscope had to be controlled manually, seriously embarrassing the delicate and critical manoeuvre that he had still to make as, towards 7 a.m., he crept towards the last obstacle of all — the triple anti-torpedo net surrounding the great ship.

He knew that, close to the shore, a small gate in the net was usually left open in daylight hours to enable very small craft to visit the *Tirpitz*.

Inside the Net

Meanwhile on board the unsuspecting *Tirpitz* the normal life of a big warship pursued its orderly tenor. She lay stern-first to the shore beneath the shadow of a towering black cliff that jutted sharply out into the fiord like the bows of a monstrous ship, and within a semicircle of mountains scattered with patches of snow among brown and green mosses on which the reindeer fed. The new day flooded the fiord with light and *Tirpitz* began to stir into life in the deep arctic silence. Hands were called at 6 a.m. and went about their duties. The hydrophonic listening posts closed. The anti-aircraft defences and the anti-sabotage watches afloat and ashore were set. *The small gate in the anti-torpedo net was opened.*

Then suddenly events moved quickly.

Towards the gap, risking observation by the guard-boat, *X6* held her underwater course. By great good fortune, a small coastal vessel, just discernible in Cameron's almost opaque periscope, appeared ahead of her, evidently making for the gate. *X6* followed her and at a minute or two past 7 o'clock passed safely through. She had now only to turn very sharply to port and dive beneath the keel of the *Tirpitz*, a cable's length away. A mere 200 yards. Proceeding blind, however, she went straight ahead and a minute later all hands were thrown violently forward as she ran aground on the north shore.

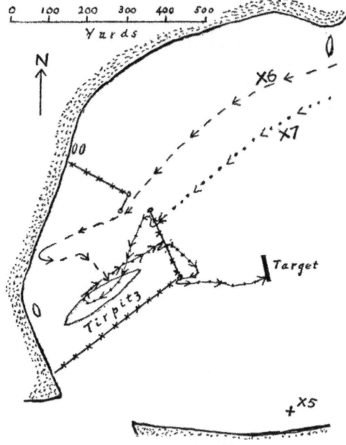

The midgets' attack on *Tirpitz*.

It was a hair-raising moment on the very threshold of the enemy stronghold. The slightest loss of nerve would bring disaster. Quick thinking and brisk orders were demanded.

Cameron was obliged to break surface and go astern. Lorrimer at the diving controls and Kendall at the helm, intent and keyed-up, responded instantly. On surfacing, Cameron beheld *Tirpitz* on his port quarter (his left rear). *Tirpitz* saw him too, but, as he dived again instantly, he was taken to be a porpoise.

A whole series of instant crises followed. On going astern to get clear of the shore and to face about to his target, Cameron found himself groping blindly, for the impact of grounding and the subsequent violent turn had put his gyro compass out of action and completely flooded the periscope. He was thus forced to surface once more and was filled with elation to find himself only 30 yards abeam of his prey.

Very nearly home now. Cameron had only to dive beneath the shadow of the big ship and drop his explosives. No more obstacles now.

But once again the sorely harassed *X6* struck some underwater obstruction. Cameron feared that he might have passed right under the ship and hit the net on her farther side. Manoeuvring by mere instinct, he got clear but was obliged to surface yet a third time to see where he was and found himself almost right under the steep flare of the battleship's port bow, abreast of her huge forward gun-turret. By now he had been identified beyond doubt by the enemy and, as he came up this time, he was greeted with a fusillade of musketry and grenades, but was fortunately too close for any heavier weapons to depress sufficiently. No chance now of making a getaway; but the tenacious Cameron was still determined to press home his attack. Once more he responded quickly to the crisis. Instantly he backed until the stern of *X6* was actually scraping the hull of *Tirpitz*. There at last he dropped his four tons of explosives to the sea-bed, pre-set to go off at the agreed hour of 8.30. Then, with remarkable presence of mind, he opened his inboard vents to scuttle the boat, so that she should not fall into enemy hands, and, as the water rose to their knees, ordered all hands out on to the casing, himself last, taking care to bring his pipe with him. *X6* had accomplished her mission.

As she started to sink, a German motor launch that had lain alongside the battleship darted up and took off the weary, bedraggled but triumphant submariners. The Germans then made an attempt to seize the midget and take her in tow, but they were too late; *X6* dipped her bows and quickly slid below to join her explosive charges at the bottom.

All over Kaa Fiord, and on board *Tirpitz* in particular, the alarm had been raised with a vengeance. Surprise was mingled with bewilderment. What could these four men have been up to? How could they possibly have penetrated the tight security measures? At first they were thought to be Norwegians, for it was impossible for a midget like *X6* to have crossed a thousand miles of the North Sea. It was some time before the Germans began to appreciate that the danger might be from underwater charges. Hands were ordered to action stations and the anti-aircraft gun crews 'closed up'. Orders were given to close all watertight doors and to raise steam. Divers were ordered to inspect the hull for limpet mines and the ship prepared to put to sea before the time-fuses might be actuated.

Before this could be done, however, *X7* was sighted at 7.40. It was the first intimation that more than one enemy craft was at work and the picture was not at all to the liking of the Germans. How many more were there? Did any of these pygmy craft carry torpedoes to attack a ship on the move? The German commander therefore ordered *Tirpitz* to stay put. The gate in the submarine net was tardily closed, but the most significant precaution taken was to shift the position of the ship slightly at her moorings. This was done by heaving on her starboard cable, so that her bows were swung bodily round in that direction for a short distance, but just enough to modify the violence of the shock she was soon to sustain.

Meanwhile, only five minutes behind Cameron, *X7* had been creeping in. Godfrey Place had decided not to chance entering through the gate in the anti-torpedo net, but to penetrate by passing right underneath the net. He had counted on the evidence of the air photos that the net would not be more than 50 feet deep and he therefore ordered '75 ft'.

At that depth, however, *X7* was caught. By going full-astern and blowing to full buoyancy, she broke clear, but by that process inevitably rose to the surface. She dived again at once and went down to 95 feet, but was once more fouled, for what she now struck was the undisclosed third net anchored to the floor of the sea. There followed another desperate five minutes of 'wriggling and blowing' and she began to rise. Her violent movements, however, had put the gyro compass out of action again and Place could not tell what his position was. He therefore stopped the motor and allowed *X7* to come right up to the surface for 'a good look round'.

To his surprise, he found that, by some lucky chance, he had somehow got right inside the net. There was *Tirpitz*, only 30 yards away and the time was 7.20.

Instantly he dived to 40 feet and *X7* struck the *Tirpitz* at full speed on the port beam. Thence she slid gently under the keel, the overhead glass port showing that she was in full shadow of the big ship, and dropped her first charge. Here, at 60 feet she paused to correct her trim, then, dead slow, crept under the keel of the *Tirpitz* towards her stem and dropped her second charge beneath the ship's stern gun-turrets, as nearly as Place could judge. Like Cameron's, both charges were fused to detonate at 8.30. Without any knowledge of one another's movements, each had dropped his explosives within a few minutes of the other.

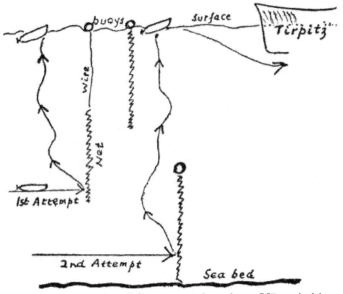

Underwater sectional diagram to show how *X7* probably penetrated the three nets of the *Tirpitz*. From a sketch by Admiral Place.

His mission fulfilled, Place turned about to withdraw. Hoping to make the spot at which he had gained entry through the anti-torpedo net, he could do no more than guess his course and once more ran full-tilt into the net, but this time it happened to be the middle one, nearest to the surface.

He was now faced with a critical situation. He had no idea where he was and all the blowing that he had been obliged to do had emptied two of the three compressed air bottles and a large part of the third. If he could not get clear before the explosion, *X7* was likely to be cracked open by the shock. He was entangled in that net for nearly three-quarters of an hour, using the technique of going full ahead and then full astern, blowing economically. The last air bottle was exhausted and he was obliged to bring the compressor into use, a desperate measure by which compressed air was made from what air there was in the submarine itself.

With the minutes flying past some new stratagem was urgently needed. No use hoping to get through by chance as before. Somehow *X7* wriggled out of the entanglement. Place at once resolved to carry out the desperate ruse that had occurred to him. He ordered No. 1 tank to be blown to full buoyancy. As he hoped, this brought the submarine to the surface very close to the net, with a bow-up angle of some 35°. She then belly-flopped down to an angle of 10° right on top of the net, and a burst of speed carried her clean over.

She was spotted by *Tirpitz* of course and dived again at once, but was so blind that she unknowingly swung hard astarboard and went into the net again, this time on the outside of it and farther along. While she was so caught there was a stupendous explosion as the underwater bombs went off beneath the *Tirpitz*. The shock waves flung *X7* clear of the net, whereupon Place was disappointed to see that *Tirpitz* was still afloat.

Havoc

Afloat yes, but in a sorry mess. With a terrific roar the whole great ship (according to one of the crew later taken prisoner) 'heaved up out of the water and bounced back again'. In the more prosaic terms of *Tirpitz*'s own log, 'The ship vibrates strongly, in a vertical direction and sways slightly, between her anchors.' She continued to quiver and sway for several minutes. All four charges must have gone off almost simultaneously, the first one detonating the others — what the log called 'two heavy consecutive detonations at one-tenth of a second interval'.

Instantly the ship was in an uproar. All the lights went out and all the complicated electric circuits by which a big warship fights, navigates and has her being were wrecked. Fire extinguishers were wrenched from their brackets and started hissing foam. Broken glass littered every deck. Men were flung violently off their feet; one was killed and 40 injured. All three engines, the rudder installations, dynamo control room, shafts, bearings and other gear were damaged very severely. Water poured in aft, and oil poured out. Two of the huge 15-inch gun-turrets, each weighing some 2,000 tons, were lifted clean off their enormous roller bearings and stuck fast, rendering the guns useless.

The full severity of these injuries was not yet apparent, but the immediate havoc was such that the captain of the *Tirpitz* (it is said) flew into a rage and ordered the crew of the *X6*, in accordance with Hitler's order, to be shot as 'saboteurs', but more seemly counsels prevailed. Other German reactions were likewise swift and angry. What other perils lurked beneath the still waters of the fiord?

One was immediately apparent, for *X7* was now seen floundering about outside the net. *Tirpitz* opened fire on her with one of her 5.9-inch guns at maximum depression and with machine-guns. The five destroyers and every other available craft in the fiord were ordered to hunt down whatever underwater craft there might be and depth-charges were dropped indiscriminately all over the place, the echoes of their explosions rolling back and forth among the cliffs and mountains and their shock-waves throbbing throughout the water.

An unhappy victim was *X5*, of whose progress hitherto we know nothing. Henty-Creer, however, had successfully brought her to a point 500 yards off the starboard bow of the *Tirpitz* and was no doubt about to make his attack (or conceivably had already made it). He surfaced, supposedly to see what was happening, was spotted and, under the anxious gaze of the captive Cameron and his shipmates, *Tirpitz* opened fire on him with her 5.9-inch guns at 8.45 a.m. and *X5* went down. Not content with this, the Germans ordered away a vessel that plastered the locality with depth-charges.

About the same time *X7* also met her destiny. The shock of the explosion that had blown her clear of the net had also caused her some damage. Water was leaking in, so Place took her to the bottom for an examination. The water in the boat surged to the stern when her bows were put down and back again as she sat on the bottom. With the depth-charges still exploding uncomfortably near, Place held a quick parley with Whittam. Water was still leaking in. The compressor, the gauges and both compasses were out of action and the craft was impossible to control. It was clearly the end. There was nothing that could be done except to surface and surrender. Better to face the gun-fire than to be destroyed below.

Place therefore took *X7* to the surface for the last time. The Germans opened fire on her again, with machine-guns and some sort of light artillery. With a jocular remark, Place clambered out through the W-and-D and found himself close alongside a very large floating screen; it was a target of the kind used for gunnery practice at sea. Spouts of water were splashing up all round and a few bullets rattled on the hull of *X7*. Place, unhurt, stripped off his white sweater and began to wave it in token of surrender. In case he should get killed, he had left orders with Whittam that, if he received no further orders or signals, he was to submerge and the crew were to get out by the Davis Escape Gear.

The Germans stopped shooting, however, and Place was about to call down to Whittam when he noticed that *X7*, which was very heavy with the water within her and riding only an inch or two above the surface, had nudged her bows beneath the gunnery target, so that water was lapping into the W-and-D. He immediately closed the hatch and jumped on to the target, continuing to wave.

So heavy was *X7* that even this small inrush of water made her sink. Place knew, however, that she was in competent hands and that his shipmates were well trained in the escape procedure. But all did not go well. As the W-and-D allowed only one man to get away, they would have to put on the Davis escape gear and slip out by both hatches. The prerequisite for escape by this means was to flood the submarine until the pressure inside equalled that of the sea outside. In *X* craft there were no scuttling valves for quick flooding, so the need was to open everything that would give access to water. As the water slowly rose and reached the batteries the lights went out and chlorine gas was given off. So, in complete darkness but in good order, the three men donned their escape gear and began to breathe oxygen. Then they waited and waited as, far too slowly, the ice-cold water reached their chests.

What went wrong then is not clear. All that is certain is that Whittam and Whitley died at the bottom of Kaa Fiord. Only Bob Aitken, who was the most experienced diver and the least exhausted, made good his escape, managing to open a hatch with the last ounce of his strength and reaching the surface in a prostrate condition some time afterwards.[29]

---

[29] Admiral Place himself said afterwards to the author: 'I don't know why Bill and Whitley were unsuccessful; probably they were

Snow began to fall, dropping a silent white curtain upon the Arctic drama, but not abating the turbulence within the *Tirpitz*. Thither Place and Aitken were taken, to join their comrades of *X6*. All were unshaven and unkempt, Place in little more than his underwear. The angry and astonished Germans pressed them hard with questions without avail, but otherwise treated them correctly before sending them off as prisoners of war to Germany.

The Germans had very good cause to be angry, for the damage to *Tirpitz* was very severe indeed. For six vital months she was useless as a man-of-war and, in fact never fully recovered. Such was the measure of the achievement of two of the world's tiniest craft, which, in a triumph of fortitude and tenacity, had overcome all the most modern devices that ingenuity could contrive to frustrate them. The great ship, pride of the German Navy, never fought an action, and became a heavy liability instead of an asset. The distortion of her frame by the underwater bombs permanently impaired her speed and she never went to sea again except to change her anchorage.

Before long she began to be harried from the air, suffering more damage, and finally, fourteen months later, in a brilliant attack by RAF Lancasters of Nos. 9 and 617 Squadrons, led by Wing-Commander J. B. Tait, her inglorious life was brought to a violent end in Tromso Fiord by super-heavy bombs in eight devastating minutes.

As for *Scharnhorst*, we have seen that she had left her moorings as the midgets were entering Alten Fiord. Even had she stayed, however, she would have escaped attack, for *X10*

---

overcome by carbon-dioxide poisoning from their physical exertions. We were all pretty tired by now and the pressure inside the boat was considerable.'

was bedevilled with troubles of every sort. She was spotted just outside Kaa Fiord when the Germans mounted their frantic hunt after the big explosion, but she escaped destruction. Her mechanical problems were so serious, however, that Kenneth Hudspeth had to abandon his mission and, after ten very precarious days hiding among the scattered islands, succeeded in rejoining his big brethren out to sea — the only one to do so. On the return passage to Scotland very severe weather made it necessary to scuttle *X10*, so that all six that had set out from Loch Cairnbawn were now beneath the waves.

Scharnhorst, however, had only another three months to live. On Christmas Day, 1943, she sailed out with a force of destroyers to attack a British convoy bound for Russia, but was intercepted by a force under the masterly leadership of Admiral Sir Bruce Fraser and sent to the bottom after a dramatic battle amid tumultuous seas in the Arctic night.

In due course came news of the awards of the Victoria Cross to Godfrey Place, Donald Cameron, of the DSO to Lorrimer, Kendall and Aitken and of the Conspicuous Gallantry Medal to Goddard. For those who died there were no awards except in the memories of their shipmates and their friends.

9: GURKHAS AND YORKSHIREMEN AT IMPHAL

The Gurkhas[30] are what Shakespeare might have called, as he did the English, 'this happy breed of men'. They are not Indians, but come from the mountain villages of the far Himalayan Kingdom of Nepal. Their skin is light brown and, in general, their stature inclines to be small, their figure firmly built, with well developed leg muscles.

Like many mountain races, the Gurkhas make first-class soldiers, brave and hardy. Born to a Spartan existence in their inhospitable mountains, remote from the rest of the world, they are accustomed to hard living, to enduring privation with cheerful stoicism, and to being self-reliant and resourceful in storm as in calm.

Usually illiterate before enlistment, the Gurkha has a keen natural intelligence. Religion is apt to sit lightly on his shoulders but a strain of fatalism flows through his being. When roused, as he easily can be, he 'sees red' in the factual sense of the term, for his eyes become bloodshot and he is then a dangerous man. He is imbued with his native maxim that 'it is better to die than be a coward'. Many of their names incorporate the term *bahadur*, meaning 'brave'. The second part of their names is that of their clan, tribe or other sub-division.

In battle the Gurkha charges with the cry *Ayo Gurkhali* ('the Gurkhas are upon you'). His favourite weapon is the broad, curved, heavy blade of the *kukri*, 16 inches long, equally

---

[30] The older spelling *Goorkha* is phonetically more correct, with the r rolled, and is still retained by one of the Gurkha regiments. In the Indian Army of today the spelling is *Gorkha*.

effective for cleaving skulls as for chopping wood. He is of particular value in mountain warfare, for he scrambles up steep hills with the agility of a goat, leaving the plainsman puffing and blowing below, and on the farther slope slides down and drops like a stone in the feat known as 'khud-racing'. To the British soldier, however, the abiding impression of 'Johnny Gurkha' is his cheerfulness. Whether stunned by the heat of the desert or stuck fast in the mud of the monsoon, a grin is readily evoked.

Although not Indians, the Gurkhas were recruited as volunteers into the Indian Army, the term 'India' meaning the whole of the sub-continent under British rule until its regrettable partition in 1947 (see Appendix F). Their officers were all British, except for a complement of Viceroy-Commissioned Officers of their own race. All Gurkhas were classed as Riflemen.

It is with these likeable mountain peasants that we shall be mainly concerned in this chapter as we turn to the arduous scenes of the Burma campaign that raged among its mountain jungles and malaria-infected valleys. These were undoubtedly the toughest physical campaigns of the whole of the Second World War, in which the 'Forgotten Army' struggled against a vicious enemy, with a low priority in arms and equipment, in a fierce and remote terrain that was virtually roadless.

The reader will not here find himself in a sophisticated theatre of war, with massive tank forces, powerful concentrations of artillery, saturating air attacks and modern engineering equipment. Certainly there were tanks, guns, aircraft and engineers, but it was predominantly a war of infantry, in which the most valuable and frequently the only means of transport were the mule, the jeep and the man with a load on his back. Physical endurance rated high in the qualities of the fighting soldier. He had no 'comforts'. He was often short of rations and when he was wounded his journey back to hospital was often long, distressing and dangerous. The sick and wounded had always to be carefully guarded, for the Japanese simply murdered out of hand any who fell into their hands. To the other hazards of war were added the trials of malaria, dysentery, jungle fever and the sores resulting from the bloodsucking leeches. In the monsoon the conditions became utterly abominable.

The Black Cats

The Japanese had launched their startling act of 'centrifugal aggression' in December 1941. One of their conquests was Burma, where they slowly drove back a half-trained and poorly equipped British-Indian force for 1,000 miles northwards to the Indian frontier. The British forces then reorganized and began to re-train behind the great mountain barrier that divided Burma from India, and in due course they became formulated as Fourteenth Army, destined to share with Eighth Army, of Desert fame, the highest renown of all British field armies. Its name and fame are imperishably linked with its great commander, the bulldog General Bill Slim. Of the three separate fronts under his direction we have to note only the Central Front. This was covered by 4th Corps, under Lt-General Geoffry Scoones, and supported by 221 Group, RAF, under AVM Stanley Vincent.

The corps gathered in the high plateau at Imphal, in the far-remote and semi-independent state of Manipur. The plateau now became a very large military establishment and was vital ground to the whole of the Allied operations in that sector of the World War. All around Imphal there stretched mountains of great scenic beauty, clad to their peaks with fine trees and adorned with sumptuous rhododendrons and magnolias, but often entangled with dense undergrowth and tough, creeping lianas that made penetration of its untrodden steeps a sore trial. The lower slopes were often matted with elephant grass, 12 feet high, through which the rate of progress was half a mile an hour; and everywhere were dense thickets of bamboo, twice as high again, crackling in a wind like musketry.

For two long years there was no large-scale fighting on the Central Front. The enemy had no intention of invading India, and the British had not yet the means of conquering Burma. A distance of some 200 miles separated the main forces. Scoones, however, in preparation for an ultimate offensive and to keep contact with the enemy, sent two divisions southwards to build such roads as they could over the mountains and the torrents, for there was no road of any sort from India into Burma.

One of these routes was allotted to Douglas Gracey's 20th Indian Division, who hacked and fought a tortuous way for some 60 miles to the village of Tamu. The other, allotted to 17th Indian Light Division, ran a fairly easy course at first out of Imphal, across flat paddy-fields and through thatched villages, embowered in mangoes, bananas and bamboos, before resolving itself into a narrow track that corkscrewed its way vertiginously through thick mountain jungle for 162 miles until it reached the remote mountain village of Tiddim, from which the road took its name. Thence, a mere cat-walk now, it ventured for a few more hair-raising miles, at altitudes of up to 10,000 feet, to the still more distant police-post known as Fort White.

It is with a part of this 17th Division that our narrative in this chapter will be concerned. Having fought the Japanese from the moment of their invasion of Burma, it was thus a thoroughly experienced division, living up to its symbol of a black cat with its tail well up. Its commander was Major-General 'Punch' Cowan, a man of rock-like calm with piercing blue eyes, fond of his pipe and cigar, a former Scottish hockey international. His nickname was derived from his profile, which resembled that of the celebrated old gentleman.

That part of 17th Division with which we shall be particularly concerned was 48th Indian Infantry Brigade, which had made its name already in the Burma retreat under the strong leadership of Brigadier Ronnie Cameron, a man of tall, rugged build, blue-eyed, fearless, outspoken, with a profound knowledge and love of the Gurkha. At the time when our narrative begins, the three battalions in his brigade were the 9th Border Regiment (from Cumberland and Westmorland) and two Gurkha battalions, who between them were to win four Victoria Crosses. The 2nd/5th Royal Gurkha Rifles was commanded by Osborne Hedley, an erect and soldierly figure, steady and unshakeable. The 1st/7th Gurkha Rifles was led for a considerable time by James Robertson, an Army boxer, fearless and calm in action.

The other brigade in Cowan's division was the 63rd, a hard-fighting all-Gurkha Brigade, commanded until January 1944 by Brigadier A. E. Cumming, who had won the VC in the disastrous Malayan campaign, and afterwards by Guy Burton, another cool-thinking pipe-smoker.

The division had also three unbrigaded infantry battalions, of which we should specially note the 1st Battalion West Yorkshire Regiment, in whose ranks also a VC would be won, as we shall see.

The Black Cats' four artillery regiments were commanded by the lively little figure of Brigadier the Baron de Robeck, known as 'Baron Bombard'. His regiment operated in conditions extremely difficult for artillery and we must remember them ever in the picture in these stirring events. One of these regiments (129th Field Regiment, commanded by Charles Younger) achieved a distinction of a peculiar sort; two of the fitter-gunners devised an ingenious means of reducing the width of the 25-pdr axle to that of a jeep, thus enabling the guns to reach positions that would otherwise have been impossible.[31]

Mountain VC

Among the lofty peaks of Fort White, in extremely arduous conditions, Cameron's 48th Brigade fought a series of fierce and rigorous actions in the spring of 1943 and here, led by Osborne Hedley, 2nd/5th Royal Gurkha Rifles won the first of their three Victoria Crosses.

In the ranks of this battalion was a havildar (sergeant) named Gaje Ghale. He was a round-faced, quiet but smiling soldier, immaculate in his turn-out and wearing a neat, black moustache. He commanded a platoon of young soldiers, and neither he nor they had yet been under fire. At the end of May he was moving with his platoon still farther on from Fort White to recapture a stockade (or old staging post) that had been lost to the enemy.

The key to possession of this stockade was a narrow ridge almost devoid of vegetation, that sloped away steeply on both flanks. Along the crest of the ridge were three excrescences, like the knuckles of a closed fist. The first two were taken without difficulty, but the farthest, known as Basha East, a quarter of a mile distant, was strongly manned by the Japanese, and the first attempts to seize it failed.

---

[31] The other artillery regiments were 21st and 29th Mountain and 82nd Light AA/A-tk.

On the afternoon of 27 May another assault was made. A weak company, only two platoons strong, one of which was led by Gaje Ghale, attacked astride the main ridge under Captain Villiers Dennys, with two companies of 1st/4th Gurkhas moving along the steep slope on their right. On the crest there was almost no cover whatsoever, and the Japanese held their fire until the Gurkhas were within 200 yards, when they opened up with all weapons.

The fire served merely to accelerate the impetus of the Gurkhas. Led by Dennys swinging his walking-stick and waving his men on, they charged up the knoll, reached the top, wavered there under a hail of fire and fell back. Again Dennys led them on, with a like result. Yet a third time they dashed up, stormed into the enemy position, fought the enemy hand-to-hand and forced them out. Basha East was won.

Throughout this spirited action Havildar Gaje Ghale had been an inspiration to his young platoon, and it was the flame of his example that led them on in this their first action. The platoon had already been under fire from mortar bombs while preparing for the attack, but when Dennys gave the signal, Gaje rallied them cheerfully and led them forward full of heart.

In many places the ridge astride which the platoon had to make its approach was no more than five yards wide and upon this narrow frontage, as the Gurkhas drew near, the Japanese concentrated the main weight of their artillery, mortars and their twelve machine-guns, but Gaje raced through without hesitation. At 20 yards or so from the enemy he was wounded in the arm, chest and leg by a grenade, but he took no heed and led his men straight in to close grips, when a bitter hand-to-hand fight ensued, which the halvidar dominated by his dazzling courage. Covered in blood, he led again in the second and third assaults, hurling hand-grenades with shrewd effect, and ever calling out *Ayo Gurkhali!*

When at last Basha East was secured he set his men at once to consolidating the position, still under vicious fire, refusing to go back to the medical aid post until ordered to do so by Dennys. Thus a large share in the success of this fine little action in those remote hills was the due of the gallant havildar, who in course of time was awarded the VC. Dennys, himself hit in the leg, won a fully merited Military Cross.

All this time their comrades of the 1st/4th, moving with difficulty athwart the steep slope on their right, had turned uphill and won their objective in gallant style, after one of their platoons had been reduced to six men.

U-Go

All through that year of 1943 the British were making ready for an offensive, to be launched along these slender slipways of the Tiddim and Tamu roads in 1944. The Japanese, of course, were well aware of this and were moved to forestall the British intention by launching their own offensive first.

Their force on this central front was their 15th Army, numbering about 110,000 men, led by the fire-eating General Renya Mutaguchi, an iron and ruthless militarist.[32] His plan was given the code name *U-Go*. Its purposes were to annihilate 4th Corps and to seize the high, undefended mountain ridge at Kohima, 130 miles farther north of Imphal, where the Japanese would have an impregnable defensive position.

Like all Japanese plans, Mutaguchi's was highly audacious and aimed at cutting in behind the British by means of columns moving very fast by unexpected routes. Surprise, speed and encirclement were always their precepts. One

---

[32] All Japanese names are here given in European style.

division was to penetrate straight to distant Kohima across what was believed to be 'impossible' jungle country, while other columns converged on Imphal from the east, south and south-west. Mutaguchi expected the whole strangulation to be completed in five weeks, well in advance of the monsoon, when normally all armies stopped fighting.

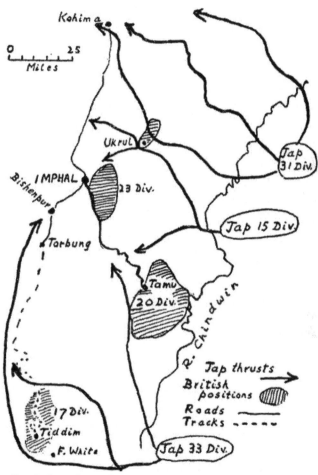

Imphal: outline of enemy plan for operation *U-Go*.

Scoones, of course, did not fail to see the signs and the plan that he made was to withdraw 17th and 20th Divisions from their distant roadheads and to fight the Japanese on ground of his own choosing at Imphal. It was an application of the Napoleonic tactics of *Reculer pour mieux sauter*. No one, however, expected that the enemy would be so crazy as to march on far Kohima, and what happened there is a separate story that formed one of the great epics of the war.[33]

The withdrawals from Tiddim and Tamu, Slim ordered, were not to take place till the last possible moment, and 17th Division, clinging to their frontal position as long as they could, had a very near squeak. The Japanese in front of them were the 33rd Division, probably the most formidable Japanese division in Burma, whose emblem was a white tiger and whom they had been fighting for more than two years. Their commander, Lt-General Yanagida, was highly critical of Mutaguchi's plan, but pursued his allotted part in it with vigour. His orders were to cut in behind 17th Division, surround and annihilate it and then march on Imphal.

Starting on 7 March and moving unseen along the wooded hilltops parallel with the Tiddim road, the White Tigers had planted no fewer than four road-blocks behind the backs of the Black Cats within a week. Their speed, dash and audacity took everyone by surprise. The withdrawal of Cowan's division over some 180 miles of extremely stiff country was therefore one of savage fighting in arduous conditions, the details of which do not concern this narrative. To relieve the strain on them, Scoones sent help from his reserve division, the 23rd, and Cowan's much-tried troops at last reached Imphal on 5 April.

---

[33] Narrated in the author's *Springboard to Victory*.

Four of the five weeks that Mutaguchi had allotted for his victory of annihilation had already passed. The White Tiger division was now in bad shape. Yanagida, standing in the shattered village of Ningthoukhong, soon to be the scene of two Victoria Crosses, thought it hopeless to pursue the offensive, though Imphal was now only 22 miles away. The furious Mutaguchi accordingly sacked him very soon afterwards, replacing him by a member of his own military sect, Lt-General Tanaka, who redressed the lack of hair on his pate by enormous black, wing-like moustaches.

Only now, as 17th Division withdrew through 23rd, did the real battle for the vital Imphal plain begin. It was to rage with ferocity for another three months on the three main sectors that gave or denied access to it: to the south-west, astride the Tiddim road beyond the village of Bishenpur (with which this narrative will be solely concerned); to the south, where desperate and bloody battles were fought among the bristling crags of 20th Division's Tamu road; and to the north-east, where a dangerous enemy thrust was parried only just in time.

As the fighting continued, its severity was accompanied by the physical ordeal of the monsoon. In late April occasional but heavy rainstorms burst, known as the 'mango showers', for it was at that season that the fruit fell from the big dark-green mango trees. About the middle of May the main monsoon began to rage, making life a misery for all outdoors. The rain crashed down with terrific violence, beating upon all surfaces with the roar of a waterfall and often pouring down without cessation for ten days. Dry water-courses became torrents. Paddy-fields and all flat surfaces were swamped. Hillsides, upon which so much fighting was to be done, became mud-slides. Clothing and blankets were permanently wet; boots, saddlery and equipment became mouldered overnight.

Weapon-pits and every hole in the ground were full of water. Between the deluges a thick white mist rose from the hot wet soil. The leeches, coming out in swarms, were a sore affliction. Men suffered again from the complaint of the First World War known as 'trench feet'. The resourceful Gurkhas, however, wrapped newspaper round their feet and rigged up bunks above the water-line by cutting down the ubiquitous bamboos.

Hammer and Anvil

Bishenpur, south-western gateway to Imphal and 16 miles distant from it, was a sizeable village on the Tiddim road, embowered in trees and standing at an altitude of about 2,600 feet. As 48th Brigade marched towards it in early April in the first mango showers, they noted the strong contrasts of the surrounding terrain. To its east were the swampy, impassable outskirts of Lake Logtak, fringed with reeds and haunted by wildfowl. To the west lay a flat zone of paddy-fields not yet flooded by the monsoon rains, and, farther west still the ground rose sharply to massive jungle-clad mountains ranging in height up to 5,846 feet at the Point so named. Twisting its way through this western mountain barrier there ran a rough track that led from Bishenpur westwards to the distant town of Silchar. Thus there were two approaches to the vital Bishenpur gateway.

The Japanese, foiled in their approach by the Tiddim road, took to these wild hills, hoping to sneak down north of the Silchar track; but they were fiercely halted in a series of sanguinary conflicts by 32nd Indian Brigade, led by the enormous figure of 'Long Mac' MacKenzie, temporarily under Cowan's command. Cowan's own division were allowed no rest after the gruelling withdrawal, and became committed to a whole series of bitter and critical defensive battles that raged for three months in two main sectors — up in the high peaks commanding the Silchar track and in the swampy lowlands astride the Tiddim road south of Bishenpur. The divisional artillery was skilfully grouped in the 'Gunner Box', just west of Bishenpur whence, amid the stench of dead mules, they could support the infantry in any quarter.

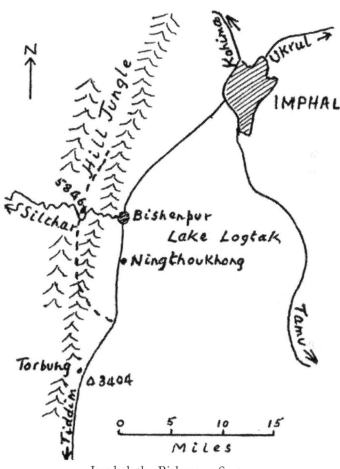

Imphal: the Bishenpur Sector.

It was astride the Tiddim road that 48th Brigade became desperately involved early in May. Mutaguchi, his divisions halted everywhere, gave priority to the White Tigers (now commanded by the moustachioed Tanaka), sent them strong reinforcements of infantry, tanks, artillery, with extra bomber support, and ordered them in sharp terms to capture Imphal. There followed a dramatic clash which constituted 48th Brigade's finest hour but which we must regretfully pass over all too lightly.

It happened that, at the very moment when the enemy was about to mount his intensified assault, Cowan launched a boldly conceived counter-offensive down the Tiddim road. It was a copy of the Japanese hammer-and-anvil tactics, under the code name *Ayo*. The Japanese held the fateful village of Ningthoukhong and were pressing hard. In vile weather Cameron took out his two Gurkha battalions and two batteries of mountain artillery in a wide left hook by night through difficult country and set up a road-block well behind the enemy at a hill that commanded the Tiddim road near the village of Torbung. Guy Burton was then to drive down from the north with his 63rd Brigade, acting as hammer to Cameron's anvil.

At that moment, however, the Japanese began their own offensive by an audacious thrust towards Bishenpur from the Silchar sector and very nearly overran Cowan's divisional headquarters. Burton's strike had to be called off but Cameron held his Torbung defile in an iron grip, beating off repeated attacks, including tank attacks, inflicting very severe casualties and blocking the passage forward of the enraged Tanaka himself. In abominable weather and amid a mass of stinking corpses the Gurkhas held their road-block for eight days until it became obvious that Burton's hammer could not strike.

Then, carrying their wounded with them, they fought their way out through the intervening enemy for another week, repeatedly attacked on all sides. Captain Terence Altham's company, having captured a village, was cut off and isolated for a day, but fought their way out at close quarters. Finally, reaching Ningthoukhong, which was much too firmly held by the Japanese, the brigade adroitly by-passed it by wading through the reeds of Lake Logtak by night and joined hands with the 1st West Yorkshires in their swampy desolation to the north of it.

The Gurkhas' casualties had been very heavy, including three COs: two of 2nd/5th, one killed and another wounded in quick succession, and James Robertson of 1st/7th, dangerously wounded. Ronnie Cameron himself was wounded and was succeeded in command of the brigade by Osborne Hedley. So hard-pressed for officers were 2nd/5th that a temporary CO had to be found from outside, and fortunately one was available in the person of 'John' Eustace, who was to lead them during the most illustrious weeks in the history of 5th Royal Gurkhas.

Before we leave *Ayo* we must take note of how 1st/7th had seen off Japanese tanks without the aid of anti-tank guns. Their weapons, used at extremely close quarters, were the Molotov cocktail, which was not found very reliable, the obsolete Boyes rifle and a contrivance, now almost forgotten, known as a Piat ('Projector Infantry Anti-Tank'), with which a Victoria Cross was soon to be won. It was a type of 'spigot mortar', fired from the shoulder and propelling a projectile that contained a 'hollow charge' explosive capable of burning through armour plate. The Piat called for plenty of guts and cunning on the part of the operator, who had to manoeuvre within about 30 yards of his quarry before he could kill; and he had to be sure

279

of a kill with the first shot, for the missile was projected by a very powerful spring that had to be recompressed with the foot, which usually meant standing up.

Sergeant Turner

The battle of attrition went on, a gruesome, fierce, exhausting and bewildering battle, sometimes among the swamped paddy-fields and the wreckage of the thatched villages along the Tiddim road and sometimes in the lofty hills clustered below Point 5846. The rain thrashed down for days on end, with storms of dazzling lightning, accompanied by thunder that merged with gun-blast and shell-burst. Desperate exhortations poured from the Japanese commanders to their troops, most of whom, filthy, diseased and underfed, still fought with suicidal abandon. Yet Tanaka was not satisfied and drove his soldiers mercilessly. In an almost hysterical Order of the Day[34] he demanded that officers should draw their swords and execute on the spot any soldier who showed himself fainthearted.

After *Ayo* 48th Brigade, despite their exhausted condition and their thin ranks, were pushed straight into the line again astride the Tiddim road, where they took post in the battle-scarred village of Ningthoukhong. There they found themselves in the very good company of 1st West Yorkshires, who, as we have noted earlier, were one of the Division's unbrigaded battalions, but under Hedley's command for this operation. They were led by the tall, unruffled, much-loved Lt-Colonel Bill Cooper, another habitual pipe-smoker, one of whose sergeants was to be the next to win a Victoria Cross.

---

[34] Found soon afterwards on the body of a dead Japanese officer by Captain Pat Gouldsbury, Adjutant of 2nd/5th RGR.

Engaged in the drive southward as hammer to 48 Brigade's anvil in *Ayo*, the West Yorkshires had experienced a gruelling time under arduous conditions at a village farther back called Potsangbam, inevitably known to British troops as Tots-and-Pans'. Fighting in deluges of rain, and suffering from stomach troubles aggravated by short rations, they had driven the Japanese back on to Ningthoukhong, but had suffered heavy casualties, the more serious because of the acute shortage of British reinforcements. Their effective strength now was only two companies. In C Company, with whom we shall be chiefly concerned, only 39 of all ranks answered to their names and Captain J. Scrutton was the only officer, with the company sergeant-major as second-in-command. All the platoons were commanded by sergeants.

Because of his weakness Cooper had been lent two companies of 2nd/5th RGR on coming up against the nasty village of Ningthoukhong. About 350 yards in his rear, separated from him by flooded paddy, was a support position, occupied by the remainder of the 2nd/5th and the 3-inch mortars of both battalions. As a convenient method of coordinating all supporting fire, tactical control forward was vested in Eustace, the new and temporary CO of 2nd/5th.

Ningthoukhong was a large village some four miles from Bishenpur, sited mainly on the east side of the Tiddim road, which was here embanked some ten feet high, with deep ditches filled with water at the foot of the embankments and putrefied by a number of floating Japanese corpses. To the feast the village was bounded by Lake Logtak. To the west, below the level of the embanked road, were large stretches of open paddy-fields, now flooded, and beyond them the jungle-clad hills, where lay Tanaka's divisional headquarters. The village was bisected by a small stream about 20 feet wide, that flowed from west to east, not large enough to create an obstacle, and the bridge that carried the Tiddim road across it had been destroyed.

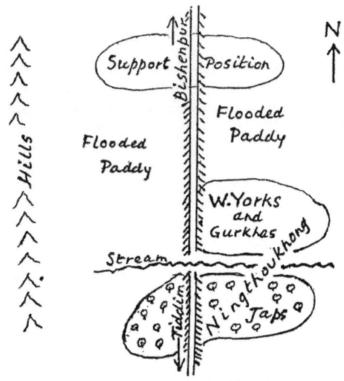

Diagram of situation at Ningthoukhong in June.

The southern part of the village was held by the Japanese. Here, although most of the bamboo houses had been badly smashed, the Japs had the advantage of excellent cover from the many trees and shrubs which give shade and privacy in all the villages of those regions but which now concealed the Japanese snipers. Here also the Japanese had the advantage of support from their light, lime-green tanks and the extra force of artillery, including heavy artillery, which Mutaguchi had allotted to Tanaka to force his way through. Some of this artillery was up in the hills to the west, whence it dominated Ningthoukhong and the surrounding country.

In contrast, the British position, lying to the north of the stream, had been completely flattened by bombing and shelling. No houses were left standing and the only cover from fire was an occasional bush or small clump of bamboo or the low retaining walls between fields. The monsoon and the pulverizing by high explosives had made the place as sodden and pitted with water-filled shell-holes as a battlefield of the First World War, so that the very stiff actions that now followed were fought by troops scrambling about in water and mud. Since digging was impossible, they built up breastworks as defences. Even so, officers and men were often standing up to the middle in water for hours. Leeches and trench feet afflicted the troops. Clouds of flies infested the air, giving place at night to swarms of particularly vicious mosquitoes, which pierced through clothing as with stilettos. The tropic heat added to the discomforts, so that the air was hot, humid and oppressive. From the hills to the west and from the plain to the south the Japanese high-velocity 'whizz-bangs' arrived and detonated without audible warning.

It was in these squalid and miasmic conditions that the West Yorkshires had taken up their watery stations. In their ranks was a sergeant named Hanson Victor Turner. Born in North Ormsby in Yorkshire, he was 30 years of age and had been a bus conductor in the service of Halifax Corporation before the war. He lived at Copley, Halifax, where he had a wife and little daughter of five. He was one's idea of a typical Yorkshireman — fair-haired, sturdy, rather short, good-humoured, dogged and thoroughly trustworthy. He was also, declared his friend,

Sergeant Stanley Harrison, to the author, a man of integrity and 'always correct in whatever he did'. Though only an 'acting' sergeant, not a substantive one, he had been given command of a platoon, which had shrunk through casualties to something less than 20 men. In the previous fighting he had already proved his worth by his steady bearing and his confident handling of his little command.

On the night of 6 June Scrutton had posted him in the critical angle formed by the stream and the embanked road at Ningthoukhong. On his right and left respectively were the platoons commanded by Sergeants Harrison and Helliwell, both much attenuated but thoroughly to be trusted. None of them had any means of communication with company headquarters, which lay some 80 yards in the rear.

The night, now clear, began quietly, but soon after midnight the look-outs heard sounds of increasing activity beyond the stream and roused their commanders. Harrison at once shot up a Very light, which disclosed a considerable body of the enemy assembling together, with two or three light tanks in the rear of them. The sergeants ordered their platoons to stand to arms.

Very soon afterwards the Japanese infantry were seen splashing into the stream and the battle erupted right along the miry front in all the nervous tensions of night fighting. Turner's four light machine-guns burst into life. The grenades flew, the artillery shells and mortar bombs crashed down. Almost from the beginning it was apparent that the enemy was making his main effort against that critical corner that Turner held. About a hundred men swarmed quickly across the stream, crept up under cover of the bank and began to lob grenades into his platoon at 20 yards range with deadly effect. Three of his Bren-guns were destroyed, several men killed or wounded and his position was in peril of being overrun.

It was in this situation that the crisis brought out the man. All the submerged qualities of a natural leader rose to the surface. He knew that, if he gave way, the whole battalion position would be lost. Holding his men together firmly and crisply, he made a quick redisposition to better advantage, brought his Bren-gun to bear effectively and sent volleys of grenades showering over the bank. The enemy halted.

Turner's stock of grenades, however, had fallen low. In the pause that ensued, Harrison, away on his right, saw his dark form jump up from his trench, heard him shout to his men 'Stay where you are' and watched him double back to company headquarters. He went himself because it was very dangerous. In two or three minutes he was back again, loaded with grenades. On the way he had been hit by a bullet or shell splinter, but took no notice.

Thus replenished, the platoon began a long and stubborn battle of defence in the dark. For a full two hours, the enemy, heard but not seen and bent upon breaking into the battalion's main position, pressed their attack against the dwindling platoon. But Turner was very much in command of the situation. With firm orders, personal example and skilful dispositions, he infused his little band with his own spirit. Unshaken by casualties, they held their ground.

Absolutely isolated, Sergeant Turner was fighting a lone battle in the night at very close quarters, under conditions that would have tested any man's nerve. A second and a third time he doubled back to company headquarters for more grenades and was again wounded. He found that the whole company was now officerless, Scrutton himself having been severely hit. In this situation Turner knew that he had to hold on at all costs.

Before dawn of the new day a fresh point of pressure by the Japanese gave evidence that they were trying to creep round to outflank the platoon. Turner now had only nine or ten men left, but something had to be done to remove the new threat. His training and his instincts told him that the right course was to counter-attack. As it was vital that his men should hold their ground, he decided that he would counter-attack himself, alone.

Ordering his men to stand fast and give him covering fire, he collected all the grenades he could carry, sallied out in the half-dark and attacked with devastating effect at a range of a few yards, meeting the enemy face to face beyond the bank. When his supply of grenades was exhausted, he went back for more and returned to the offensive. Again there were high-pitched cries and sounds of hurried splashing movements. Five times did Turner make his attacks, each time single-handed. The effect was dramatic and the enemy's manoeuvre withered away, but the sergeant went out against them yet a sixth time. It was his last sally, for in the act of throwing another missile he was killed. When his body was found next morning near the stream 30 dead Japanese were counted in front of his platoon post.

It was the turning point of the action. After Turner's attack the Japanese pressure petered out. Major H. H. Crofton declared afterwards that the enemy's attempt to penetrate the defences came within an ace of succeeding and that it was Turner who saved the day. Colonel Eustace, Captain D. D. Parkin (of the adjacent A Company) and Sergeants Harrison and Helliwell (both of whom also fought stoutly) say the like. Harrison declared, to the author, 'I myself am proud to have known and fought with him.' The two sergeants both say that, having run out of grenades, Turner began throwing 2-inch mortar bombs and that a bomb was in his hand when his body was found next day. This sounds strange, for bombs are not actuated by being thrown; possibly Turner thought that they would nevertheless serve as deterrents.

A tablet in Halifax Town Hall serves as a reminder to succeeding generations of his soldierly conduct. Awards of the DSO went to Captain Scrutton, of the Distinguished Conduct Medal to Private B. Smith and of the Military Medal to Lance-Corporal A. Coates and Private Bradley.

At dawn on 7 June, when the ground was swathed in a waist-high mist, the Japanese redoubled their attack against the West Yorkshires. This time they gave weight to their assault with five tanks. Cooper unfortunately had no anti-tank guns but his men resisted stubbornly, their naturally good morale fortified by the nonchalant figure of Bill Cooper himself, going about with a rifle slung from his shoulder, puffing his pipe, and with a comforting word for every man. Gradually, however, his thin companies, their ranks further depleted by some 60 casualties, and under severe pressure from enemy tanks, were obliged to give ground a little where penetration was threatened. The strength of the battalion was now only 130 effectives. Eustace thereupon came up from the support position with an additional company of Gurkhas to counter-attack, but found that the Japanese had abandoned the sector that they had gained, leaving 100 dead as tribute to the West Yorkshires. There was more drenching rain and the sodden, sleepy air was tainted with offensive smells.

Ganju Lama

In the watery dawn of 12 June, as the flights of duck were taking off from the lake, the White Tigers burst across the stream in another shock attack of particular violence, under orders that it was to be pressed to the death. The assault was

287

preceded by a bombardment by heavy artillery, massed mortars and tanks firing from concealed positions. The infantry, accompanied by five tanks, then bore down on the Gurkhas. The tanks, using a firm track, drove along the front of the defences, firing at the Gurkhas at point-blank range with their 47-mm guns. The young reinforcements whom the Gurkhas had just received had a sudden and shattering introduction to battle. Two platoons were overrun and a company was obliged to withdraw. One of the only two antitank guns (of 82nd Regiment, RA) was knocked out by a direct hit, but the other, as soon as it could be brought to bear by Lieutenant Robertson, quickly destroyed two of the tanks outright; the other three tanks, in taking avoiding action, got stuck in the mud, but they still contrived to direct damaging fire.

Not until these tanks had been destroyed or immobilized was the enemy penetration halted. Their inroad extended to a depth of 200 yards and a length of 300. A steady artillery fire continued to pour down on the Gurkhas in the humid heat. All telephone lines were cut and the radio links failed. The companies stabilized on the new perimeter after four hours of stiff and costly fighting, skilfully protected throughout by the screen of artillery fire put down by Captain John Hanchet, the cool and gallant gunner forward observation officer of 129th Field Regiment, who, himself in danger of being overrun, had dropped his fire step by step as the Gurkha platoon had gradually withdrawn, and who still stuck to his post with an enemy tank 25 yards from him.

Twice the Japs attempted to assail the new position, but were broken up by the guns and by Hurricanes of the RAF. Defence, however, was not enough. The lost ground had to be recovered. Eustace was too weak to counter-attack and accordingly Hedley sent him up two companies of 1st/7th

Gurkhas. In one of these companies was a rifleman named Ganju Lama who was to be the next in 48th Brigade's roll of VCs. Son of an orthodox lama of Sikkim, he was a large man for a Gurkha, well-built and strong. As one of the battalion's Piat-gunners, he was a picked man and had already won the Military Medal for his daring in stalking Japanese tanks in Operation *Ayo*.

Eustace sent in the counter-attack by 1st/7th at 2.30 p.m., supported by an artillery barrage. The Japs immediately put down a counter-barrage, but the Gurkhas raced through, only to be checked by the three concealed enemy tanks, which, though immobilized, had come to life again and covered all the lines of advance. The moment was critical. As the troops checked, Ganju saw that the moment had come for him to set out on another tank-hunting mission. He tucked his Piat under his arm and, on his own initiative, crawled forward through the mud. He was soon spotted and a concentration of fire burst upon him. He was hit in the leg and both arms, his left wrist being broken. Notwithstanding what one might think an impossible handicap, he struggled forward. He knew that he had to get within 30 yards of each tank before he could be sure of a kill; so to 30 yards he went. With his first bolt he clean knocked out the nearest tank. Standing up, he recocked and reloaded his Piat, crawled on to the next tank, still under fire, and knocked out that one too.

He was about to attack the third one when he saw it hit and destroyed by Robertson's remaining 2-pdr behind him. But he did not consider his mission finished. There were still the tank crews to be dealt with. Such as survived had leapt out and were ready to fight. Ganju therefore calmly returned to his company, said, 'Give me some grenades,' sallied forth again and polished off the tank crews. His audacious feat enabled the 1st/7th to regain the whole of the lost ground, in which they counted 70 more dead Japanese.

Talking to the author years later, Lord Mountbatten, then the Supreme Commander in that zone, said that, in the conditions that prevailed, he thought this was perhaps the finest of all the Burma VCs.

Stiff fighting went on for some time in the miasmic squalor of Ningthoukhong and its rotting corpses. Other units came in and 48th Brigade was ordered to a different scene. They had suffered another 225 casualties and in 2nd/5th only four British officers remained out of the establishment of sixteen. Hedley reported to Cowan that they would not be fit to fight again unless they could have a rest, but that was not to be.[35]

At Mortar Bluff

The scene now shifts from the swampy desolation of the Tiddim road up into the high jungle hills clustering below Point 5846, north of the Silchar track, which, as we have noted earlier, approached Bishenpur from the west, and where two more VCs were to be won in quick succession under tense conditions.

Tanaka, having been baulked first on the Tiddim road and then again on the Silchar track, had passed on yet higher and farther up into the hills, beyond Point 5846, and it was from there that he had made his dangerous foray behind Cowan's headquarters in April. For nearly three months he had been trying to batter his way down into the plain by one route or the other. Now, in the third week of June, reinforced by the greater part of a brigade of fresh troops from another division,

---

[35] The equally trying operations at Potsangban and elsewhere have been omitted, being outside our main narrative.

he swung his main effort up into the highlands once more, probing at various points to find a way through.

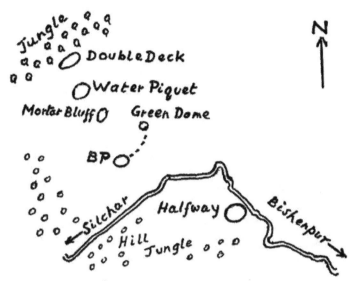

Objectives of 2nd/5th Royal Gurkhas in the heights above the Silchar track. The dotted line shows the covered route taken for the recapture of Mortar Bluff.

He was being held back by 'Long Mac' Mackenzie's 32nd Brigade, fighting stiff sections in extremely tough conditions, sometimes dependent on parachute drops for their supplies. Much dispersed in piqueting this wild, upland country and much exhausted and weakened in numbers, the brigade could not prevent some penetration by the Japanese probes, and Cowan sent in 48th to relieve them, hard-tried though they also had been.

A feature of these hills, due no doubt to the monsoon winds, was that they were heavily forested on the western sides of their main ranges, right up to the crest, Point 5846 itself wearing a crown of dense bamboo, but relatively bare on the eastern slopes, so that there was only limited cover for troops attacking from that quarter, whereas Tanaka's troops enjoyed the cover of the jungle.

When the 2nd/5th and their supporting gunners moved out from Bishenpur they found themselves in a contorted, knobbly terrain through which the Silchar track twisted its way up. Escaping the occasional shell, they halted first at an elevated feature just south of the track known as Halfway House, which became the advanced headquarters of the battalion, still commanded by Eustace.

Looking north-west from there, they were confronted by a long upward slope rising several hundred feet higher to the jungle-crowned crest nearly two miles away, with the intermediate terrain broken by a series of knolls and bluffs erupting from the main hillside and almost completely bare of tree cover. They constituted, one may say, a flight of giant steps to the summit, at an average height of about 5,000 feet. Tactically important to both sides, each had been viciously fought for.

The first of these barren and exposed hillocks north of Halfway House was known as BP Piquet, named after a very gallant officer of 1st/4th Gurkhas who had been killed there in the earlier fighting by 63rd Brigade. Beyond came Mortar Bluff and then Water Piquet, so named because it had protected a water-point used by one of MacKenzie's battalions. Farther on still, a little short of the wooded crest, was Double Deck. Each of these features was completely isolated and nothing in the nature of continuous defences or mutually supporting posts was possible.

When Hedley and Eustace, accompanied by Major Peter Brown, a battery commander of 129th Field Regiment, arrived at Halfway House on the morning of 25 June (sniped at on the way by a Japanese gun), they found that the two farthest features, Double Deck and Water Piquet, were in the hands of the enemy. Mortar Bluff was held by the 7th/10th Baluch Regiment and BP Piquet had just been recaptured by the 1st Northamptonshires. Despite the altitude, the air was very hot, humid and sleepy.

A plan was made for 2nd/5th to relieve the garrisons of BP and Mortar Bluff, as a preliminary step to the capture of Water Piquet. Accordingly, that same afternoon a company, together with some 3-inch mortars, moved up to BP under the command of Captain D. F. Little, a resolute and spirited officer who, to make good the shortage in 2nd/5th, had been borrowed from the Gurkha Parachute Battalion and who had already proved his worth at Ningthoukhong. At the same time an augmented platoon of 41 men went about a mile farther on still to Mortar Bluff. The reliefs were effected without serious enemy interference.

The force for Mortar Bluff was commanded by a subedar named Netrabahadur Thapa. He was a well-built, typical Gurkha, highly professional, with a strong and infectious personality, yet of a jolly disposition and always ready with a joke, popular and very much trusted. His Gurkhas shook themselves out and settled into the weapon-pits that they had taken over from the Baluchs. The subedar went round them all, examining their fields of fire, checking ammunition, closely examining the country all around him and testing his telephone link to Eustace in the rear. He had no artillery officer with him but was able to call for prearranged defensive fire from a battery of mountain guns near Halfway House, from the rest of the divisional artillery in the Gunner Box near Bishenpur and from the mortars at BP.

Night fell soon after 5.30, with threatening clouds, and it became extremely dark. At 7 o'clock a deluge of rain fell like a cataract. The Gurkhas stood to their weapons, peering through the blinding curtain of rain. At 8 o'clock they were assailed by shell-fire and two minutes later attacked by a screaming horde of Japanese, who materialized at a range of only a few yards. The Gurkhas met them with grenades and small arms and Netrabahadur called for the guns. The shells of the 3.7-inch mountain howitzers crashed down within a minute, supplemented by the mortar-bombs from BP. The Japanese attack was quickly broken and they retreated behind the curtain of rain. Very soon no sound could be heard but the heavy drumming of the rain on the jungle vegetation and on the steel helmets of the watching Gurkhas.

Netrabahadur knew very well, however, that another attack was to be expected. He went round his posts and reported to Eustace by telephone. Though soaked to the skin, he was in buoyant form and his young soldiers, many of them recent reinforcements, drew strength from his cheerful confidence and his assured professionalism. There was a long pause and the night dragged on, while the rain still beat down with blinding vehemence. The weapon-pits were full of water and the weapons difficult to hold.

The second attack came in at 1.30 a.m. on the 26th. It was made from a different quarter and in greater strength. In one sector two of the Gurkhas' Bren-guns were put out of action, one by a hit and the other by jamming. The enemy dashed in and secured a foothold. It was a moment of deadly peril. Of the 16 men holding that sector, 12 were killed or wounded. The subedar hurried across and, with a shower of grenades, himself scattered the enemy and arrested the penetration. Then he swiftly improvised a new front. In the rain-sodden night the

294

hilltop became the scene of tense and deadly conflict at very close quarters with grenade, kukri and bayonet. The Gurkhas could not throw out the enemy, but they held their ground against a continuous series of attacks that went on all the rest of the night.

Netrabahadur, kukri in hand, was everywhere, encouraging his soldiers, making dispositions to meet a new situation, and tending the wounded. He knew that he was beyond all reach of aid, but so good were his dispositions and so infectious his example that not a man moved from his trench and not a yard more ground was given. He was utterly calm and from time to time sent clear, objective and professional reports back to Eustace, for miraculously the telephone line held till nearly the end.

Ammunition began to run short. Netrabahadur asked Eustace for replenishment, but when he appreciated that there would be some delay before it could reach him, he called for the fire of his supporting artillery to come down on his own position. This courageous act had an immediate effect. The Japanese faltered and began to withdraw. Unhappily, the mountain guns also were short of ammunition and had to reduce their rate of fire and then cease altogether. The little garrison's casualties mounted severely as the night wore on. Soon more than half of them were dead or wounded, but still the remainder kept the enemy at bay.

By now Netrabahadur knew that the supplies of his own ammunition were on the way from BP. They were being carried up by a section of eight men whose own mission was dangerous enough. At 4 a.m. the section ran into the Japs on the perimeter of Mortar Bluff, were attacked and every man killed or wounded.

All was not yet lost, however. Netrabahadur — still ruled by the magnificent fighting spirit that inspired him all that night — himself dashed out and, assailing with his kukri the Japanese who had trapped the carrying party, retrieved the ammunition.

He quickly distributed it and, with such men as he could spare from the handful left alive, he led a fierce little counterattack at 4.15 a.m. In the melee he clove the skull of a Japanese with his kukri but was himself shot in the mouth. He tried to collect himself, but a minute later was killed by a grenade. His body was found next morning, lying beside the Japanese with the cleft skull.

By this time only six of the garrison were left out of the original 42, the senior being a havildar named Lachimbahadur Thapa. Realizing that daylight would disclose the weakness of his position and that its capture would then be inevitable, he collected as many wounded as his men could carry and withdrew safely and skilfully through the darkness and therein to BP Piquet.

For this shining act of valour and fortitude, one of the most remarkable in the whole war, the subedar was in due course awarded the Victoria Cross.

And Water Piquet

That same night the Japanese had attacked BP also, but Little's company had repulsed them decisively. When he learnt of the fate of Mortar Bluff, Little sent out a detachment to secure a small knoll not far from it known as Green Dome, the lee of which would provide some cover under which troops could form up for the next operation.

The plan to go right through to the capture of Water Piquet had now to be quickly revised in the last cold and rain-sodden hour before dawn. Mortar Bluff had first to be retaken. This task Eustace allotted to a company led by the spirited Lieutenant J. P. Henderson. When he had accomplished it another company was to go for Water Piquet and then press on to the still higher Double Deck.

The rain had stopped but the whole countryside was drenched. The air was heavy with moisture and the men were wet through. As the first light of day began to give shadowy shape to the hills, the companies detailed for the attacks moved up to BP over the sodden ground. There a final reconnaissance was made while the battalion halted under what was believed to be safe cover. As they waited, a Japanese gun opened fire and the very first shell landed in the middle of the battalion headquarters, where it killed six officers and men and wounded several more.

Henderson's company, using a route fairly free from observation, advanced to Green Dome and formed up in the dead ground behind it for their attack on Mortar Bluff, which was being bombarded by the divisional artillery and the 5.5-inch guns of 8th Medium Regiment. The sun had come out in strength and the saturated ground was steaming. At 9.50 a.m. Henderson's company stepped out for the assault and the guns lifted. The men had first to slither down the muddy forward slopes of Green Dome, cross a small saddle and then ascend a fairly steep incline to Mortar Bluff itself.

The whole 250 yards was totally devoid of cover and inevitably the leading platoon drew fire from every weapon that the Japanese had. Some men began to falter, but the young officer led them like a veteran, crossed the exposed saddle and stormed up the slippery ascent to Mortar Bluff.

Foremost in breaking that dangerous pause in the assault was a slim, very young naik (corporal) named Agansing Rai. Quite unlike Netrabahadur, he had a serious, rather shy and retiring nature, but was remarkably self-reliant and not lacking in a quiet sense of humour. He had earned his two stripes, despite youth, by serious application to his job.

Leading a section of eight men, Agansing was the first to reach the barbed wire surrounding the crown of Mortar bluff. Tearing his way through, he led his section straight at a machine-gun that had caused most of the casualties, firing his tommy-gun as he went and heedless of the stream of its bullets. The enemy detachment was swiftly overcome, Agansing himself killing three out of the four.

The company then surged forward across Mortar Bluff, but was assailed at very short range by a 37-mm gun sited in concealment among bushes a little way beyond the bluff, as well as by fire from Water Piquet. Again, and quite on his own initiative, Agansing led his section straight for the gun. Intense fire reduced his section to himself and two other men. The three, forming themselves into an arrow-head, attacked at the double, closed with the five men of the gun detachment and killed them all, three of them again falling to the aim of the naik.

The three men then returned quickly to Mortar Bluff, just in time for yet another splendid little exploit, for such was the impetus of Henderson and his company that, not content with the capture of his assigned objective, he swept on, pursuing what was left of the enemy, and launched himself against the farther objective of Water Piquet, 300 yards away, which had been assigned to the other company.

As they neared Water Piquet, they were met by machine-gun fire and showers of grenades from one of those formidable bunkers which the Japanese were well known to hold to the death. It was certainly to the death this time, for once more Agansing went out on a dangerous mission, and this time he went alone, supported only by the covering fire of his Bren-gunner. He went for the bunker with a tommy-gun in one hand and a grenade in the other. Bearing a charmed life amid the bullets and grenades directed against him, he raced up to the bunker and, in a very remarkable feat of daring, discharged his grenade and tommy-gun right into the aperture, killing all within it. The remainder of the garrison of Water Piquet then fled.

The exploit of Agansing Rai was another example of how personal gallantry can smooth the path to tactical success. The shy naik saw the obstacles that imperilled the mission and went straight for them on his own initiative. His was also a rare example of a VC being won without ever a wound.

There remained the yet farther and higher objective known as Double Deck. The uphill assault, carried out by the other company with what was described as 'considerable ferocity', and preceded by a skilfully controlled artillery bombardment, was an instant success under the strong leadership of another very fine subedar named Dhirbahadur Gurung. There he led his men on farther still to hunt down whatever Japs were still left in the hilltop jungle, where they captured two field-guns and where the subedar won the Military Cross. For the first time on this front, the Japanese were seen to abandon their weapons and run.

Very soon afterwards there took place an encounter which reveals the spirit of the brave and soldierly Gurkha and which provides a fitting occasion for us to say goodbye to him. Peter Brown, the battery commander from 129th Field Regiment, was walking up to Water Piquet to establish a new observation post when he saw coming towards him a Gurkha soldier with his head bandaged, his right arm in a sling and limping from a third wound in his leg. In his left hand he was carrying his rifle and his pack. A few paces from the officer the Gurkha halted, put his rifle and pack on the ground and gave a model salute with his left hand. 'Never,' said Brown afterwards, 'did I return a compliment with more pride.'

So ended the most momentous 24 hours in the history of 2nd/5th Royal Gurkha Rifles, in which they had suffered yet another 35 casualties but had won two of their three VCs. It was almost the end of the great Kohima-Imphal battle. Mutaguchi had made his last desperate attempt to reach Imphal. On the jungle tracks by which his 31st Division had penetrated to far Kohima the Japanese troops, for the first time in their history, were reeling back in ignominious rout in the merciless rain, throwing away their arms, crazed, dying of hunger or disease and drowning in the oozy puddles into which they stumbled and from which they had not the strength to lift their heads. British forces, fighting southwards from Kohima and northwards from Imphal, had joined hands and the main road was reopened and the siege of Imphal ended. On other sectors, despite last-hour outbursts, the enemy was being rounded up or driven back.

On the Black Cats' sector, the newer enemy troops still exhibited a ferocious spirit, but the old White Tigers were in desperate straits. Defeated again and again in close combat, decimated, wasted with dysentery and malaria, emaciated, sometimes reduced to eating grass and slugs, driven back into battle with gaping wounds by remorseless officers, ejected from stretchers and made to crawl into action on their bellies, they were a spent force, yet some of them were tigers still, quite willing to be driven to the slaughter-house. But Mutaguchi, 'withholding my tears', his hour of disgrace at hand, was at last obliged to retreat, in the most crushing and humiliating defeat ever suffered by the Japanese army.

For 17th Indian Light Division there was only another week or so of mountain scrapping and they then went back to India to enjoy an honourably-won rest and to recruit themselves to take part in Slim's great offensive into Burma on which, in the masterly tactics of the Battle of Mandalay-Meiktile, he smashed the remaining Japanese armies and marched victoriously back to Rangoon. The Black Cats, finishing the war near the point where they had begun it, had won seven Victoria Crosses in the Burma War. Of these, if we include Sergeant Turner's while under command, five had been won by 48th Indian Brigade. Four of them had been won in the space of three weeks. All were won not only by the most impressive valour but also by soldierly skill.

It may be observed that Ganju's, Agansing's and Gaje's feats were performed in daylight and in hot blood during an assault. Sergeant Turner's repeated sorties were lone acts, in the dark, deliberately calculated over a long period and while his platoon was under sustained pressure. It is, of course, impossible to discriminate between acts of supreme valour in their different circumstances, but, if a 'rating' were possible among the bravest of the brave, Sergeant Turner must be placed very high.

To Netrabahadur must certainly be awarded one of the highest places in the Valhalla of brave men. He sustained attack after attack by overwhelming numbers, rallying and sustaining his garrison, growing less and less by casualties, in pitch darkness, in pouring monsoon rain, fighting hand-to-hand with the enemy inside his position, and this for a matter of hours beyond all reach of aid or support. And throughout this time, as long as communications lasted, he gave absolutely calm, coherent and professional reports by telephone. It was a prolonged, isolated and splendid effort of leadership.

Some months later, at a touching ceremony before the whole paraded battalion, the subedar's shy young widow, accompanied by their little daughter, with Eustace leading them both by the hand, received her husband's VC at the hands of Field-Marshal Lord Wavell, Viceroy of India.

10: THE MIDGETS AT SINGAPORE

By midsummer of 1945 the Second World War was approaching its grand climax. In Europe a devastated Germany had surrendered and Hitler was dead. Italy had long ago capitulated and had become almost an ally. In the Pacific the Allied forces, American-led, were surging steadily through the maze of islands in the Pacific, ejecting the Japanese from their far-flung conquests one by one. In Burma the British Fourteenth Army, under the brilliant leadership of Bill Slim, had already swept victoriously across jungle and paddy-field and recaptured Rangoon itself.

But all was not yet over. There was no sign yet of a Japanese collapse. Fighting tenaciously, they still held half 'the gorgeous East in fee'. Britain, though sorely tried through six hard years, had made ready for yet one more effort and had begun to augment the forces that she had in the Far East. Among them there was 14th Submarine Flotilla, led by Captain W. R. Fell, who had long been a champion of miniature underwater craft, first the 'human torpedo' or Chariot and then the midget submarine. In his flotilla were six ocean-going submarines and six midgets of improved type, manned by experienced crews, many of whom had already taken part in the expedition against *Tirpitz*.

These new midgets were called *XE* craft. In addition to mechanical improvements, they had been modified to withstand the severe physiological conditions of tropical climates, which would otherwise have been beyond human tolerance. A ventilating system, a device for extracting carbon dioxide and a small refrigerator to some extent tempered the excessive heat and humidity that made men and equipment sweat profusely. There were also a small domestic refrigerator for food and an increased supply of fresh water.

A further alteration enabled the XE craft to carry two types of explosive charges — one very large underwater bomb on one side of the hull, as before, and a large magazine on the other side in which was stored a supply of 'limpet' mines, which were smallish mines designed to be attached to an enemy's ship's bottom by magnets. We shall see these in use.

All Allied forces in the Pacific were under American command and the midget submarines suffered a severe blow when they found themselves cold-shouldered by the US Navy. Arriving in Australian waters at the end of April, and looking very smart in tropical rig, the flotilla was plunged in gloom. 'Tiny' Fell fought hard for them, flying all over the place to urge their employment. The only sympathetic ear he found was that of Rear-Admiral James Fife, commander of the US 7th Submarine Fleet, but, even he could offer them no target.

The flotilla was, indeed, on the point of being disbanded when an American naval staff-officer inquired casually if the XE craft could cut submarine cables. The Japanese wireless codes had long ago been broken, but they still had secure telegraphic links from Tokyo to Singapore. A high priority was given to the task of cutting them, but no one had yet suggested the means. Fell jumped at the chance and at once set his midgets to work to evolve a technique for this unexpected mission. Two gallant young officers lost their lives in these experiments before the problem was solved. Fell then flew off to the Philippines again to put his plan before Admiral Fife, who, having read them, said: 'What about having a crack at the two 10,000-ton cruisers in Singapore?'[36]

---

[36] *The Sea Our Shield* by W. R. Fell.

Thus were set in motion two series of operations that were to prove the versatility of the midgets and were to be signalized by the award of the Victoria Cross to two of the very smallest men of their crews. In July the flotilla sailed north to join Admiral Fife in the Philippines, just won back from the Japanese, and at last felt themselves back in the war again. The cable-cutting operations fell to *XE4*, under the Australian Lieutenant Max Shean, and to *XE5*, under Lieutenant Percy Westmacott, both of whom had already distinguished themselves in audacious exploits with *X* craft in Norwegian waters, where Westmacott had blown up a big floating dock.

Shean, starting from Borneo, was required to sail, under tow, 700 miles across the South China Sea to Saigon in South Vietnam (Indo-China) and there cut the Singapore and Hong Kong cables; while Westmacott, sailing from an anchorage near Manila, was to make the 650 miles passage to Hong Kong and sever the links with Japan itself. Both were operations of exceptional daring in enemy waters and of particular danger to the divers, who would be required to emerge from their craft, identify and sever the cables with heavy cutters, the natural perils being enormously increased by the risk of oxygen poisoning from the severe physical effort involved.

XE4's mission was a brilliant success. Under the noses of a Japanese defensive post ashore only 100 yards away, Shean searched the coral rock of the sea bottom with a grapnel. Sub-Lieutenant A. H. Bergius swam out, found the cables and cut them, with the most satisfying results. *XE5*, however, after a perilous passage to Hong Kong, found the water of Telegraph Bay foul with mud, her diver sinking into bottomless slime. After four full days and nights, Westmacott was obliged to withdraw.

To *XE1* and *XE3* fell what had the appearance of a far more warlike mission. It was they who were to 'have a crack' at the two Japanese cruisers, *Takao* and *Myoko*, lying in the apparently secure waters of Singapore. With others of the flotilla, they sailed south from the Philippines to the island paradise of Labuan, near the northern tip of Borneo. It was 26 July. At only 5 degrees north of the equator, the tropic sun beat down with its utmost intensity. The lush vegetation ashore formed a fringe to a placid sea of deep blue, seemingly at variance with the manifestations of man's wrath evident on every hand. To the crews of the midgets, the steamy heat promised a severe ordeal of endurance cramped in a very hot, stuffy and humid air, immersed in a sea that registered more than 80° Fahrenheit.

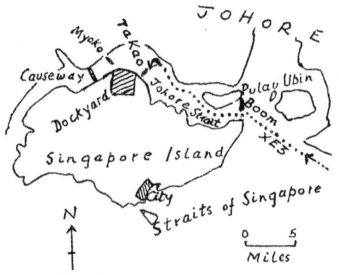

The Attack on *Takao* by *XE3*. Width of Johore Strait slightly enlarged.

Singapore is a flat island, about the size and shape of the Isle of Wight, lying off Johore, a state which forms the tip of the Malay Peninsula. It is almost on the equator. The famous city of the same name, built by the British out of a swamp, is at the southern extremity. The island is separated from the mainland by the Johore Strait, averaging a mile or so wide. Here, on the northern shore of the island and facing the mainland, is the great naval dockyard, also British-built.

Takao and *Myoko* were anchored close to the dockyard, the former a trifle to its east and the latter to the west, close to the causeway that links the island with Johore. Both were heavy cruisers mounting ten 8-inch guns as their main armament, but, having been already damaged, were serving primarily as floating forts to defend the dockyard. Neither of them was protected by an anti-torpedo net. The only approach to the ships was by the eastern arm of the Johore Strait. Its entrance from the open sea was barred by a 'boom' or anti-submarine net, and from that point a raiding vessel would have to travel some 11 miles of much-used water to reach *Takao*, and a further two to reach *Myoko*.

This was the proposition that faced *XE1* and *XE3* as they lay for a few hours off the small island of Labuan. The former was commanded by the bearded Lieutenant Jack Smart who had commanded the passage crew of the unfortunate *X8* in the *Tirpitz* expedition. With him were Sub-Lieutenant Harold Harper and two other old hands of the *Tirpitz* days in ERA Fishleigh and Leading Seaman Pomeroy. Their target was *Myoko*, beyond the dockyard.

XE3, allotted to the destruction of *Takao*, was manned by a quite remarkable little ship's company, and it is with them that we shall be mainly concerned. Her commander was Lieutenant

307

Ian Fraser who, as we have noted earlier, was 'a mere shrimp of a man'. Standing only 5 feet 4 inches, he was obviously called 'Tich'. A lively, high-spirited bantam of 23 years, he sparkled with energy and ingenuity and was a first-rate seaman. He had been a cadet in the training ship *Conway* and, having failed to pass the entrance examination for the Navy, had joined the Blue Star Line and then the Royal Naval Reserve as a midshipman shortly before the war. He had already won the DSC while serving with the celebrated 10th Submarine Flotilla in the Mediterranean. Like Godfrey Place and Don Cameron, Fraser had married a girl in the Wrens, who, at the time of the attack on the *Takao*, had just given birth to their first baby.

Fraser's No. 1 was Sub-Lieutenant W. J. L. Smith, a New Zealander, and obviously known as 'Kiwi'. He was an experienced *X* craft hand, but new to *XE3*. The senior rating was Engine-Room Artificer Charles Reid, a highly trained hand of the regular service, utterly reliable and calm and of remarkable stamina. He was helmsman of the boat, sitting at the steering wheel, just in front of Smith. The fourth hand, and the most experienced of all as a midget submariner, was Leading Seaman 'Mick' Magennis, who had been in the passage crew of Place's *X7* in the *Tirpitz* expedition. Magennis was the ship's diver, for which his aptitude as a swimmer equipped him well. When not so employed he operated the main ballast tanks and the periscope motor, also acting as electrician. Scarcely any taller than Fraser, he was, by temperament as well as size, ideally suited to life in a midget, being wiry, resilient, nimble and full of guts. Hailing from Belfast, the son of a Scot and an Irishwoman, he was 25 years old and had had about ten years' service in the Navy, having joined as a boy, but, being somewhat impatient of the formalism of big ships, had never found his true niche until he joined the midgets almost at their creation.

A bare five hours after their arrival at Labuan, the little expedition sailed at 2 p.m. on 26 July, setting a course approximately WSW. *XE1* was under tow by *Spark* and *XE3* (her passage crew commanded by Frank Ogden) by *Stygian*. A passage of some 700 miles faced them, for the last 40 of which the midgets would be on their own. All four craft were fully submerged by day, but *Spark* and *Stygian* came to the surface at night. On this occasion each midget carried a magazine of limpet mines on her starboard side and an underwater charge of increased power on the other.

The long passage went smoothly enough and well before dawn on 30 July the attack crews of the midgets were paddled out by rubber dinghy and took over from the sweating passage crews, but all four submarines continued their passage fully submerged for another whole day. Not until 11 p.m., when the expedition had reached the eastern end of the Straits of Singapore, were the *XE* craft surfaced and their tows slipped, to continue on their missions alone. Before long Smart became seriously impeded by other craft, so that Fraser went ahead at some point, and it is on *XE3* that attention now becomes focused.

Fraser had memorized every inch of his course and needed only to be told by Kiwi Smith the distance run as recorded by the Chernakeef Log. He was dressed in khaki shirt and shorts and, in case of capture by the barbarous enemy, was careful to make his status as a naval officer as prominent as possible.

As *Stygian* faded from her vision astern, *XE3* shaped course at 240 degrees across the Straits of Singapore for the coast of Johore, making good about five knots on her main diesel engine. Trimmed right down, a mere pencil line on the water's dark face, she was almost invisible. The sea was dead-calm, the night warm, still, very quiet, very dark and, even at a distance of some miles from the land, was embalmed with the hot, spicy, bitter-sweet aroma of the East, like the smell of stale curry.

For the greater part of the night Fraser sat out on the casing on the edge of the after-hatch, his legs dangling down inside. From there he peered out into a night of black velvet through his night binoculars for hour after hour, from time to time passing orders quietly to the control room. Within, all was dark except for the red glow of the instrument lights. There was no conversation, each man absorbed in his job. All that bothered Fraser was the bright glitter of phosphorescence that shimmered at the bull-nosed bow and the frothing stern.

Except for the hum of the engines everything was dead quiet. The little company felt very much alone in that silent and hostile sea. Disregarding the numerous minefields, they slid safely over them all. After about two hours a partial moon rode the sky, turning the sea to gunmetal and the tree-fringed coast of Johore into a line of charcoal against an oyster sky. Along that coast, from which vague sounds were audible, *XE3* moved as quietly as possible at a good speed. She had a duel with time, for she had to get through the anti-submarine net and reach *Takao* before the tide began to ebb at noon, otherwise there would not be enough depth of water to get beneath her keel.

Just before 3 a.m. there was a moment of acute anxiety when Fraser nearly ran into a fishing boat, believing it to be a buoy that he wanted to identify to fix his position. He swung swiftly away just in time, still on the surface. Soon afterwards the low-lying coast of Singapore Island began darkly to resolve itself straight ahead, and its smell to come more sharply to the nose.

Fraser began to shape to starboard for the entrance of Johore Strait. Almost at once a large ship, with a smaller one in company, began to bear down on him. Fraser at once gave the order to dive to 40 feet and slid down from the hatch. At 36 feet, however, the boat hit the sea-bed with a series of dragging bumps and it was immediately evident that the Chernakeef Log had been damaged. This was a serious navigational inconvenience, but the revolutions of the propeller shaft would still give a fair guide. Fraser kept the boat down there for half an hour while the log was taken in, and then he surfaced very cautiously.

To his alarm the two enemy ships were still there, and closer. He was obliged to dive again at once but continued on course at slow speed, with the batteries at minimum power.

When he judged that he was near the anti-submarine boom at the entrance of Johore Strait, with time in hand, Fraser decided to give the crew a short rest, for Smith and Magennis were drowsy with fatigue after some 30 hours' concentration in the hot and stagnant atmosphere of the control room. Only Reid, always responding instantly and exactly to all helm orders, seemed in good shape. So Fraser took *XE3* to the bottom again and issued Benzedrine tablets to Smith, Magennis and himself, and they all rested while the chronometer ticked and the oxygen hissed away quietly. After three-quarters of an hour, the tablets having taken effect, all turned back to their instruments, much refreshed, as Fraser gave the order: 'Stand by to get under way.'

Into the Strait

Just before dawn on the 31st, Fraser surfaced with the utmost caution, expecting to find the boom close ahead, but, on taking three or four bearings, was disconcerted to find that he was still 3½ miles short of it. He would now have to negotiate the boom in full daylight and would have to hurry to reach *Takao* before the tide fell too far. All now felt the immediacy of the hour. They were about to enter narrow waters infested by the enemy. From here onwards they would have to be underwater for 15 or more hours and knew that they were to be faced, not only with danger but also with a severe trial of physical and nervous fortitude. Magennis made ready to don his diving suit in case he had to get out and cut the anti-submarine net. He and his shipmates waited expectantly for orders. They soon came:

'Stand by to dive.'

'Aye, aye, sir. Ready to dive, sir.'

'Dive, dive, dive; 40 feet.'

Then: 'Steer 290 degrees.'

XE3 slipped smoothly below on her quiet electric motor. An hour or so later Fraser took her up to 10 feet and began taking a series of quick glimpses through the periscope. Very soon he could discern the line of buoys from which the antisubmarine net was suspended, with a guard-boat stationed at the entrance to the narrow gate. From now on he was very much tensed, snapping out his orders sharply. The sea was dead calm, so that the slightest ripple must have been evident to watchful eyes. To Magennis the orders 'Up periscope' and 'Down periscope' followed each other in rapid sequence.

Fortune favoured them. Not only was the gate open, but also the enemy watch was negligent. Going dead-slow, *XE3* crept safely through at 10.30. She was at last in Johore Strait, with Singapore on her port hand and the small island of Pulau Ubin to starboard, the channel here being only about 500 yards wide. Mangrove swamps fledged the low-lying shores for much of the way, but the little glass window in the dome of the control room showed that the water in the middle of the channel was jade-green, quite translucent and shimmering in the tropic heat. Very careful navigation was needed, for the deep-water channel was narrow and the tide strong on the bends. Smith began to have difficulty with the trimming as the density of the water showed sharp variations. *XE3* crept along noiselessly underwater at a trifle over three knots, occasionally rising to periscope depth for a quick peep. She still had 11 miles to go and could not now reach *Takao* until well after high water, but there should still be water enough.

When the tide began to ebb, *XE3* was still only halfway along the strait, and her speed was slackened by the turn. Her crew were bathed in perspiration and breathing heavily, the air saturated and foul. Fraser ordered Magennis to get into his diving suit, a sore trial in the cramped space and the heavy atmosphere. Magennis was red in the face, panting for breath and streaming with sweat as he struggled bit by bit into the awkward rubber gear.

At 12.30 Fraser once more ordered 'Up periscope' and exclaimed: 'There she is!'

Takao was at last in sight, three miles away. Fraser called the other three to the periscope in turn to have a good look at their prey. All were filled with excitement. *Takao* lay exactly as they had expected, with her stern close to the Singapore shore and her bows pointing out into mid-channel. She looked formidable enough with her banked turrets of big guns and her bristling secondary' armament, among which rose two lattice-work masts, like Eiffel towers. Beyond her several other ships lay at anchor with a number of small craft plying busily among them.

The timing was going to be critical. *Takao* was lying in very shallow water and the undulating contours of the sea-bed were such that at low tide her stern and bows were aground but there was a trough of deeper water under her amidships. To reach that trough *XE3* would have to cross the sandbank on which the cruiser's bows were resting without being seen. Having worked out his method of doing so, Fraser stood over towards the northern shore, then turned to port and, at eight minutes past two, gave the order: 'Stand by to start the attack.'

A mile to go now. The equatorial sun was high and hot, the water dangerously clear, with 10 feet of underwater visibility. Inside *XE3* there was a taut atmosphere, each man intent on his own instruments, ready to respond to orders instantly, the oxygen cylinders hissing an undertone to the drama. Fraser, small though he was, was kneeling at the periscope, frequently ordering it up or down, his commands crisp and firm. Smith needed all his attention to keep the boat at the right depth in the changing buoyancy of the water. Reid, utterly reliable, was concentrating on keeping a precise course, knowing that the slightest error could take them away from the target. Magennis, now clothed in his diving suit except for the hood and breathing apparatus, was converting Fraser's periscope readings into ranges by means of the slide-rule.

When the range had shortened to 400 yards, Fraser ordered 'Up periscope' for a last look round. To his horror he found that a Japanese cutter, crammed with sailors obviously going on shore leave, was only 40 feet from his starboard bow. Immediately he went as deep as the shallow water allowed, but even so the cutter passed within a foot or two of the periscope. 'I do not know,' wrote Fraser afterwards, 'why they did not see us.'

XE3 moved on underwater dead-slow, touched bottom lightly and scraped along the gravelly sea-bed as she crossed the dangerous sandbank, with only 10 feet of water, brightly and alarmingly sunlit, above her. Very near now.

Too near, in fact. With a loud clang, *XE3* crashed straight into *Takao*'s hull. Something had gone amiss. She should have been below the cruiser's keel amidships but instead, with only 13 feet on the depth-gauge, she had hit the ship too far forward, where she was resting on the sandbank. In that sandbank *XE3* was jammed.

There followed a fearful tussle with rudder, motor and hydroplane. For ten minutes the boat wriggled and thrust ahead and astern, with her propeller thrashing. She was like a motor-car stuck in the mud and driven by a blind man. All kept their heads, however, and soon the boat was wrenched clear. Fraser would have been entirely justified in dropping his explosives there and then, but he was determined to strike his target where he would do the utmost possible damage. At considerable risk, he took the boat right out into deep water again, 1,000 yards away, and made a fresh attack, aiming to get into the trough of deep water below his enemy amidships.

It was already past 3 o'clock when he began his second strike, the water falling lower and lower. But this time he was successful. From the bright, sunlit water showing in the overhead glass port the boat slid into the blackness which showed that she was right beneath at last. Using his short night periscope, Fraser manoeuvred a little till be was under the keel itself. This brought the boat right down to the sea-bed, with the keel of *Takao* only a foot or so above her. There Fraser stopped the motor and again gave each man a chance to have a good look through the overhead port into the dark, cavernous space above.

What they saw was a hull that seemed to be pressing down on them and heavily fouled by a dense drapery of seaweed and encrusted with barnacles and shells. That would not have mattered if Fraser had been content merely to drop his big depth-charge, but he intended to plaster his enemy with limpet mines also. Before the magnets of the limpets could cling to the cruiser's hull, all that mess would have to be cleared away down to the bare steel.

Magennis Swims Out

It was now Magennis's great hour, in which he was to accomplish a feat unique in submarine history. The little diver sat ready in his suit, bathed in sweat. With Fraser's help he donned his hood and breathing gear, crawled into the wet-and-dry compartment and waited for it to flood. Attempting then to emerge, he found that the hatch would not open more than halfway, its lid coming into contact with the hull of the cruiser. There was no chance of its being opened farther, for *XE3* was already sitting on the sea-bed. So tight was the fit that if the tide fell much farther the midget must have been crushed by the cruiser.

Magennis, however, was not to be outdone. Taking a fearful risk, he inhaled oxygen deeply, slipped off the bulky breathing set and just managed to squeeze his small body through the aperture, before replacing his artificial lung. It was a daring and unprecedented act. Floating away, he found himself, as it were, in a dark underwater cave, its roof festooned with a canopy of weeds. Using his diver's knife he began to cut away the weeds and the clinging shellfish. Many of the shells were very sharp and cut his hands. Little bubbles floated up, caused by a small leak in his breathing gear. He went about his work methodically, without haste, while his shipmates sweated with anxiety and heat.

He then extracted six limpet mines from the magazine on the starboard side, laying them on the casing. The limpets weighed 200 lb. each and, although buoyant, were of an awkward shape and difficult to handle. He was soon feeling the strain of these underwater exertions, breathing heavily. Taking his limpets one at a time, he swam out along the keel, placing them in groups, about 50 feet apart. The task of fixing proved to be very difficult and exhausting, the danger of oxygen poisoning near at hand. The sides of the cruiser below water were very steep and the magnets of the limpets not strong enough, so that some of them slipped off and he had to swim off to recover them. Having set the firing mechanisms to work, but too exhausted to pull out the countermining pins, he swam back to *XE3* and gave the 'thumbs-up' sign to Fraser, who was able to watch much of his activity. Then he wriggled back through the lid of the W-and-D and, having dried out there, crawled into the stewy atmosphere of the control room. He had been out for a full half-hour and was absolutely dead-beat.

All was by no means over yet. The big 4-ton explosive charge on the port side was cast off without much trouble by the wheeled mechanism inboard and there were grunts of most profound satisfaction when the crew heard it touch bottom with a dull thud. Like the limpets, it had been pre-set to go off in six hours' time. There remained, however, the big limpet magazine on the starboard side, itself weighing 2 tons. This dead weight must also be discarded for the boat to be manoeuvrable, but all the efforts of the crew could not dislodge it. Fraser, haunted by the risk of being crushed beneath the cruiser as the tide fell farther still, and beginning to show at last the results of a prolonged and acute nervous strain, was very much on edge. It was now past 4 o'clock. Get out they must, somehow.

The cruiser's keel was now actually touching the midget's casing just aft of the periscope standard, so that she could not get free by going astern. Fraser therefore gave the order for 'Half ahead', but XE3 did not budge. He ordered 'Full ahead' and still she did not move. He ordered maximum power, with no better result. Under that black menacing giant the boat seemed to be completely trapped.

He tried every trick in the submariner's book and had almost given up hope when, quite suddenly, grinding along the gravel beneath her, XE3 began to move. In a minute or two she was free, but the weight of the limpet magazine on her starboard side, now flooded with water, at once began to take effect, swinging the boat's head in that direction, so that Reid, calm and steady as ever at the helm, had to report: 'Can't control her, sir.'

Nevertheless, she crept out of the dread black cavern and slewed round into clearer water, where Fraser stopped her on the bottom. She was only some 30 feet from *Takao* and, at 17 feet, obviously at risk of being seen, but Fraser decided that the dead weight of the limpet magazine must be got rid of as soon as possible. The normal method having failed, this was another task for the diver. Fraser looked doubtfully at the exhausted Magennis. Could he ask him so soon to carry out another dangerous and laborious task? The others having little diving experience, Fraser decided to go out himself, but the tenacious Magennis look aggrieved and said: 'I'll be all right as soon as I've got my wind, sir.'

Five minutes later he rose to his knees and, armed with a giant spanner, crawled to the W-and-D and floated away through the hatch in a foam of bubbles that gave the watching Fraser acute anxiety. His anxiety was increased as, in the dead silence of the control room, he listened to the banging and clanging as Magennis wrenched and levered with his spanner to unseat the heavy magazine. Any moment he expected a shower of depth-charges to be launched from *Takao*. Magennis, however, was quite calm and practical, doing the job in his own way. At last the magazine was freed and fell to the bottom.

The gallant little diver then swam back to safety. Fraser ordered a course of 90 degrees and *XE3* began her passage home. Just before midnight, dazed with fatigue after 46 nerve-straining hours, Fraser scarcely able to stand, Smith pale and drooping, they made their rendezvous with *Stygian* at the appointed spot in the Straits of Singapore.

Meanwhile, Jack Smart's crew in *XE1* had been beset with difficulties and arrived in Johore Strait too late to attack *Myoko*. He therefore decided to reinforce the attack on *Takao* and, being now unable to get underneath her, dropped his charges close alongside.

It must be said that the result was disappointing. Certainly a very large hole was torn in *Takao*'s bottom and serious damage was done to her fighting gear; very probably she would have sunk if she had been in deep water. What was less satisfactory was to learn (after some time) that the operation did not appear to have been necessary, for an American submarine had previously damaged *Takao*'s stern fairly severely at sea, a fact that had not been disclosed to the British submariners. Possibly the Americans themselves had been unaware of the extent of the damage and wanted the midgets to make sure of her.

When this became known later, it left a taste of ashes in the mouths of the gallant young men who had undergone this ordeal, but the facts did nothing at all to undervalue the richly deserved awards of the Victoria Cross to 'Tich' Fraser and

Mick Magennis. Kiwi Smith was awarded the DSO and Reid the Conspicuous Gallantry Medal.

APPENDIX A: ROLL OF VICTORIA CROSS AWARDS 1939-45

Some abbreviations:

RAFVR: Royal Air Force Volunteer Reserve.

RCAF: Royal Canadian Air Force; similarly for Royal Australian and Royal New Zealand Air Forces.

att.: attached.

Bn: Battalion.

R: Royal.

X signifies a posthumous award.

X Aaron, Flt Sgt A. L. RAFVR, 218 Sqn RAF; Italy, 12/8/43.

X Abdul Hafiz, Jemadar, 3/9 Jat Rgt; Burma, 6/4/44.

Agansing Rai, Rifleman, 2/5 R. Gurkha Rifles; Burma, 26/6/44.

Ali Haidar, Sepoy, 6/13 Frontier Force Rifles; Italy, 6/4/45.

X Allmand, Capt. M., att. 6 Gurkha Rifles; Burma, 11-23/6/44.

Anderson, Lt-Col. C. G. W.; 2/9 Australian Infantry; Malaya, 18-22/1/42.

X Anderson, Pte E., East Yorkshire Rgt; Wadi Akarit, 6/4/43.

Anderson, Major J. T. McK., Argyll and Sutherland Highlanders; Tunisia, 23/4/43.

Annard, 2nd-Lt R. W., Durham Light Infantry; Belgium, 15-16/5/40.

X Barton, Pilot Off. C. J., RAFVR, 578 Sqn RAF; Nuremberg, 20/3/44.

X Baskeyfield, Sgt J. D., S. Staffordshire Rgt; Arnhem, 20/9/44.

X Bates, Cpl S., R. Norfolk Rgt; Normandy, 6/8/44.

X Bazalgette, Sqn Ldr I. W., RAFVR, 635 Sqn RAF; Normandy,

4/8/44.

Beattie, Lt-Cdr S. H., RN; St Nazaire Raid, 27/3/42.

X Beeley, Rifleman, J., King's R. Rifle Corps; *Crusader*, 21/11/41.

Bhanbhagta Gurung, Rifleman, 3/2 Gurkha Rifles; Burma, 5/3/45.

Bhanduri Ram, Sepoy, 10 Baluch Rgt; Burma, 22/11/44.

X Blaker, Major F. G., Highland Light Infantry, att. 9 Gurkha Rifles; Burma, 9/7/44.

Brunt, Capt. J. H. C., Sherwood Foresters, att. 6 Lincolns; Italy, 9/12/44.

Burton, Pte R. H., Duke of Wellington's Rgt; Italy, 8/10/44.

Cain, Major R. H., R. Northumberland Fus., att. S. Staffs.; Arnhem, 19-25/9/44.

X Cairns, Lt G. A., Somerset Light Inf., att. 1st S. Staffs.; Burma (Chindit ops), 13/3/44.

Campbell, Brig. J. C., R. Artillery and General Staff; *Crusader*, 21-23/11/41.

X Campbell, Flying Off. K., RAFVR, 22 Sqn RAF; Brest Harbour, 6/4/41.

Campbell, Lt-Col. L. MacL., Argyll and Sutherland Highlanders; Wadi Akarit, 6/4/43.

Chapman, Cpl E. T., Monmouthshire Rgt; Germany, 2/4/45.

X Charlton, Guardsman E. T., Irish Gds; Germany, 21/4/45.

Cheshire, Wing Cdr G. L. RAF; sustained leadership and gallantry in bombing ops, 1940-4.

X Chhelu Ram, Havildar-major, 6th Rajputana Rifles; Tunisia, 19/4/43.

X Chowne, Lt A., 2 Bn Australian Inf.; New Guinea, 25/3/45.

X Clarke, Lt W. A. S., The Loyals; Tunisia, 23/4/43.

X Cosens, Sgt A., Queen's Own Rifles of Canada; Holland, 25/2/45.

Cruickshank, Flying Off. J. A., RAFVR, 210 Sqn RAF; the Atlantic, 17/7/44.

Cumming, Lt-Col. A. E., 12 Frontier Force Rgt; Malaya, 3/1/42.

Currie, Major D. V., 29 Canadian Recce Rgt; Normandy, 18-20/8/44.

Cutler, Lt A. R., R. Australian Artillery; Syria, 19/6 to 6/7/41.

Derrick, Sgt T. C., 48 Bn Australian Inf.; S.W. Pacific, 23/11/43.

X Donnini, Fusilier D., R. Scots Fus.; Germany, 18/1/45.

X Durrant, Sgt T. F., R. Engineers and No. 1 Cdo; St Nazaire, 27/3/42.

Eardley, Sgt G. H., K.O. Shropshire Light Inf; Overloon, 16/10/44.

X Edmondson, Cpl J. H., 17 Bn Australian Inf.; Tobruk, 13/4/41.

Edwards, Wing Cdr H. I., 105 Sqn RAF; Bremen, 4/7/41 (first man in this war to win VC, DSO and DFC).

Elliott, Sgt K., 22 NZ Bn; Ruweisat, 15/7/42.

Ervine-Andrews, Capt. H. M., E. Lancs Rgt; Dunkirk, 31/5/40.

X Esmonde, Lt-Cdr E., RN; torpedo-bomber attack on German battle-cruisers, off Dover, 12/1/42.

X Fazal Din, Naik, 7/10 Baluch Rgt; Burma, 2/3/45.

X Fegen, Capt. E. S. F., RN; Atlantic, 5/11/40.

Foote, Lt-Col. H. R. B., R. Tank Rgt; Gazala, 27/5 to 6/6/42.

Foote, Rev. J. W., Canadian Army Chaplain; Dieppe, 19/8/42.

Fraser, Lt I. E., RNR.; Singapore, 31/7/45.

X French, Cpl A., 9 Bn Australian Inf; New Guinea, 4/9/42.

X Furness, Lt the Hon. C., Welch Gds; France, 23/5/40.

Gaje Ghale, Havildar, 5 R. Gurkha Rifles; Burma, 24-27/5/43.

Ganju Lama, Rifleman, 7 Gurkha Rifles; Burma, 12/6/44.

Gardner, Capt. P. J., R. Tank Rgt; *Crusader*, 23/11/41.

X Garland, Flying Off. D.E., 12 Sqn RAF; Belgium, 12/5/40.

Gian Singh, Naik, 4/15 Punjab Rgt; Burma, 2/3/45.

Gibson, Wing Cdr G. P., RAF, 617 Sqn; Mohne and Eder Dams, 16-17/5/43.

Gordon, Pte J. H., Australian Inf.; Syria, 10/7/41.

Gould, Petty Off. T. W.; HM Submarine *Thrasher*, off Crete, 16/2/42.

X Gratwick, Pte P. E., 48 Bn Australian Inf.; El Alamein, 25-26/10/42.

X Gray, Lt R. H., R, Canadian Naval Volunteer Res.; Far East, 9/8/45.

X Gray, Sgt T., 12 Sqn RAF; F/O Garland's observer, above.

X Grayburn, Lt J. H., Parachute Rgt; Arnhem, 17-20/9/44.

Gristock, Warrant Off. G., R. Norfolk Rgt; France, 21/5/40.

X Gunn, 2nd-Lt G. W., R. Horse Artillery; *Crusader*, 21/11/41.

X Gurney, Pte A. S., 48 Bn Australian Inf; Tel el Eisa, 22/7/42.

X Hannah, Sgt J., RAFVR, 83 Sqn RAF; over Antwerp, 15/9/40.

X Harden, L/Cpl H. E., R. Army Medical Corps, att. R. Marine Cdos, 23/1/45.

X Harman, L/Cpl J. P., R. West Kent Rgt; Kohima, 8-9/4/44.

X Harper, Cpl J. W., York and Lancaster Rgt; NW Europe, 29/9/44.

Hinton, Sgt J. D., 20 NZ Bn; Greece, 28-29/4/44.

X Hoey, Major C. F., R. Lincolnshire Rgt; Arakan, 16/2/44.

Hollis, Company Sgt-maj. S. E., The Green Howards; Normandy, 6/6/44.

X Hornell, Flt Lt D. E., 162 Sqn RCAF; Atlantic, 25/6/44.

X Horwood, Lt A. G., The Queen's Rgt, att. Northamptonshire Rgt; Arakan, 18-20/1/44.

Hulme, Sgt A. C., 23 NZ Bn; Crete, 20-28/5/41.
X Hunter, Cpl T. P., 43 R. Marine Cdo; Italy, 2/4/45.

X Jackman, Capt. J. J. B., R. Northumberland Fus.; *Crusader*, 25/11/41.
Jackson, Sgt N. C., RAFVR, 106 Sqn RAF; Germany, 26/4/44.
Jamieson, Capt. D., R. Norfolk Rgt; Normandy, 7-8/8/44.
Jefferson, Fusilier F. A., Lancashire Fus.; Cassino, 16/5/44.

X Karanjeet Singh Judge, Lt, 15 Punjab Rgt; Burma, 18/3/45.
Kelliher, Pte R., 4 Bn Australian Inf.; New Guinea, 13/9/43.
Kamal Ram, Sepoy, 3/8 Punjab Rgt; Cassino, 12/5/44.
Kenna, Pte E., 4 Bn Australian Inf.; New Guinea, 15/5/45.
Kennealey, L/Cpl J. P., Irish Gds; Tunisia, 28-30/4/43.
X Keyes, Lt-Gol. G. C. T., R. Armoured Corps; Western Desert, 17-18/11/41.
X Kibby, Sgt W. H., 48 Bn Australian Inf.; El Alamein, 25-26/10/42.
X Kingsbury, Pte B. S., 14 Bn Australian Inf.; New Guinea, 29/8/42.
X Knowland, Lt G. A., R. Norfolk Rgt, att. Army Cdos; Arakan, 31 /1/45.

Lachhiman Gurung, Rifleman, 4/8 Gurkha Rifles; Burma, 12-13/5/45.
Lalbahadur Thapa, Subedar, 2 Gurkha Rifles; Wadi Akarit, 6/4/43.
X Lassen, Major A. F. E. V. S., a Dane serving with the Army Commandos; Italy, 8/4/45.
X Leaky, Sgt N. G., 6 King's African Rifles; Abyssinia, 19/5/41.
Learoyd, Flt Lt R. A. B., 49 Sqn RAF; Dortmund-Ems Canal, 12/8/40.

Le Patourel, Capt. H. W., Hampshire Rgt; Tunisia, 3/12/42.

Liddell, Capt. I. O., Coldstream Gds; Germany, 3/4/45. Killed soon afterwards.

X Linton, Cdr J. W., RN; HM Submarine *Turbulent*, continuous operations 1939-43.

X Lord, Flt Lt D. A. S., 171 Sqn RAF; over Arnhem, 19/9/44.

X Lyell, Capt. the Lord, Scots Gds; Tunisia, 22-27/4/43.

X Mackey, Cpl J. B., Australian Pioneer Bn; North Borneo, 12/5/45.

Magennis, Ldg Seaman J. J.; Singapore, 31/7/45.

Mahoney, Major J. K., Westminster Rgt (Canada); Cassino, 24/5/44.

X Malcolm, Wing Cdr H. G., 18 Sqn RAF; N. Africa, 4/12/42.

X Manser, Flying Off. L. T., RAFVR, 50 Sqn RAF; Cologne, 30/5/42.

X Mantle, Ldg Seaman J. F.; Portland (England), 4/7/40.

Merritt, Lt-Col. C. C. I., S. Saskatchewan Rgt; Dieppe, 19/8/42.

X Middleton, Flt Sgt R. H., RAAF, 149 Sqn RAF; Italy, 29/11/42.

Miers, Cdr A. C. C., RN; HM Submarine *Torbay*, 5/3/42.

X Mynarski, Pilot Off. A. C., 419 Sqn RCAF; Cambrai, 12/6/44.

X Mitchell, Pte G. A., London Scottish; Italy, 23/1/44.

Namdeo Jadhao, Sepoy, 1/5 Manratta L. I.; Italy, 9/4/45.

Nand Singh, Naik, 1/11 Sikhs; Arakan, 11-12/3/44.

X Netrabahadur Thapa, Subedar, 2/5 R. Gurkha Rifles; Imphal, 25-26/6/44.

Nettleton, Sqn Ldr J. D., 44 (Rhodesia) Sqn RAF; Augsburg, 17/4/42.

Newman, Lt-Col. A. C., Essex Rgt and 2 Cdo; St. Nazaire, 27/3/42.

X Newton, Flt Lt W. E., 22 Sqn RAAF; New Guinea, 16/3/43.

X Ngarimu, 2nd-Lt M. N. a K., 28 NZ Bn; Mareth Line, 20-21/3/43.

Nicholls, L/Cpl H., Grenadier Gds; Belgium, 21/5/40.

Nicholson, Flt Lt J. B., 249 Sqn RAF; Battle of Britain, 16/8/40.

Norton, Lt G. R., South African Forces, att. Hampshire Rgt; Italy, 31/8/44.

X Osborn, Warrant Off. J. R., Winnipeg Grenadiers; Hong Kong, 19/12/41.

X Palmer, Sqn Ldr R. A. M., RAFVR, 109 Sqn RAF; Germany, 23/12/44.

Parkash Singh, Havildar, 8 Punjab Rgt; Burma, 6-19/1/43.

X Parkash Singh, Jemadar, 13 Frontier Force Rifles; Burma, 16-17/2/45.

Partridge, Ptc F. J., 8 Bn Australian Inf.; Bougainville, Solomon Isles, 29/7/45.

Peters, Capt. F. T., RN; HMS *Walney*, Oran, 8/11/42. Place, Lt B. C. G., RN; attack on *Tirpitz*, 22/9/43. Porteous, Capt. P. A., R. Artillery and 4 Cdo; Dieppe, 19/8/42.

Premindra Singh Bhagat, 2nd-Lt, Indian Engineers; Abyssinia, 1/2/41.

Queripel, Capt. L. E., R. Sussex, att. Parachute Rgt; Arnhem, 19/9/44.

X Ram Sarup Singh, Subedar, 2/1 Punjab Rgt; Burma, 25/10/44.

X Randle, Capt. J. N., R. Norfolk Rgt; Kohima, 4-6/5/44.

Rattey, Cpl R. R., 25 Bn Australian Inf.; Solomon Isles, 22/3/45.

X Raymond, Lt G., R. Engineers; Burma, 21/3/45.

Reid, Flt Lt W., RAFVR, 61 Sqn RAF; Dusseldorf, 3/11/43.

X Richpal Ram, Subedar, 6 Rajputana Rifles; Eritrea, 7-12/2/41.

Roberts, Lt P. S. W., RN; HM Submarine *Thrasher*, off Crete, 16/2/42.

X Rogers, Sgt M. A. W., Wiltshire Rgt; Italy, 3/6/44.

X Roope, Lt-Cdr G. B.; in HMS *Glowworm* against German pocket-battleship *Hipper*, off Norway, 8/4/40.

Ryder, Cdr R. E. D., RN; St Nazaire, 27/3/42.

X Sefanaia, Sukanaivalu, Cpl, Fiji Military Forces; Bougainville, Solomon Isles, 23/6/44.

X Savage, Able Seaman W. A.; St Nazaire, 27/3/42.

X Scarf, Sqn Ldr A. S. K., 62 Sqn RAF; Malaya, 9/12/41.

X Seagrim, Lt-Gol. D. A., The Green Howards; Mareth Line, 20-21/3/43.

X Sephton, Petty Off. A. E.; off Crete, 18/5/41.

X Sher Bahadur Thapa, Rifleman, 1/9 Gurkhas; Italy, 18/9/44.

Sherbrooke, Capt. R. St. V., RN; North Cape (Russian convoy), 31/12/42.

X Sher Shah, L/Naik, 7/6 Punjab Rgt; Arakan, 19/1/45.

Sidney, Major the Hon. W. P. (Lord De L'Isle and Dudley), Grenadier Gds; Italy, 7-8/2/44.

Smith, Pte E. A., Seaforth Highlanders of Canada; Italy, 21/10/44.

Smythe, Sgt Q. G. M., R. Natal Carbineers; Gazala, 5/6/42.

Stannard, Lt-Cdr R. B., RNR; off Norway, May-June, 40.

Starcevitch, Pte L. T., 43 Bn Australian Inf.; N. Borneo, 28/6/45.

X Stokes, Pte J., K. O. Shropshire Light Infantry; Germany, 1/3/45.

X Swales, Capt. E., South African Air Forces (582 Sqn RAF); Germany, 23/2/45.

X Thaman Gurung, Rifleman, 1/5 Gurkha Rifles; Italy, 10/11/44.

X Thompson, Flt Sgt G., RAFVR, 9 Sqn RAF; Dortmund-Ems Canal, 1/6/45.

Tilston, Major F. A., Essex Scottish Rgt, Canadian Army; Germany, 1/3/45.

Topham, Cpl F. G., medical orderly, 1st Canadian Parachute Rgt; Germany, 24/3/45.

Trent, Sqn Ldr L. H., 487 Sqn RNZAF; Amsterdam, 3/5/43.

X Trigg, Flying Off. L. A., RNZAF, 200 Sqn RAF; the Atlantic, 11/8/43.

Triquet, Major P., R. 22e Rgt, Canadian Army; Italy, 14/12/43.

Tulbahadur Pun, Rifleman, 6 Gurkha Rifles; Burma, 23/6/44.

X Turner, Sgt H. V., W. Yorkshire Rgt; Imphal, 6/6/44.

Turner, Lt-Col. V. B., Rifle Brigade; El Alamein, 27/10/42.

Umrao Singh, Havildar, Indian Artillery; Arakan, 15/12/44.

Upham, 2nd-Lt C. H., 20 NZ Bn; Crete, 22-30/5/41.

Upham, Capt, BAR to the VC; Western Desert, 27/6 to 14/7/42.

Wakeford, Capt. R., Hampshire Rgt; Cassino, 12/5/44.

X Wakenshaw, Pte A. H., Durham Light Inf.; Western Desert, 27/6/42.

Wanklyn, Lt-Cdr M. D., RN; HM Submarine *Upholder*, 24/5/41.

X Warburton-Lee, Capt. B. A. W., RN; HMS *Hardy*, Norway, 10/4/40.

Ward, Sgt J. A., RNZAF, 75 (NZ) Sqn, RAF; Holland, 7/7/41.

Watkins, Lt T., Welch Rgt; Normandy, 16/8/44.

X Weston, Lt W. B., The Green Howards, att. 1st W. Yorks Rgt; Burma, 3/3/45.

X Wilkinson, Lt T., RNR; HMS *Li Wo*, Far East, 14/2/42.

Wilson, Capt. E. C. T., E. Surrey Rgt; Somaliland, 11-15/8/40.

Wright, Company Sgt-maj. P. H.; Coldstream Gds; Italy, 25/9/43.

X Yeshwant Ghadge, Naik, 5 Mahratta L. I.; Italy, 10/7/44.

APPENDIX B: AWARDS SINCE 1945

Korea

Carne, Lt-Col. J. P., 1st Gloucestershire Rgt; Imjin River, 22-23/4/51.

X Curtis, Lt P. K. E., 1st Duke of Cornwall's Light Infantry, att. 1st Gloucesters; same action.

X Muir, Major Kenneth, 1st Argyll and Sutherland Highlanders; Songju, 23/9/50.

Speakman, Pte W., 1st Black Watch, att. King's Own Scottish Borderers; 4/11 /51.

Borneo

Rambahadur Limbu, 10th Gurkha Rifles; 21/11/65. This was in the 'confrontation' war, when Sukarno, the flamboyant dictator of Indonesia, attempted to grab the territories of North Borneo, Sarawak and Brunei, which were under British protection.

Vietnam

The following awards were won by members of the 'training teams' of the Royal Australian Infantry seconded to units of the South Vietnam forces in the war against the Viet Cong. All were for repeated acts of courageous leadership in desperate situations and for rescuing wounded from the enemy.

X Badcoe, Major P. J.; 23/2 to 7/4/67.

Payne, Warrant Officer Keith; 24/5/69.

Simpson, Warrant Officer R. S.; 6-11/5/69.

X Wheatley, Warrant Officer K. A.; 13/11/65.

APPENDIX C: PRINCIPAL WITNESSES

For the general background of events, the official histories of the United Kingdom, New Zealand, South Africa, Australia and Rhodesia and other standard works have been accepted, those of the old Dominions being particularly valuable. For greater detail the archives of several branches of the Ministry of Defence have been searched for original and unpublished evidence.

More valuable still (because at first hand) have been the personal narratives of the individual informants recorded below, many of whom have been most generous of their time and labour in helping to reconstruct half-forgotten and unchronicled incidents and many of whom have checked the relevant parts of my manuscript.

Rear-Admiral Place (Chairman of the Victoria Cross and George Cross Association), Colonel Eustace and Brigadier Hely have been unsparing. Long, detailed and valuable memoranda have been provided by Brigadier Wills, Marshal of the Royal Air Force Sir John Slessor, Major-General Wimberley, Major Bingham, Mr Gouldsbury, Major Derek Lloyd, Lt-Col. Sell, and my old comrade Major Savory of Rhodesia, just before he died. To all these I record my thanks. A few books of special value are also mentioned.

CRETE
Brigadier J. T. Burrows, CBE, DSO; Brigadier J. H. G. Wills, CBE; Brigadier A. F. Hely, CB, CBE, DSO; Lt-Commander Paul Whatley; Lt-Commander John Wingate, DSC.

NZ War History Branch: *Crete* (by D. N. Davin).

I. McD. G. Stewart: *The Struggle for Crete.*
Howard Kippenberger: *Infantry Brigadier.*
Roy Farran: *Winged Dagger* (Collins).
Hector Bolitho: *The Galloping Third* (John Murray).
G. Sims: *HMS Coventry, Anti-Aircraft Cruiser.*

BATTLE OF THE ATLANTIC
Marshal of the Royal Air Force Sir John Slessor, GCB, DSO,
MC, and his book *The Central Blue.*
George Pollock: *The Jervis Bay* (William Kimber).

CRUSADER
Brigadier A. F. Hely, CB, CBE, DSO; Brigadier H. A. Hardy,
MBE, MG; Major Guy Savory, MC; Captain P. J. Gardner, VC,
MC; Major T. A. Bird, DSO, MC; Mr P. T. Flower; Major
Charles Bingham; Major W. J. M. Tabrum; Lt-Col. H. A. Hope,
OBE, MC; Lt-Col. M. D. B. Lister; Major Derek Lloyd, MC;
Colonel W. C. H. Sanderson; Mr A. A. Banks; Lt-Col. R. A.
Wyrly-Birch, DSO.
    Michael Carver: *Tobruk.*
    Robin Hastings: *The Rifle Brigade.*
    Dudley Clarke: *The Eleventh at War* (Michael Joseph) Robert
        Crisp: *Brazen Chariots* (Frederick Muller)
    B. H. Liddell Hart: *The Tanks.*

GAZALA
Major-General H. R. B. Foote, VC, CB, DSO; Major-General
Raymond Briggs, CB, DSO; Lt-Col. J. C. Slight, DSO; Lt-Col.
H. S. Sell, OBE, MC; Mr R. M. Grey, MM.
    Lt-General Sir Francis Tuker: *Approach to Battle.*
    Michael Carver: *Tobruk.*
    Louis Duffus: *Beyond the Laager* (Hurst and Blackett).
    B. H. Liddell Hart: *The Tanks.*

RUWEISAT
Brigadier J. T. Burrows, CBE, DSO; Brigadier T. C. Campbell, CBE, DSO, MC.
Howard Kippenberger: *Infantry Brigadier.*

WADI AKARIT
Major-General D. N. Wimberley, CB, DSO, MC, DL; Lt-Gol. D. Ramsey-Brown, MC; Major D. F. O. Russell, MC, LI D; Lt-Col. M. A. Ormsby, MC; Sergeant Jack Freeman; Dr R. F. Clark; Lt-Col. F. R. Yorke.
Lt-General Sir Francis Tuker: *Approach to Battle.*

THE MIDGET SUBMARINES
Rear-Admiral B. C. G. Place, VC, CB, DSC; Mr Ian Fraser, VC, DSC; Lt-Commander G. J. Rowe, DSC.
Rear-Admiral Sir William Jameson: *Submariners VC.*
Captain W. R. Fell: *The Sea our Shield.*
Ian Fraser: *Frogman VC.*
C. E. T. Warren and J. Benson: *Above Us the Waves.*
Leonce Peillard: *Coulez le Tirpitz.*
David Woodward: *The Tirpitz.*

IMPHAL
Colonel N. Eustace, DSO; Major-General R. C. O. Hedley, CB, CBE, DSO; Captain D. D. Parkin, DSO; Mr D. A. Gouldsbury; Colonel P. M. Brown, MC; Major-General J. A. R. Robertson, CB, CBE, DSO; Mr Terence Altham; Sergeant S. Harrison; Sergeant T. Helliwell; Major H. A. V. Spencer; Colonel W. Harris, MBE; Mr J. Fallon, MBE.

My thanks are also due to the Regimental Secretaries of many regiments, Mr D. W. King, the War Office Librarian,

Rear-Admiral P. N. Buckley, Head of the Naval Historical Library, Mr E. B. Haslam, Head of the Air Historical Branch, the Military History Society, (through Mr C. G. Andrews) and the Officers in Charge of Records for their generous help at all times.

APPENDIX D: SUBMARINE TERMINOLOGY

I am grateful to the staff of the Flag Officer Submarines for kindly assisting me in formulating these simplified definitions.

Casing. An upper deck built above the cylindrical 'pressure hull', to facilitate walking and provide a seaworthy bow.

Engine. A diesel engine for propelling the submarine on the surface.

Motor. An electric motor driven by batteries for propulsion when submerged.

Hydroplanes. Horizontal metal fins fitted astern to give the boat 'bow-up' or 'bow-down' angles, thus controlling her depth.

Ballast tanks provide the buoyancy, when emptied of water, to keep the submarine on the surface. When the main vents at the tops of these tanks are opened, seawater rushes in and the submarine dives.

Vents. Valves in the tops of the tanks to control the exit and entry of air.

To trim. To adjust the weight of the submarine by pumping and flooding to and from (a) the trimming tanks, which keep the boat level fore-and-aft; and (b) the compensating tanks, which adjust the bodily weight of the boat in changing conditions of buoyancy, so that it is in equilibrium, i.e. does not tend to rise or sink; her depth can then be controlled by the hydroplanes.

Buoyancy. A submarine that has a good 'trim' has no buoyancy. This condition can be upset by the amount of the salt content in the water, as when entering a river mouth. The flow of fresh water then reduces the density of the salt water and the submarine will tend to sink. Water is then pumped out to adjust the trim and return the boat to neutral buoyancy.

Trimmed down. Riding on the surface with the least possible exposure by partially flooding the ballast tanks; the normal practice when surfaced in enemy waters.

Gyro-compass. A gyroscope (a rotating fly-wheel mounted in gymbals) adapted to serve as a compass.

To blow to full buoyancy. To expel all the water from the main ballast tanks by means of high-pressure air carried in cylinders.

To vent. To open the main vents to allow the escape of any air that had leaked past the control valves into the main ballast tanks (as during depth-charging) and so return the boat to neutral buoyancy.

APPENDIX E: OUTLINE ORGANIZATION OF AN ARMY IN THE FIELD

In each field Army (general or lieut.-general) there were one or more army corps (lieut.-generals). Each corps normally consisted of two or more divisions (major-generals). In each infantry division there were three brigades (brigadiers), the equivalent of a brigade of artillery, the equivalents of regiments in engineers, signals, medical, transport and other services. Each infantry brigade consisted of three battalions.

Usually each corps had at least one armoured division, consisting of two armoured brigades (sometimes only one) and one brigade of motorized infantry. 'Army Tank Brigades' did not form part of the 'armoured division' and usually served in support of the infantry.

THE ARTILLERY REGIMENT

A lieutenant-colonel's command. Normally a 'field regiment' had three batteries (majors), each divided into two troops (captains) of four 25-pdr guns. RHA regiments (employed with armoured divisions) were identical, except when equipped with anti-tank guns; later RHA regiments had self-propelled guns.

Each division had three field regiments, an anti-tank and a light AA regiment. Heavier artillery was directly under corps command.

THE ARMOURED REGIMENT

Commanded by a lieutenant-colonel. Normally organized in a small headquarters squadron and three other squadrons (majors) of three troops (captains), each of five tanks, each tank commanded by a junior officer or sergeant. Establishments varied from time to time and from theatre to theatre.

THE INFANTRY BATTALION
Commanded by a lieutenant-colonel and normally consisting of four rifle companies (the main assault troops) (majors or captains) and a support company of Bren-carriers, heavy mortars, an anti-tank platoon, etc. Each rifle company was divided into three platoons (under subalterns) of four sections of seven men each. Establishments varied somewhat, however.

A term such as '4th Essex' means the fourth battalion of the Essex Regiment. In the Australian Army '2/17' means the unit of the 17th Battalion raised for the Second World War. In the Indian Army '3/1 Punjab' was the third battalion of the 1st Punjab Regiment.

APPENDIX F: A BRIEF NOTE ON THE INDIAN ARMY

The reader is reminded that during the Second World War virtually the whole of the Indian sub-continent was under British sovereignty and was not divided into the separate states of 'India' and 'Pakistan', as it unfortunately became after the grant of independence. In this book, therefore, the term 'Indian' means what it meant before 1947.

Indian Army formations and units were organized and trained in precisely the same way as the British Army. British troops formed a large part of each Indian division, including, as a rule, all the artillery and one British battalion in each infantry brigade. Until late in the war virtually all the officers in the Indian units were British. The rank and file of the Indian infantry were recruited from two sources only — the Gurkhas of Nepal (who are not Indians) and the martial races of Northern India.

The Indian soldier was known as a sepoy. The infantry non-commissioned officers were havildars (equivalent to sergeants), naiks (corporals) and lance-naiks. Above these was a grade peculiar to the Indian Army known as Viceroy's Commissioned Officers (VCOs), who were junior in status to the King's Commissioned Officers. Except in the cavalry, their ranks were those of subedar (wearing two stars) and jemadar (one star). The senior VCO was the subedar-major.

A NOTE TO THE READER

If you have enjoyed this book enough to leave a review on **Amazon** and **Goodreads**, then we would be truly grateful.
The Estate of C. E. Lucas Phillips

Sapere Books is an exciting new publisher of brilliant fiction and popular history.

To find out more about our latest releases and our monthly bargain books visit our website:
saperebooks.com

Printed in Great Britain
by Amazon

27596711R00190